SUSANNE WEIGELIN-SCHWIEDRZIK, AGNES SCHICK-CHEN,
SASCHA KLOTZBÜCHER (EDS.)

AS CHINA MEETS THE WORLD

CHINA'S CHANGING POSITION IN THE INTERNATIONAL COMMUNITY

ÖSTERREICHISCHE AKADEMIE DER WISSENSCHAFTEN
PHILOSOPHISCH-HISTORISCHE KLASSE
SITZUNGSBERICHTE, 747. BAND

BEITRÄGE ZUR KULTUR- UND GEISTESGESCHICHTE ASIENS

Nr. 50

ÖSTERREICHISCHE AKADEMIE DER WISSENSCHAFTEN
PHILOSOPHISCH-HISTORISCHE KLASSE
SITZUNGSBERICHTE, 747. BAND

Edited by
Susanne Weigelin-Schwiedrzik
Agnes Schick-Chen
Sascha Klotzbücher

As China Meets the World

China's Changing Position in the International Community

VERLAG
DER ÖSTERREICHISCHEN AKADEMIE DER WISSENSCHAFTEN
WIEN 2006

Vorgelegt von w. M. ERNST STEINKELLNER
in der Sitzung am 16. Dezember 2005

Britisch Library Cataloguing in Publication data.
A Catalogue record of this book is available from the British Library.

Die verwendete Papiersorte ist aus chlorfrei gebleichtem Zellstoff hergestellt,
frei von säurebildenden Bestandteilen und alterungsbeständig.

ISBN-13: 978-3-7001-3644-6
ISBN-10: 3-7001-3644-7

Druck: Grasl Druck & Neue Medien
Printed and bound in Austria

http://hw.oeaw.ac.at/3644-6
http://verlag.oeaw.ac.at

Contents

Susanne Weigelin-Schwiedrzik

Preface

China's integration into the international community of states has played a crucial role in its recent history. However, the story of China's transition from empire to nation has to date never been documented in book form. For this reason, the Department of East Asian Studies at the University of Vienna together with the Historical Society for 20th Century China and the Ministry of Education and Research of the Republic of Austria invited more than 100 scholars from all over the world to a conference on China's changing position in the international community called "As China Meets the World" in May 2004. The aim of this conference was to explore a wide range of aspects related to China's integration into and contact with the world so as to gain a deeper understanding of how external factors helped shaping China's internal development during the 20th century. The outcome of this exploration is that there is no internal development in China that could be understood without taking external factors into consideration. The long cherished "challenge and response" paradigm, however, is not sophisticated enough to explain the myriad of possibilities which emerge from looking at fields such as the history of ideas, of media, of science and technology just as thoroughly as a diplomatic, political and economic history. The "challenge and response" paradigm lacks the perspective of dialogue between China and the outside world, it does not motivate scholars to ask how China's inner development has contributed to reshaping the world and how active Chinese scholars and politicians have been in using the outside world in changing China from within. Today, the outside world is not only a challenge to China's internal transformation, China is a challenge to the world.

Instead of selecting papers from all the 13 different panels that took place during the conference the editors decided to focus on one aspect which has recently gained in importance but has long been neglected by China scholars. We found the papers related to China's relationship with and entry into international organizations and into the regime of international law most interesting and therefore asked those scholars who had written original papers for the conference on this question for their contributions. Although we cannot, of course, claim to have covered the whole field, we have succeeded in bringing together a number of articles that open a fresh and new perspective on this aspect of "China meeting the world".

With the conference having taken place in Vienna, our volume starts out with an analysis on the recent development of Sino-Europeans relations as reflected in recent documents both sides published in order to make their expectations known to the respective other side as well as to the public. The outcome of this analysis lays the foundation for the next two articles of the volume as it shows that the PRC government is departing from its earlier stand claiming that the Taiwan and Tibet questions were of mere internal importance allowing for no international involvement whatsoever. Both A. Tom Grunfeld and Judith Hufnagel present an analysis of these two issues which focus on the international perspective with A. Tom Grunfeld looking at the internationalization of the Tibet question resulting from world wide attention to the problem and Judith Hufnagel analyzing the relationship between the two sides of the Taiwan Strait from an international law perspective.

China's transition from empire to nation in its early phase is highlighted by two contributions to this volume. Cixi's funeral, the first ever in Chinese history to allow for representatives from other countries to participate, is described by Margareta Grieszler as a most significant signal of the Qing court's changing self perception and a starting point for a re-arrangement of rituals that is still in flux as of today. Xu Xiaoqun relates to the same process by discussing the late Qing's attempts at reforming the dynastic system in order to prevent it from collapsing. His article shows as much as any other in this volume how China's integration into the world shaped the logic of its internal transformation with internal possibilities of adaptation presiding over the selection of external elements.

China joining the world also implies China cooperating with and becoming a member of international organizations. The League of Nations has lately gained some attention, and it is in this context that Donald Jordan gives us an interesting report on the League of Nation's involvement in China's first major modernization effort of the Nanjing Decade. John K. T. Chao presents to us a meticulous account of how China first joined the United Nations as the Republic of China and member of the Anti-Axis forces and how the Republic of China later lost its seat in the General Assembly as well as the Security Council of the UN as a result of the People's Republic of China making many years of diplomatic efforts.

Finally, two articles look at different aspects of the rule of law in relation to China. Wang Dong writes on China's early attempts to cope with the regime of international law at a time when the Great Powers still looked at China as an unqualified member of the international community. Agnes Schick-Chen leads us back to the present by giving an introduction to how the discussion on the development of legal culture in China can be understood through the discourse on the rule of law versus the rule by law. In both cases, the rule of law stands out as an import from the West very difficult to integrate into Chinese culture and society.

In both cases, the imposition of Western norms turns out to be impossible. Instead, what was once regarded as an imposition has by now turned into an instrument that is used to help China gain a top position among the nations of the world.

While most contributors to this volume participated in the Vienna conference, we would like to thank others, especially Professor John K. T. Chao and Judith Hufnagel, for supplying us with a special contribution to make the collection of articles more encompassing. Dr. Wolfgang Zeidl and Dr. Sascha Klotzbücher were kind enough to translate and edit Professor Chao's article for which we would certainly like to express our thanks. We hope that our selection of articles will not only encourage more colleagues from the China field to consider focusing on diplomatic history and the history of China's foreign relations as a possible field of research. We would also appreciate if the wider public got more interested into understanding how China has during the course of the 20th century emerged as one of the world powers of tomorrow.

Susanne Weigelin-Schwiedrzik
Nele Noesselt

Striving for Symmetry in Partnership: An Analysis of Sino-EU Relations Based on the Two Recently Published Policy Papers

On October 13, 2003, the PRC government published its "*Policy Paper on the Relationship with the EU*". This was the first time in PRC history that the Chinese government made its assessment of and strategic orientation for its relationship with a foreign country or a particular region of the world known to the public. This fact alone shows how much Sino-EU relations have gained in importance and how much hope is vested into the future development of this relationship on the side of the Chinese government. The EU had published its latest policy paper under the title of "*A Maturing Partnership – Shared Interests and Challenges in EU-China Relations*" slightly earlier. In this paper, the EU underlines the maturity of its relationship to China and outlines a prospect of positive developments for the future.

This article aims at comparing the two above mentioned policy papers by giving them a close reading and putting the interpretation of the texts into a historical context as well as into the context of academic debates on EU-China relations as conducted both in China and in Europe. The idea is to explore the mutual perceptions of what both sides call a "maturing" partnership and to assess to which degree their mutual perceptions are compatible with each other.

The China Strategy of the EU

The European Community (transformed into the European Union by the Treaty of Maastricht of 1993) had already established diplomatic relations with the PRC in 1975, several years before the US had done so and as a logical consequence of several EC member states establishing or resuming diplomatic relations with the PRC since the late 1960s. However, in the beginning stages of its relationship, cooperation was confined to import export activities resulting into a Trade Treaty of 1978, renewed in 1985, and a Textile Treaty of 1979. A deepening of this relationship envisioned for the 1980s was jeopardized by the 1989 incident on Tian'anmen Square which was prompted by a halt to contacts. Since 1992 a process of normalization has taken place which has gained momentum since 1995 with the growing interest of both sides pushing the relationship to the point reflected by the two above mentioned policy papers.

The EU's China strategy is marked by a fundamental particularity which makes it different from its policies towards countries of the so called Third World and countries in Eastern Europe. This is first and foremost true for the EU's human rights policies. Safeguarding human rights, developing democracy and introducing the rule of law are basic preconditions the EU demands to be fulfilled both in cooperating with Third World as well as post-socialist countries from Eastern Europe. Although these items are also on the EU's agenda in its relationship to China, the EU does not dispose of any mechanisms to enforce its demands. The instrument of political dialogue established in 1994 does not include any sanctions in case the PRC does not comply with its rules except for the EU interrupting the relationship (as in the case of the Tian'anmen Incident of 1989) or supporting UN resolutions critical of China. Under these circumstances, however, the PRC could call off its participation in the political dialogue depriving the EU of its sole instrument through which to exert at least a certain influence on China (Baker 2002:59)'.

As a consequence of this constellation, the EU's main aim has so far been to convince the PRC government of the necessity to become a positive and active member of the international community of states by accepting and implementing international norms and standards. Simultaneously, the EU tries to accompany the process of internal transformation in the PRC by "developing an overall partnership based on dialogue and oriented towards solving practical problems" (Schubert 2002) avoiding public criticism, confrontation and sanctions. Since 1995 the EU has actively supported reforms of politics and economy in China and thus tried to influence the further development in the PRC:

> "I believe *political reform* will become increasingly irresistible as China's economy opens up to the world. Europe must keep up its support for reform not merely through high-minded statements but through practical and effective actions: *applying political pressure from the top down and helping China create a civic society, including a fully-fledged legal system, from the bottom up.*" (IP/95/731) (Italics added by the author)

Already in its 1995 policy paper "*A Long Term Policy for China-Europe Relations*" (COM (1995) 279) did the EU define human rights questions as of central importance for its cooperation with the PRC. In this paper, human rights issues occupy a sub-chapter of their own in the context of what is called "political relations". Three aims are to be achieved: integrating China into the international community, especially the WTO, supporting reforms in China, especially those related to human rights, and developing economic cooperation between China and the EU. On the top of that, the situation of the so called national minorities (Tibet), and the special situation in Hong Kong and Macau are mentioned separately (COM (1995) 279). This shows that economic interests in cooperating with China had already gained some prominence. Nevertheless, the EU passed an official resolution on December 14, 1995 criticizing the imprisonment of Wei Jingsheng (PESC/95/102) and underlining its insistence on enhancing the human rights situation in the PRC. As a result, the PRC broke off the political dialogue with the EU in 1996.

Since 1996, several EU member states such as France, Spain, Italy, Greece and Germany have refrained from supporting resolutions critical of the human rights situation in the PRC, obviously responding to the needs of more bilateral trade with the PRC. As a result of this, the EU has been unable to define a stand towards human rights issues supported unanimously by all member states (Schubert 2002). A new EU China strategy was implemented in 1998, the keyword of which was a "comprehensive partnership" to be developed between the EU and China (COM (1998) 181). This paper is also a reaction to the CCP's 15th Party Congress which decided on intensifying market reforms, as well as China's role in the Asian Financial Crisis and its involvement in solving regional problems related to Korea, Cambodia and Hong Kong (Wiessala 2002:96). At the same time, the EU stopped backing UN resolutions critical of the human rights situation in the PRC as a trade off for resuming the dialogue on human rights issues with the PRC. From this point on, the EU Parliament rather than the EU Commission has been standing at the forefront of criticism against human rights violations in the PRC, a form of criticism that has so far not had any negative impact on the EU relationship to China as it is only part of an internal discussion process and never officially forwarded to the PRC (Wiessala 2002:97).

With the help of the new concept of "comprehensive partnership" with China formulated in 1998, the political dialogue was intensified and complemented by annual summit meetings between the EU and the PRC. The first summit of this kind took place in April 1998 shortly after the publication of the second China policy on the occasion of the ASEM summit in London. It was during this summit that China's integration into the ASEM process which had started in 1996 was formally proposed underlining the EU's strategy to influence China's process of transformation through integration into international organizations. Bilateral cooperation from this time on has been organized into the very five agendas outlined in the 1998 policy paper and all strategy papers to come. These include the growing integration of China into the international community, the support for the establishment of a society in which the rule of law guarantees the safeguarding of human rights, the promotion of China's integration into the world economy, increasing financial aid from the EU and last but not least efforts to enhance the EU's visibility in the PRC (COM (1998) 181).

Since 1998, the EU has voiced its assessment of EU China relations several times. These assessments reflect the progress of the EU's ability to define its China strategy. They are documented in two important communications called "*Report on the Implementation of the Communication 'Building a Comprehensive Partnership with China*'" (COM (2000) 552) and "*EU Strategy towards China: Implementation of the 1998 Communication and Future Steps for a More Effective EU Policy*" (COM (2001) 265). The March 2002 "*Strategy Paper for China*" also does not depart from the 1998 communication, however it is characterized a shift towards focusing the cooperation on technical and financial development aid for China. For the next five years to come, the EU is willing to support China with 250 million Euros to be spent on sustainable development, on the rule of law and the expansion of civil society. "Good governance" is the primary concern of the EU's China policies, a new orientation which has already been reflected by the EU's aid to the introduction of democratic elements into the Chinese political system such as the experiments with local elections at the grassroots level in the Chinese countryside which have been going on since 1987 (Umbach/Fulda 2003:47–56).

In the summer of 2003 the European Union published its to date latest communication based on the 1995 strategy. The policy paper "*A Maturing Partnership – Shared Interests and Challenges in EU-China Relations*" is quite obviously an attempt to adapt the EU's strategy to the new situation since 2001 both in China and in the EU. The system of political dialogue is expanded in the 2003 paper (COM (2003) 533). What has already been established as regular meetings and arrangements found between the leaders of both sides since 2002 is complemented in this paper by multiple levels of coordination, transforming the top-down structure of cooperation into a more and more complex and multi-facetted system of contacts. With regard to the dialogue on human rights, the EU's policy paper states that the aims formulated in 1995 had been reached with the PRC government basically accepting the human rights mechanisms of the UN and entering the discussion on the UN convention on human rights. The next step as discussed by the EU Council during its meeting on March 18, 2003, would be for the PRC government to ratify the UN convention (PRES/03/63).

While discussions on questions concerning the implementation of human rights continue, additional mechanisms have been created to discuss questions related to the development of information society, of free trade and of nutrition safety. As far as security and technology questions are concerned, the EU and the PRC have decided to intensify their cooperation (Galileo Project) knowing that the technological cooperation would be a much easier to handle issue compared to human rights and the transformation of the political system. Visible successes in this field are expected despite the problems of defining the dividing line between the civil and the military sectors (dual use technologies) and of safeguarding intellectual property by avoiding unintended technology transfers.

Chinese Perspectives on Sino-EU Relations

Friedrich has shown that the Chinese perception of the EU and its policies does not necessarily reflect the matter of fact understanding of the situation. Instead, what academic debates in the PRC are aimed at is to develop a theoretical framework with the help of which to define China's position in the world. That is why he introduces the concept of "articulated perception" as the result of "transferring Chinese conceptions of the world order" to the analysis of the world as such (Friedrich 2000:220). Consequently, any analysis of Sino-EU relations has to take the theoretical framework into account that moulds the "articulated perception". Since the 1980s, this theoretical framework has been marked by the concepts of "independence and self reliance" as well as "multi-polarity" while the concept of triangularity which opens up the opportunity for the PRC to manœuvre between the US and Russia still persists and exerts a certain influence (Friedrich 2000:220–226).

Already since times when the PRC government used the theory of intermediate zones and later on the theory of the three worlds as its theoretical frameworks, Europe was given an important strategic position in the Chinese world order. At the time, PRC strategists knew very well that it could deploy its strengths best when acting as a third global player in situations of bipolar conflicts. During the Cold War, especially since the beginning of Ping-Pong-Diplomacy, this strategy had proven successful which is why the dissolution of the Soviet Union was perceived as a loss of international influence and strength by the Chinese government. A uni-polar world is disadvantageous to the PRC, especially as China is easily pushed into the unfavorable position of a counter pole to dominant power structures. Consequently, the PRC government reiterates the necessity of a multipolar world order, trying to act as often as possible as mediator in upcoming conflicts.

Only when several poles compete with each other, does the PRC have the possibility to choose between different options in its strategic orientation (Xi Runchang 2000:45–48). The centre of its attention is the necessity to secure a stable and peaceful situation for economic growth in terms of the overall global situation as well as of the countries in its immediate neighborhood. The development of strategic alliances, for example with the EU, the US or with India, reflects a modern understanding of international politics as well as the self assessment on the side of the PRC government of a regional power pursuing its legitimate interests as part of the international community.

The US, Europe, Russia and Japan are together with the PRC the five poles of the multi-polar system. The rise of the US as a consequence of the decline of Russia, however, threatens the continued existence of the multi-polar system. In response to this, both government and academic publications in the PRC underline that the PRC's foreign policy is still based on the "Five Principles of Peaceful Co-Existence" and therefore aimed at avoiding military conflicts in international politics (Liu Qingcai 2001:104–109).

The PRC has always encouraged the EU to take over the role of a pole in the multi-polar system underlining a common foreign policy as well as an independent defense strategy as two important preconditions for taking over this role. That is why the position of a High Representative for the Common Foreign and Security Policy, created by the Treaty of Amsterdam and currently held by Javier Solana, the role of the EU Troika as well as plans to organize a European army independent of NATO structures are seen by academics from the PRC as steps into the right direction (Feng Zhongping 2004a:51).

Even though the EU and China both officially declare that their political dialogue in its institutionalized form as well as their growing relationship is not directed against third parties, the academic discussion in the PRC reveals a slightly different perspective as it does not reiterate the idea that Sino-EU relations could be confined to fulfilling the respective self interests. Instead academic contributions to the discussion underline that strengthening relations with the EU serves the purpose of counterbalancing the hegemonic tendencies of the US.

> "As the superiority of the Sino EU strategy is reflected in the economic sphere rather than in the realm of military power, the EU and China stand for a new political and economic order as a result of reforms and not for a form of military superiority as a means to dominate the world as displayed by the US." (Liu Wenxiu 2002:71)

Chinese researchers conceive of the EU as using financial incentives as well as means of cooperation and dialogue in order to transfer its system of norms and structures to other countries. It is in this context that they cast an eye over the situation of post-socialist countries in Eastern Europe and their integration into the EU. They pay close attention to the fact that with its expansion into Eastern Europe the EU has not only enlarged its geographical space and economic power, it has also gained in importance as a focus of identification. With this gain of symbolic power the EU is prepared to apply more successfully as in the past hard power strategies vis à vis third party states, but, what is even more important, its preconditions for applying soft power strategies have been enhanced especially in multi-lateral contexts. Consequently, according to the academic discourse in the PRC, China will have to cope with the EU making stronger efforts to export its own ("capitalist") values, especially its understanding of human rights, to Asia (Wang Haixia 2003:21–22; Zeng Yuan 2001:59).

Also in security matters has the EU gained in importance since its expansion into Eastern Europe. This implies that the EU could be regarded as a potential counter player besides the US and Japan, especially if the EU decided to interfere with what China regards as the geopolitical order of Asia. That is why those researchers interested in questions of geo-strategy and security argue in favour of China developing its cooperation with the EU and the US simultaneously in order to use one to restrict the other with the aim of consolidating China's position in the region (Xiao 2004:49).

The main difference between the academic discourse in the PRC and in Europe consists in a difference of assessment regarding the importance of the EU in the realm of international relations and the implications of the human rights issue for Sino-EU relations. Only recently has the Chinese academic discourse acknowledged the weight of the EU in international politics as equaling the importance of the US, Japan and Russia (Feng Zhongping 2004a:49).This is clearly due to the progressing integration of Europe and the ongoing discussion on the European constitution. However, the two discourses do not show any sign of conversion when it comes to discussing the implications of the human rights issue for Sino-EU relations. While the EU regards the human rights issue as highly important not only as a matter of principle but also in order to avoid being labeled as only pursuing selfish economic interests, academics in the PRC tend to downgrade this problem and its relevance for the future relationship between the PRC and the EU.

The situation in Hong Kong is another aspect of Sino-EU relations the implications of which are often overlooked by researchers from the PRC. This contrasts sharply with the EU's view that the former British crown colony should be regarded as "an agent of change" helping to transfer (Western) standards of administration as well as human rights to the polity of the PRC. During his term as the last British Governor of Hong Kong as well as in his capacity as the EU's Commissioner for External Affairs Chris Patten did not miss any chance to make this point clear (Wiessala 2002:98–99). Macao, too, is seen as a model for China, especially as Macao belongs to the founding members of the WTO (Wiessala 2002:101). But neither the Chinese government nor academic discourse raises these issues. Instead, they tend to underline that there are no direct conflicts inhibiting the relations between the EU and China from progressing as contrary to China's relations with Russia and Japan there are no territorial or border conflicts involved.

The Chinese EU Policy

With its EU policy paper the PRC for the first time in the 30 year history of Sino-EU relations makes its view of this strategic partnership known to the public. No comparable strategy paper has so far been published with regard to China's relations with ASEAN states or the US, with other countries of the region or other regional organizations.

The Chinese EU policy was published on October 13, 2003 only shortly after the EU had made its own strategy paper for future relations with China known to the public (COM (2003) 533). The document is subdivided into four parts. In its introduction, it defines the position of Sino-EU relations in the realm of international politics. This is followed by remarks about "the status and the role of the EU" and a chapter on the "Chinese policy toward the EU". The final chapter is dedicated to "deepening Sino-EU relations in all fields". This is where the PRC government outlines its view for the next five years of cooperation.

In the introduction, the paper reiterates the PRC's view on a multi-polar globalised world in which peace, stability and development have to be maintained. It transfers the notion of "*xiaokang shehui*" (welfare society) from the realm of internal politics to the international field defining a fair world order of equal rights as the aim to be achieved by a "foreign policy of independence and self reliance". In this context, the EU takes over the role of a regional and global player which is economically integrated by a common currency and geographically expanded to 25 member states.

A central argument of the paper deals with the necessity of a partnership of equals, based on mutual respect (*huzhong*), mutual confidence (*huxin*), mutual advantage (*huli*), and reciprocity (*huhui*). Cooperation is asked for in the fields of politics, economy, science and technology as well as education. Social, administrative, and judicial aspects as well as the military sector are mentioned. In the realm of politics, the PRC document is mostly interested in questions of stability, both in terms of internal and regional politics. This includes problems of labour migration, social security, human resources, poverty alleviation, and pollution control. When referring to the limits of the EU's Taiwan policies, the insistence on the One-China-Principle and the EU's stand toward the issues of Tibet, Hong Kong, and Macao, the PRC paper reiterates the Chinese government's position on maintaining and safeguarding territorial integrity and sovereignty.

The issue of regional and international security is covered in a comparatively long sub- chapter of the paper. The PRC wants both sides to get involved in finding solutions for regional problems (i.e. North Korea) and to strengthen international cooperation by actively participating in UN and ASEM activities. The PRC paper also backs the fight against international terrorism as well as activities for international arms control before taking up the issue of military cooperation and lifting the EU arms embargo.

This shows that the PRC government is primarily concerned with using foreign politics as an instrument of reaching aims in the realm of internal politics. Its relations with the EU are seen as favorable in terms of economic growth and social stability. Questions of international concern are only raised if in the interest of both sides. This means that no demands are being forwarded that are not or only indirectly linked to the EU as well as no issues are being raised which are of concern only for the EU and not for China. The issues that are being raised as possible fields of cooperation read like the agenda of the PRC government for solving social problems in China. The inclusion of classical issues of development policies such as migration, poverty alleviation, pollution control, public health and similar topics reflects the new leadership's concern for questions of social stability, a political orientation that has long been asked for, but which did not form the focus of attention of the Jiang Zemin/Zhu Rongji leadership. Quite obviously, the new leadership sees these problems as major risk factors for the social and political stability of the country.

The fact that the PRC paper subsumes the Tibet problem to the possible fields of cooperation shows a slight, but important deviation from its earlier stance. While it used to insist that the Tibet question was a question of internal politics where international involvement should be rejected as an infringement of sovereignty, the PRC paper now asks for the EU's support for its Tibet as well as Taiwan policies. In contrast to its earlier stance, the PRC now tries to instrumentalise its international partners for reaching aims that had so far been explicitly left to internal politics.

The principles raised in the introduction of the paper are easily put aside as formulae without content. However, they should not be neglected as they reflect the self perception of China's position in the world. China regards itself as strong enough to demand equality in its international partnerships. External norms imposed on China therefore potentially violate the principle of equality no matter whether they relate to questions of economics or of politics. To raise certain demands and to define their fulfillment as a precondition to future collaboration as the EU tries in the case of its cooperation with Third World countries seems utterly counterproductive and will only meet with repulsion from the PRC government.

Diverging Orientations and Terminologies

The China policy as forwarded by the EU defines the aims of Sino-EU relations in two areas: on the one hand as support for "China in its transition to an open society based on the rule of law and on human rights", on the other hand as promoting the "opening of China's economy" (COM [2003] 533). The development of civil society, the establishment of an open society and progress toward a full fledged market economy are mentioned. All this taken together equals a system change for the PRC. Also in the fields of cooperation on issues of law and administration as well as what China's integration into the WTO is concerned, the EU policy defines standards and criteria for the PRC to comply with. The PRC paper is silent on these issues, preferring to stress economic growth as the result of Sino-EU relations hoped for.

The two policy papers quite obviously have conflicting policy aims. From the point of view of the PRC government, the EU's demands for fundamental change in China are the main obstacle to a "maturing partnership" which is alluded to in both papers. The EU's hope for what amounts to a system change in China violates the principle of a "partnership of equals" formulated in the Chinese paper and reveals a lack of equality which the Chinese side so urgently asks for in the introduction to its paper. Even though commentators on both sides applauded the positive development of Sino-EU relations in responding to the two policies, a closer look reveals a certain autism on both sides that is quite remote from an adequate understanding of respective particularities and respect for diverging interests. The Chinese side keeps silent on all issues that are not directly related to its economic interests and security considerations. This silence, however, does not prevent the EU from sticking to its hope of transferring its own norms to the PRC.

"Governance" is one of the keywords that are frequently used in the EU's China policy. The term refers to the problem of "governability" on two levels. When used in the sense of "global governance" it refers to the realm of regional and international politics whereas it is used in the sense of "good governance" in the context of the rule of law, of transparent administrative structures and democracy. However, the fact that this is a keyword of central importance for the EU policy paper does not mean that the Chinese paper would adopt or else respond to it (for a discussion of the concept of "governance" in the PRC see Wang Yizhou 2000:30). When looking at the academic debate in the PRC, one will easily find an answer to this lack of responsiveness: the term does not play a major role in these discussions, and it is quite difficult to find an adequate translation for the term to begin with. Two possibilities occur in the few texts related to the issue: "*shanzhi*" stands for the art of governing, *"zhili"* for rules of governing and administration. No matter what term they use all participants in the debate stress that good governance is only possible if based on the cooperation of government institutions with non government organizations. The capabilities of the state are to be complemented by the self organization of society so that the state is in a better position to maintain its rule over society. Very often the term "governance" in the sense of *"zhili"* is used when discussing questions of rural administration or of "corporate governance". However, "governance" in the sense of the EU policy does not occur in Chinese language articles on the topic. That is why, where the EU paper speaks about governance, the Chinese paper does not[1]. The human rights issue is mentioned in the EU paper as a problem of governance, while the PRC paper raises it in the context of "political dialogue". As the two papers were published consecutively, the fact that the Chinese side refrains from joining into the use of the term "good governance" has to be seen as a conscious departure from EU terminology.

When Chinese authors use the term "governance", they refer to the situation in rural areas. The EU however is focused on the situation in the more developed urban areas. During recent months, many reports about unrest in the Chinese countryside have shown that overcoming the rural urban dichotomy by ameliorating life in the Chinese countryside is a precondition to making China stable for the future. If the EU continues to overlook this problem and instead continues to focus on the situation in urban areas, its hope for a positive development in China might be jeopardized by growing unrest in Chinese villages. The development in Eastern Europe is not a model for what is happening in China. To hope that the situation in China might follow the rules of peaceful regime change in Eastern Europe means designing a future for China which is unlikely to be matched by what is going to happen. The high percentage of rural population still marks a major particularity of post-Mao China that any scenario for the future development has to take in account.

According to Minxin Pei (2002) China's governance crisis is a crisis of rural areas and structures. The loss of legitimacy and esteem for the CCP has led to a loss of state control as well as state services in the countryside. Regional disparities, a deepening divide between state and society, and a more and more obvious gap between rich and poor go along with a diminishing capacity of the CCP to maintain its power monopoly. Conflicts between state and society aggravate, as the state gets rid of its enterprises and ideologically and politically motivated mass campaigns are replaced by an orientation toward economic success, putting the CCP into a position where its claim to power monopoly in China is measured against economic growth. As long as the CCP leadership is unwilling or unable to

[1] The Chinese Policy Paper on the EU does not mention the term "*zhili*", but refers to "*guanli*", which can be translated as "managing". However, the term "*guanli*" appears only in the chapters on transport, finance and environmental issues, which in this context do not belong to the European concept of "*governance*" (*Zhongguo dui Oumeng zhengce wenjian* 2003, chapter 2.3; 2.4; 2.7).

find a solution for what some people call the negative consequences of its reform policy, the danger of growing local unrest, especially in the densely populated areas of Hunan, Henan, and Anhui might well lead to an overall destabilization of CCP rule in China (Pei 2002).

To focus on the democratization of China's urban areas complies with EU principles, however, under the given circumstances in the PRC, this strategy involves the danger that a weakened state loses control of the rural areas and cannot prevent rural society from exerting a destructive influence on the cities. There will be no space for civil society any more, and hopes for the development of a market economy will be jeopardized by social destabilization.

The Chinese policy paper develops the concept that the EU should support China's economic development and administrative capacities. It reiterates the PRC's demand for equality in the partnership time and again using wordings such as "collaboration" (*hezuo*), "exchange" (*jiaoliu*), "reciprocity" (*huhui*) and "constructive understanding" (*liaojie*) wherever possible. It does, of course, not envisage system change. Cooperation in the fields of agriculture, sustainable development and in the energy sector is welcome, but only if not damaging to the overall demand for a partnership of equals. In future, China not only wants European institutions and delegations to come to China, it also wants its own financial institutions and other facilities to become active in Europe.

On the other hand, the PRC paper picks up some of the basic issues raised by the EU Commission since 1995. The terminology of "political dialogue" and human rights appears as an integral part of the paper's vocabulary, for example. But as natural as the usage of these words seems to be, a closer look reveals that even in this domain, the two partners have a different understanding of one and the same word. For the PRC only those topics are worth mentioning under the title of "political dialogue" that are controversial and at the same time high on China's list of priorities. That is why the "One-China-Policy" and the future of Hong Kong, Macao and Tibet are subsumed in the category of "political dialogue" while problems such as illegal migration, trans-national pollution and arms export – all of vital importance for the EU – do not fall under this category. Both partners have the safeguarding of peace and international stability on their agendas, however these issues are part of what the EU calls global governance and not of "international cooperation", a term used in the PRC paper rooted in an understanding of international politics based on the concept of sovereignty.

When it comes to the problem of political transformation, the PRC side asks for an exchange of political parties and institutions avoiding the keywords the EU uses in this context. Take the keyword "civil society" as an example. The Chinese side does not use it in its paper although it has long since been established in the academic discourse in the PRC where the term is adapted to the political system so that even the mass organizations of the CCP can be included[2]. No wonder that delegations from these organizations can be exchanged under the category of "strengthening civil society".

Conflicts of Strategic Dimensions: Arms Embargo, Market Economy Status and Measures to counter Terrorism

Not only on the level of language and wording do we find diverging ideas between the EU and the PRC. The strategic partnership both sides like to herald also reveals a divergence of strategic orientations. This becomes obvious when reading the PRC based interpretations of the two policy papers.

On October 14, 2003, one day after the official publication of the PRC document, the state news agency *Xinhua* published a commentary to the Chinese policy paper. In this commentary, three aspects are underlined: China's demand for an end to the EU's arms embargo that has been in effect since the PRC government's bloody suppression of the students' movement in 1989, the demand for an officially acknowledged market economy status and China's hope for a close cooperation with the EU in fighting international terrorism (Xinhua 10/14/2003). The three aspects mentioned by Xinhua should play a key role in all other commentaries to be published and are crucial for an adequate understanding of the PRC's paper. Up until today, even academic commentaries refer to these main ideas.

An April 2005 article in the academic journal International Studies (*Guoji wenti yanjiu*) by Huo Zhengde argues that based on what Xinhua had selected as the three major aspects of the policy paper the Sino-EU relationship cannot be assessed as a "mature partnership". As long as the EU did not lift its sanctions against the PRC, the EU's policy could only be understood as an attempt to westernize (*xihua*) China by unconditionally adopting European concepts of human rights and the rule of law. In addition to criticizing the EU for its attempt to transfer its norms and models to China, Huo also mentions that the EU applies different standards when assessing counter terrorist measures. What the EU sup-

[2] See Yu Keping's study on "*civil society*" and "*good governance*", in which he analyses the changing definition of the Chinese civil society (*gongmin shehui*) and its position in the political system in relation to China's domestic development. He also refers to mass organizations of the CCP (workers' union, youth organization) in the 1990s: Yu Keping: Zhongguo gongmin shehui de xingqi ji qi dui zhili de yiyi (The rising of a Chinese civil society and its governance implications). Available online: http://www.gongfa.com/civilsocietyykp.htm (22.07.2005). See also: Yu Keping et al. (2002) (eds.): Gongmin shehui de xingqi he zhili de bianqian. Beijing: Shehui kexue wenzhai chubanshe.

ports as counter terrorism in one country is being criticized in the context of East-Turkestan, Xinjiang, Taiwan and Hong Kong (Huo Zhengde 2005:4–5).

Huo Zhengde's articles make clearer what had been left slightly vague in the above mentioned Xinhua commentary. As part of its fight against terrorism on its own territory, the PRC seems to seek support from those countries and regions like the EU and its member states which acknowledge the PRC as the only legitimate representative of the Chinese people. This includes supporting the Beijing government in its repulsion of Taiwan's demand for independence. This new turn toward internationalizing the Taiwan issue can be understood as a reaction to the EU's policies toward Russia and Chechnya. To subsume the Taiwan issue into the category of counter terrorism means that China is aimed at gaining international support even for violent steps against Taiwan. As a matter of fact, this argument was put forward quite frankly in a TV discussion broadcasted by the Chinese TV. Participants of this discussion used the term "to chechnise Taiwan" when comparing the situation in Chechnya and in Taiwan. In both cases, the demand for independence was interpreted as a form of separatism with governmental actions against it seen as measures of counter terrorism (Fenghuang 2004). When the PRC used to stress international involvement in the Taiwan question was unacceptable, the new Taiwan policy seeks the opportunity to internationalize the question in times of the international fight against terrorism. The above mentioned TV discussion was by no means a discussion on internal politics. On the contrary, it was a discussion on counter terrorist policies in Russia, on the third anniversary of 9/11 and on the problem of nuclear weapons in East Asia. Thus, the Taiwan question was raised in the context of international politics and the legitimacy of this approach underlined by outlining the scenario of a nuclear armed Taiwan demanding independence. Looking at Taiwan's independence from this angle, the argument goes, it is quite clear that it is for the benefit of the international community to support China's claim for national unity even if forwarded by force.

If this interpretation of the situation is correct, it forces us to look at the partnership between the EU and China from a different angle. What seemed to be a lack of equality in the partnership to the disadvantage of the PRC turns out to be a chance for China to treat its endurance of the EU's insistence on system change for the EU's support for China's policy against Taiwan. In both cases, demands are being raised that are over-demanding which again reveals the "mature partnership" to be a dream for the future rather than an adequate description of the status quo. Only if the EU goes so far as to unconditionally support the PRC in whatever measure it might take to "safeguard national unity" the precondition of the Chinese side for a further deepening of the partnership is fulfilled. And only if the PRC is willing to undergo system change is the ground set for what the EU envisages as the future of the relationship of equals.

The Xinhua commentary also sees international terrorism as the main threat to peace and stability (Xinhua 10/14/2003). As the EU has a similar assessment of the international situation, this opens up the opportunity to cooperate on an international level and for the PRC to be an acknowledged participant of the worldwide fight against terrorism. This again supports the PRC's claim to act as mediator in regional conflicts related to terrorism. It is in this context that Feng Zhongping analyses the EU's stand toward talks with North Korea and comes to the conclusion that in contrast to the US, the EU does not favor a policy of isolating North Korea. Instead it prefers dialogue as a means of avoiding military conflict in East Asia. Consequently, with China participating in the North Korea talks, it can lend support to the EU's stand and thus underline its role as a stabilizing factor in the region. To some degree, this situation adds to the attractiveness of a "deepened partnership between the EU and the PRC" especially as the EU is still weakened in its international activities by a lack of common strategy for East Asia (Feng Zhongping 2004b).

Besides striving for international support for its Taiwan policy and for unequivocal commitment to its One-China-Policy the PRC aims at a normalization of Sino-EU relations by demanding a lift of the arms embargo and for acknowledgement of its market economy status. This becomes very clear when taking the fact into account that the PRC's strategy paper refrains from voicing an overall assessment of Sino-EU relations at the end of the paper, but finishes it with a rather abrupt reference to the EU's arms embargo. Quite obviously, the market economy status and the lift of the arms embargo are two major preconditions to a deepening of the relationship (*Zhongguo dui Oumeng zhengce wenjian* 2003).

The arms embargo is also raised as an issue by several authoritative commentaries published together with the internet version of the PRC document. All of these commentaries refer to the problem of the arms embargo either in their titles or in their texts[3]. Only if the EU complies with the PRC's demands and puts an end to the sanctions as well as trade restrictions, these commentaries say, is it possible for the partnership to develop positively. The then Chinese ambassador in Germany Ma Congrong puts this idea into the following words:

> "The continuation of the embargo was 'discriminating', Ma said. 'It's an embarrassment. It hinders the relationship. We cannot have a normal relationship with the EU as long as the embargo is in place.' " (International Herald Tribune 04/06/2005).

---

[3] See for example *Renmin Ribao* (10/29/2003): "*Jiechu dui Hua junshoujinling – Tuidong Zhong-Ou guanxi wending fazhan: Zhonggou shouci fabiao dui Oumeng zhengce wenjian*" (Lifting the arms embargo – Promoting the stable development of Sino-EU relations: China issues its first policy paper on the EU).

In the eyes of China's Prime Minister Hu Jintao, the arms embargo is "a product of the Cold War" (*lengzhan chanwu*). It has to be removed to put an end to the "discrimination (*qishi*) of China" (*Xinhua* 12/8/2004). The idea of partnership, says Hu Jintao, excludes the privilege of one side to punish the other through sanctions. Thus the PRC should not be misconceived as being passive in its partnership with the EU, to the contrary, China wants to actively mould the partnership according to its own requirements.

It is important to note that the Chinese side likes to underline that the lifting of the arms embargo is but a symbolic act of only minor practical consequences. It is widely known that the PRC imports products from the EU which are needed for the modernization of its army. To downgrade the political meaning of lifting the arms embargo therefore mostly serves the purpose of refuting the argument that Taiwan's security could be affected by this move. Symbolic might also mean that rather than helping the PRC to buy more weapons for its army, the EU's lift of the arms embargo could be counted as a major diplomatic success for China's foreign policy and its strive for "equality", "normalization" and multiple options in international politics. Not symbolic, but clearly practical would be the result of lifting the arms embargo if the PRC used its success to convince Russia to continue selling weapons and to reconsider the sales conditions in the face of growing competition from EU member states (Umbach 2005b:75).

Apart from the problem of the arms embargo, Chinese commentaries raise yet another problem impeding the partnership of equals (Xinhua 10/14/2003): The EU has not yet acknowledged China as a country with a full fledged market economy even though by the year 2005 the EU had grown to be the most important trade partner of China, ranking first before the US and Japan (Renmin Ribao 4/29/2005). The PRC has already tried to gain acknowledgement of its "market economy status" since 1998 when it was taken from the EU's list of "non market economy" countries. Every time the EU rejected the request on the basis of its examinations having shown deficits in four our of five areas under scrutiny: in the banking sector, concerning property rights and insolvency regulations, corporate governance and the reduction of state involvement into companies (MEMO/04/163).

The 2004 Summit: a Deepening of Partnership?

After the EU-China Summit in The Hague in December 2004 both sides reiterated their interest in intensifying cooperation. The EU showed its acknowledgement for the PRC's continuing reform efforts and regarded its own strategies for China as successful. On this basis, the EU made certain concessions while the Chinese side tried to flatter its partner by underlining the growing importance of the EU as a result of its expansion into Eastern Europe (Joint Statement 12/8/2004). However, the Chinese Prime Minister Hu Jintao did not miss the chance to explain China's principles of international politics and to renew, even before the summit, the demand to lift the arms embargo and to comply with the One-China-Principle. Thus he did not refrain from criticizing members of the EU parliament who keep in close contact with President Chen Shuibian. The latter had been rejected the necessary visa procedures for a visit to Europe which had been planned for the spring of 2005. However, in spite of diplomatic pressures from the PRC a video conference took place on March 1, 2005 in which members of the EU parliament discussed the consequences of the PRC's Anti-Secession Law for Taiwan with Chen Shuibian.

China's demand for a partnership of equals was reiterated underlining that future cooperation should be based on understanding (*xianghu liaojie*) and confidence (*xianghu xinren*) (Ministry of Foreign Affairs PRC 12/10/2004), indirectly hinting at the transfer of norms and standards to be unacceptable for the Chinese side.

An agreement was signed during the summit on the non-proliferation of weapons of mass destruction and on arms control. As Chris Patten already explained before the summit, these two agreements as well as the acknowledgement of the international code of conduct were necessary preconditions to be fulfilled before the lifting of the arms embargo could come into effect. Additionally, Chris Patten asked for progress in questions of human rights (SPEECH/04/483,11/16/2004). Thus, he was referring to the code of conduct for arms exports from EU member states that had been in existence since 1998. However, a global agreement which had been discussed by the EU Parliament before the summit in The Hague is still pending.

Some EU member states, among them France and Germany, backed the demands raised by the Chinese side in its 2003 policy asking for a lifting of the arms embargo as a sign of normalization and deepening of partnership. This argument, however, was met with severe criticism from NGOs since the National People's Congress passed the Anti-Secession-Law in March 2005 (*Fan fenlie guojia fa* 03/14/2005). They regard lifting the arms embargo as a wrong signal in times of tightening relations across the straits and ask for progress in human rights issues as well. Otherwise, an aggravation of the human rights situation and threats of violence against Taiwan and against national minorities on the mainland would be the bitter consequence of the EU's decision. If the EU accepted these consequences, major damage for its image and trustworthiness could not be excluded (Report on Human Rights 36, Gesellschaft für bedrohte Völker GFBV:2004).

While France and Germany continue to support the call for a lift of the arms embargo, Great Britain sides with the US in voicing its reservations. However, as the UK seems to prefer not to "solve" the arms embargo dilemma during the British EU presidency, a shift in the strategic orientations of the UK and its participation in a new discussion on a code of conduct as necessary preconditions for a lifting of the embargo are likely to occur.

The US have in the meantime threatened with sanctions against the EU in case the decision in favor of lifting the embargo should be taken, the argument being that this decision would contribute to a further tightening of tensions between Taiwan and the mainland and to destabilizing East Asia (Umbach 2005a:49). The US regards its interests as violated and criticizes the Sino-EU cooperation in the field of satellite technology (Galileo) and the export of "dual use" technologies (Umbach 2004).

The EU faces criticism both from inside and outside regarding the lifting of the arms embargo. That is the reason why the decision which had originally been planned for June 2005 has been postponed indefinitely. On a supra-national level, however, the EU continues to comply with the PRC's demand without, of course, giving an exact date, when the High Representative for the EU's Common Foreign and Security Policy, Javier Solana, says:

> "It is our aim to totally normalize relations with China and to lift the last sanctions that have been in effect since the Tian'anmen-Incident in 1989. China has a new generation of leaders, and in future we should be able to avoid sanctions. With regards to the embargo, this is a political and not a military decision." (Handelsblatt 04/15/16/17/2005)

Umbach argues in his analysis of the arms embargo issue that the outcome of the summit in The Hague shows how the contents of the strategy papers and the reality of Sino-EU relations gape enormously. The EU did not use the opportunity to relate the lifting of the embargo to the demand of having the UN Convention on Human Rights ratified by the Chinese side. Additionally, he criticizes the fact that the EU simply ignores security issues in its policies toward China and takes decisions solely based on economic considerations. As a consequence, compromises are found at Taiwan's expense and the so called "strategic partnership" is asymmetric in the sense of a "multi-lateral kowtow" of EU members to the PRC (Umbach 2005b). His statement shows that the above mentioned asymmetry in Sino-EU relations is not only perceived by the Chinese side, it can also be argued to exist if looked at through the angle of EU interests. This assessment of Sino-EU relations casts even more doubts on the validity of what is called "a maturing partnership" in both policy papers!

With regard to economy and trade, the summit discussed the necessity of compliance with WTO rules and with the TRIPS agreement (safeguarding of intellectual property), and a treaty against smuggle and illegal copying of trademark products was signed. The President of the EU Commission, José Manuel Barroso, underlined in his press release China's responsibility as a global player in sticking to a moderate and stable export orientation and developing close ties with the EU (SPEECH/04/523). As a plan for the future, both sides agreed on designing a new framework program for the development of Sino-EU relations and for deepening mutual understanding through the instrument of political dialogue.

Since December 2004, the PRC government has been waiting for the acknowledgement of market economy status in vain. The EU stresses that it is not due to political considerations, but due to lacking technical preconditions that this step has still not been taken (MEMO 04/163), the Chinese side refers to several anti-dumping charges put forward against China by the EU, criticizing the EU for its protectionist tendencies (Huo Zhengde 2005). In case of acknowledging China's market economy status, the WTO rules would not make these measures impossible, but at least more difficult to pursue. China is also unhappy about the situation because Russia was granted market economy status in May and June 2002 by the EU and the US.

With President Barroso stressing China's responsibility as a global player, the EU reveals its strategic orientations in the realm of economics. In early 2005, the global quota system for textile products expired and the export of Chinese T-shirts to the EU market grew by 187% during the first four months of the year (if compared to the year 2004) (FAZ 06/10/2005). On June 10, 2005, the EU and China signed a textile agreement in which the Chinese side compromised on the issue by promising to self restrict its export to the EU (MEMO 05/201). Peter Mandelson, the responsible commissioner for trade, saw in this step a sign for the possibility of intensifying the Sino-EU partnership in the future:

> "Today's agreement is a significant demonstration that China is entering the global economy as a responsible and valued partner [...] China is entitled to reap the comparative advantages and its WTO accession, while managing its integration into the global economy in a way that avoids fear of China , and in a way that does not provoke a protectionist backlash by European industry and the general public." (SPEECH/05/344:10-06-2005)

The PRC's concessions should not let us forget that there are still some unresolved issues obstructing the partnership. When the EU Troika visited China in June 2005, the PRC government did not rest to reiterate that the lift of the arms embargo was still pending thus criticizing the EU's position in the Taiwan issue.

Conclusion

The two policy papers discussed in this article reflect a growing interest of both sides to deepen the relationship. The EU policy stresses its access to the Chinese market and the possibility to gain in international influence by cooperating with China. However, the EU cannot influence the situation in China as much as it has done so in Eastern Europe and in Third World developing countries. Nevertheless, the EU likes to refer to the positive experience of transformation in Eastern Europe since the end of the Cold War and to positive results in its cooperation with Third World countries. Despite the overall positive assessment of the relationship, the Chinese side still fears a transfer of norms and standards connected with the EU's financial support and technological cooperation. This is an obstacle to the development of the partnership although the EU has never tried to define the PRC's compliance with norms it had demanded from Eastern European countries as a precondition to cooperation, but refers to the system of political dialogue as a means of reaching rapprochement in areas of dissent.

The Chinese side does not refrain from putting forward demands that are difficult to fulfill for the EU. As a reaction to the EU asking for an open society and a full fledged market economy, the PRC tries to use its relationship with the EU as support for its Taiwan policies and for enhancing its position as a regional power in East Asia. In this context, China's demand for the lifting of the arms embargo is of crucial importance. The PRC government is trying to get the same kind of support against Taiwan's "separatism" as Putin for his policies in Chechnya. If the EU complies with these demands, the asymmetry of the partnership as perceived by the Chinese side is healed. If not, as happened on the occasion of the last major summits, the reality of the partnership cannot develop to the level that is described in the two EU policies.

The two policies show fundamental differences in their strategic orientations. Even though both speak positively of cooperation their stance in many crucial questions are quite divergent. This is especially obvious when the EU stresses the necessity of a system change in China to be supported by its soft power strategy while China is interested in the EU as support to its effort of attaining economic growth and political stability simultaneously. For China, complying with its demands for a One-China Policy and acknowledging equality in the partnership are two necessary preconditions to be fulfilled for future cooperation. This means that the strategic orientations of the two partners do not reflect mutual respect and understanding to a degree that should be expected if both sides speak of a mature partnership. Instead, both sides cling to their respective interests and speak in positive terms of a good collaboration that is, as we have shown, blind to what the other side is concerned with.

That is why the political dialogue both sides seem to applaud has not yet shown results that really stand for a deepening of mutual understanding. This becomes very clear when we see that the EU's concept of supporting change in China through integration into international organizations is met with severe criticism. In addition, the specific challenges politics in China have to face up to do not seem to have made enough influence on the EU's China policy. The PRC counters the EU's demand for system change by asking for support for its Taiwan policy as a means of healing the asymmetry of Sino-EU relations has so far not attracted enough attention.

Susanne Weigelin-Schwiedrzik and Nele Noesselt, Department of East Asian Studies, University of Vienna

References

Baker, Philip (2002): Human Rights, Europe and the People's Republic of China. In: The China Quarterly (Mar. 2002), 45–63.

COM (1995) 279: A Long Term Policy for China-Europe Relations. http://europa.eu.int/comm/external_relations/china/com95_279en.pdf (January 20, 2005).

COM (1998) 181: Building a Comprehensive Partnership with China. http://europa.eu.int/comm/external_relations/china/com_98/index.htm (January 20, 2005).

COM (2000) 552: Report on the Implementation of the Communication "Building a Comprehensive Partnership with China". http://europa.eu.int/comm/external_relations/china/report_2000.htm (January 20, 2005).

COM (2001) 252: The European Union's Role in Promoting Human Rights and Democratization in Third Countries. http://europa.eu.int/eur-lex/en/com/pdf/2001/en_501PC0252.pdf (January 20, 2005).

COM (2001) 265: EU Strategy towards China: Implementation of the 1998 Communication and future steps for a more effective EU Policy. http://europa.eu.int/comm/external_relations/china/com01_265.pdf (January 20, 2005).

COM (2003) 533: A Maturing Partnership – Shared Interests and Challenges in EU-China Relations.http://europa.eu.int/comm/external_relations/china/com_03_533/com_533_en.pdf (January 20, 2005).

Fan fenlie guojia fa (03/14/2005). 反分裂国家法 (Anti-Secession Law). http://www.china.org.cn/chinese/PI-c/810355.htm (June 25, 2005).

FAZ (06/10/2005): EU und China legen Handelsstreit über Textilien bei. (EU and China Settle Trade Dispute over Textiles). http://www.faz.net/s/Rub28FC768942F34C5B8297CC6E16FFC8B4/Doc~E6880397FC4294616BF16E243AC52E35F~ATpl~Ecommon~Scontent.html (June 27, 2005).

Fenghuang (2004): 俄罗斯反恐 (Counter-terrorist Measures in Russia) http://www.phoenixtv.com/home/fhkp/html/489/singlepage326097.html (July 17, 2005).

Feng Zhongping (冯仲平) (2004a): 中国对欧盟政策文件初析 (A First Analysis on China's Policy Paper on the EU). In: 外交学院学报 (Journal of China Foreign Studies University) 75 (Mar. 2004), 49–53.

Feng Zhongping (冯仲平) (2004b): 欧盟在六方会谈门口外张望 (The EU's Outsider Perspective on the Six-Party-Talks). In: 世界知识 (World Affairs) 5/2004. http://www.qikan.com.cn/gbqikan/mag.asp?issn=0583-0176&year=2004&periodnum=5 (June 27, 2005).

Friedrich, Stefan (2000): China und die Europäische Union (China and the European Union). Hamburg: Institut für Asienkunde.

Gesellschaft für Bedrohte Völker GFBV (2004): Report on Human Rights 36. Plädoyer für eine neue Chinapolitik der Europäischen Union (For a new EU Policy Towards China). http://www-alt.gfbv.de/dokus/dokinh.htm (July 20, 2005).

Handelsblatt (04/15/16/17/2005):Wir wollen keineswegs mehr Waffen nach China liefern. (In no Case Do We Want to Sell More Weapons to China.) [Interview with Javier Solana], 8.

Huo Zhengde (火正德) (2005): 论中欧战略关系 (On the Strategic Relations between China and the EU). In: 国际问题研究 (International Studies) 2, 1–6.

International Herald Tribune (04/06/2005): China Lobbies EU Over Arms Embargo (by Dempsey, Judy). http://www.iht.com/articles/2005/04/05/news/diplo.html (April 10, 2005).

IP/95/731: Commission Launches New Policy on China. (EC Press Release July 5, 1995). http://europa.eu.int/rapid/pressReleasesAction.do?reference=IP/95/731&format=HTML&aged=1&language=EN&guiLanguage=en (April 10, 2005).

Joint Statement (12/08/2004): Joint Statement of the 7th EU-China Summit. http://europa.eu.int/comm/external_relations/china/summit_1204/conclusions.pdf (January 10, 2005).

Liu Qingcai (刘清才) (2001): 中俄美大国战略关系与中国的外交选择 (On Strategic Relations Between the Great Powers China, Russia and the US and China's Strategic Choice in Foreign Diplomacy). In: 吉林大学社会科学学报 (Jilin University Journal, Social Science Edition) 6 (Nov. 2001), 104–109.

Liu Wenxiu (刘文秀) (2002): 中国 – 欧盟的'全面伙伴关系'的内涵与定位 (Status and Meaning of the China-EU 'Comprehensive partnership'). In: 山东大学学报 (Journal of Shandong University) 2 (Mar. 2002), 68–73.

MEMO/04/163: China – Market Economic Status in Trade Defense Investigations (28.6.2004). http://europa.eu.int/rapid/pressReleasesAction.do?reference=MEMO/04/163&format=HTML&aged=1&language=EN&guiLanguage=en (25.3.2005) (April 10, 2005).

MEMO/05/201: EU-China Textile Agreement (06/10/2005). http://europa.eu.int/rapid/pressReleasesAction.do?reference=MEMO/05/201&format=HTML&aged=1&language=EN&guiLanguage=en (March 25, 2005).

Ministry of Foreign Affairs PRC (12/10/2004): 开创中欧友好合作的新局面：李肇星谈温家宝出访欧洲成果 (A New Perspective of Friendly Cooperation between China and Europe: Li Zhaoxing on the Results of Wen Jiaobaos State Visit to Europe. http://www.fmprc.gov.cn/chn/wjb/zzjg/xos/dqzzywt/t174025.htm (June 06, 2005).

Pei, Minxin (2002): China's Governance Crisis. In: Foreign Affairs (Sept.-Oct. 2002). http://www.gbcc.org.uk/iss23analysis.htm (March 18, 2005).

PESC/95/102: Declaration by the Presidency on Behalf of the European Union in Support of the Chinese Dissident, Mr. Wei Jing Xeng [sic! Wei Jingsheng] (12/14/1995). http://europa.eu.int/rapid/pressReleasesAction.do?reference=PESC/95/102&format=HTML&aged=1&language=EN&guiLanguage=en (March 18, 2005).

PRES/03/63: 2495th Council Meeting – External Relations – Brussels, 18 March 2003, (03/18/2003). http://europa.eu.int/rapid/pressReleasesAction.do?reference=PRES/03/63&format=HTML&aged=1&language=EN&guiLanguage=en (March 25, 2005).

Renmin Ribao (10/29/2003): 呼吁解除对华军售禁令 – 推动中欧关系稳定发展：中国首次发表对欧盟政策文件 (Lifting the Arms Embargo – Promoting the Stable Development of Sino-EU Relations: China Issues its First Policy on the EU). http://www.people.com.cn/GB/guandian/8213/8309/28296/2158767.html (May 20, 2005)

Renmin Ribao (04/29/2005): Still Two “Bottlenecks“ for Sino-European Relations.http://english.people.com.cn/200504/29/eng20050429_183228.html (March 25, 2005).

Schubert, Gunter (2002): China und die Europäische Union im Kontext der GASP. (China and the European Union in the Context of the CFSP.) In: Aus Politik und Zeitgeschichte (B19-20/2002).

SPEECH/04/483: The Rt. Hon. Chris Patten: Lifting of the Arms Embargo on China: The Rueda Report on Arms Exports. Strasbourg, November 16, 2004. (01/16/2004). http://europa.eu.int/rapid/pressReleasesAction.do?reference=SPEECH/04/483&format=HTML&aged=1&language=EN&guiLanguage=en (March 25, 2005).

SPEECH/04/523: José Manuel Barroso: Press Conference of 7th EU-China Summit. The Hague, December 8, 2004. http://europa.eu.int/rapid/pressReleasesAction.do?reference=MEMO/05/201&format=HTML&aged=1&language=EN&guiLanguage=en04/523&format=HTML&aged=1&language=EN&guiLanguage=en (March 25, 2005).

SPEECH/05/344: Peter Mandelson: Statement to the press following EU-China negotiations on textiles. Shanghai, June 10, 2005 (06/12/2005). http://europa.eu.int/rapid/pressReleasesAction.do?reference=MEMO/05/201&format=HTML&aged=1&language=EN&guiLanguage=en (June 25, 2005).

Umbach, Frank and Andreas Fulda (2003): Zur Zukunft der EU-China-Beziehungen im 21. Jahrhundert: Einige grundsätzliche Anmerkungen zum “China Country Strategy Paper: 2002–2006“ der Europäischen Kommission vom 1.März 2002 und den Perspektiven einer GASP der EU gegenüber China. (The Future of EU-China Relations in the 21th Century: Some Basic Annotations on the “China Country Strategy Paper: 2002–2006“, issued by the EU Commission on March 1, 2002 and the Perspectives of a CSFP towards China.) In: ASIEN (Oct. 2003) 89, 47–56.

Umbach, Frank (2004): EU’s links with China Pose New Threat to Transatlantic Relations. In: European Affairs 2 (2004), 38–47. http://www.europeanaffairs.org/current_issue/ 2004_spring/2004_spring_38.php4 (April 25, 2005).

Umbach, Frank (2005a): The Debate over Lifting the EU Arms Embargo on China and its Transatlantic Implications. In: CSIS/PMG (Ed.): Reviewing the Transatlantic Partnership. U.S. German Bilateral Dialogue. Conference Report, Washington D.C., October 2004, Washington D.C. 2005, 45–52. http://www.csis.org/europe/rtp_report.pdf (March 25, 2005).

Umbach, Frank (2005b): Strategic Partnership or Multilateral Kotau? EU-China Relations and the Lifting of the (arms) Embargo. In: Internationale Politik 3 (März 2005), 70–77. http://www.dgap.org/Publikationen/Asien/ (June 27, 2005).

Wang Haixia (王海霞) (2003): 欧盟东扩及其对中国的影响 (The Eastern Enlargement of the EU and its Consequences for China). In: 当代世界 (The Contemporary World) 10 (2003), 21–22.

Wang Yizhou (王逸舟) (2000): 社民社会与中国外交 (Civil Society and China’s Foreign Relations). In: 中国社会科学 (Social Sciences in China) 3 (2000), 28–38.

Wiessala, Georg (2002): The European Union and Asian Countries. London: Sheffield Academic Press.

Xi Runchang (郗润昌) (2000): 多极格局框架并未向单极逆转 (A Multipolar Structure and no Development Towards an unipolar World). In: 和平与发展 (Peace and Development) 2 (2000), 45–48.

Xiao Gang (肖刚) (2004): 面向21世纪中叶的中国外交战略 (China’s Foreign Strategy for the Mid-21st Century). In: 广东外语外贸大学学报 (Journal of Guangdong University of Foreign Studies) 1 (Jan. 2004), 47–52.

Xinhua (10/14/2003): 中国希望通过首份对欧政策文件推动双边关系. (With the First Policy Paper on the EU China hopes to Deepen Bilateral Relations). http://news.xinhuanet.com/zhengfu/2003-10/14/content_1121475.htm (April 28, 2005).

Xinhua (12/08/2004): 温家宝：对华军售禁令是冷战产物. (Wen Jiabao: The Arms Embargo is a Product of the Cold War).http://news.xinhuanet.com/world/2004-12/08/content_2306746.htm (June 18, 2005).

Yu Keping (俞可平）(2002): 中国公民社会的兴起及其对治理的意义 (The Rising of a Chinese Civil Society and its Governance Implications). In: Yu Keping (俞可平）et al. (ed.): 公民社会的兴起和治理的变迁 (The Rising of a Chinese Civil Society and its Development in Governance). Beijing: Shehui kexue wenzhai chubanshe. http://www.gongfa.com/civilsocietyykp.htm (July 22, 2005).

Zeng Yuan (曾元) (2004): 欧盟东扩及其对华关系前瞻 (The Eastern Enlargement of the EU and the Future of [the EU's] Relations with China) . In:东南亚研究 (Southeast Asian Studies) 3 (2004), 55–59.

Zhongguo dui Oumeng zhengce wenjian (10/13/2003): 中国对欧盟政策文件 (China's Policy Paper on the Relationship with the EU). http://www.fmprc.gov.cn/chn/wjb/zzjg/xos/dqzzywt/t27700.htm (July 27, 2005). English version: http://www.fmprc.gov.cn/eng/wjb/zzjg/xos/dqzzywt/t27708.htm (July 27, 2005).

A. Tom Grunfeld

The Advantages and Perils of Globalization: The Case of Tibet

Introduction

A 2001 study conducted by Leiden University and the Washington DC-based Institute for International Mediation and Conflict Resolution identified 126 high-intensity conflicts (defined as large-scale armed conflicts causing more than 1000 deaths) from mid-1999 to mid-2000, 78 low intensity conflicts (100–1000 deaths) and 178 violent political conflicts (less than 100 deaths) (Bob 2002). Yet, except for – at best – a fleeting newspaper account, only a handful ever caught the world's attention.

Historically an astonishing small number of insurgencies gained much notoriety and, even less, ultimately succeeded. Most were largely forgotten by all but the most diligent scholars and, of course, the participants and victims.

This lack of attention raises two interesting questions: why do some groups manage to gain international sympathy, publicity, access to opinion makers and politicians, and funding when so many others remain relatively obscure regardless of the righteousness of their causes and does international recognition help these groups achieve their goals?

Why was the struggle for East Timorese independence, to take but one obvious example, so well known and documented when similar undertakings in other parts of Indonesia (Aceh, the Moluccas and Irian Jaya come quickly to mind) remain largely invisible to the world community? Who succeeds in this "[...] harsh, Darwinian marketplace where legions of desperate groups vie for scare attention, sympathy and money?" (Bob 2001:321)

Undoubtedly, the single most important element in the globalization of conflicts has been technology. The advent of cell phones, e-mail, the world-wide web, inexpensive and comprehensive air travel and instant media access have made global transportation, communications, international conferencing and visits to the conflict sites themselves easier than ever and, as a consequence, have transformed international political and social relations by breaking down geographic, cultural and political barriers (Kluver). Whether these developments have led to a greater measure of success for political struggles is open to question but what we can be sure of is that more of these campaigns than ever before have made appearances in the world's media.

While violence will guarantee publicity and keep a cause in the public eye, it is not a very useful long-term strategy and few groups are willing to go that far. For non-violent (or semi-violent) groups the vehicle to recognition is often an international Non-Governmental Organization (NGO). NGOs created by the activists can render international legitimacy while established NGOs can provide public relations and organizational skills, connections to people who can generate interest and, especially, money; for it is money, above all else, that is the ineluctable component for publicity, media events, foreign lobbying trips, and mass campaigns.[1]

The successes of a handful of social and political movements in using international support to either help achieve victory (the anti-apartheid movement, East Timor) or, at the very least, achieve a very high profile (Tibetan independence, Zapatistas in Chiapas, Mexico) have spurred others to try and replicate these endeavors. To that end some organizations have decided to become proactive in their pursuit of wider recognition for lesser known movements.

For example, the Hague-based Unrepresented Nations and Peoples Organization (UNPO), which champions several dozen indigenous peoples struggling for recognition and varying forms of sovereignty from native Hawaiians in the U.S. to Hungarians in Romania to the Ogoni in Nigeria, holds intensive week-long media and diplomacy training sessions replete with mock media interviews and role playing. The UNPO was established in 1991 by, among others, Michael van Walt van Praag and Lodi G. Gyari; both of whom had extensive experience marketing the Tibetan exile struggle for independence (Bob 2001).[2]

The key to a successful media campaign – whether it is intended to sell toothpaste or an insurgency – is marketing. As far as public relations goes, "marketing trumps justice." Sadly, the righteousness of a cause seems to be of little import. Just look at the many famines that occur regularly without adequate response until – and if – the international media and NGOs become involved. One crucial caveat about marketing a political cause. Unlike a commercial product, marketing success is not the ultimate goal. Activists are not interested in acquiring personal fortunes or market share but solely to use marketing as a means to achieving their goals.

Marketing of a political cause requires some necessary ingredients to be successful: 1. a charismatic leader who can speak a western language, preferably

---

[1] There is a study to be done of national NGOs and their activities on behalf of local political movements. My case study, however, addresses international NGOs only.

[2] See further http://www.unpo.org/.

English ("major international NGOs," observes one scholar of this phenomenon, "often look for a figure who neatly embodies their own ideals, meets the pragmatic requirements of a 'test case,' or fulfills romantic Western notions of rebellion – in short, a leader who seems to mirror their own central values." (Bob 2002), 2. an easily understood and compelling narrative, 3. the demonization of one's opponent, 4. unity among the people engaged in the struggle, and 5. international legitimacy.

No conflict has been as successful at this marketing strategy as the struggle of the Dalai Lama and his fellow Tibetan exiles for Tibetan independence. Even the most widely recognized conflicts such as East Timor, Northern Ireland, Bosnia, Palestine, etc. have not been able to generate the support and positive media attention that the Tibetans have realized. Their experience in achieving world-wide recognition and acclaim – even if they have not, and probably will not, succeed in achieving independence – will likely be a model to emulate for many years to come.

Some Tibetan History

Tibetans were in a unique position in that their history allowed for an easily constructed highly favorable narrative. Western fantasies about Tibet began as early as the 18th century when, in the midst of European exploration and colonization of the world, a few remote corners of the globe were spared European conquest and no inaccessible part of the world conjured up as much fantasy and mystery than did Tibet. The more isolated it seemed, the more cachet and intrigue it incurred[3] and the more attempts were made to breach its defenses. Missionaries, diplomats, spies, adventurers and the spiritually inclined routinely attempted the journey and just as routinely failed.[4] Geographic hurdles, the lack of colonization, Tibet's peripheral status politically and economically and political constraints all kept Westerners out and created the mystique about Tibet that remains to this day. It is important to note that it was only Westerners who were barred; Asians frequented Tibet's monasteries and bazaars in large numbers including merchants and pilgrims from western China, Mongolia, from northern India, Nepal and even as far away as Russia.

The Tibet of the Western imagination is, according to Orville Schell (2000:243), "the most powerful utopian myth of a largely dystopian century,"

---

[3] "There was, indeed, something seductively perverse about the Promethean and very Western impulse to trespass where not welcomed." (Schell 2000:148) After the British/Indian military reached Lhasa in 1904, the Indian Viceroy, Lord Curzon, wrote Sven Hedin, the explorer who had repeatedly failed to reach the fabled city, "I am almost ashamed of having destroyed the virginity of the bride to whom you aspired." (Bishop 1993:36)

[4] For a brief description of many of these hardy individuals see Schell 2000:1–40 or Meyer/Brysac 1999.

and, indeed, according to Laurie Hovell McMillan (2001:X), "[...] a dream from which the English-speaking West has not entirely awoken [...]."[5] In the latter part of the nineteenth, and through the first half of the twentieth century, it was British diplomats and colonial officials who were most interested in Tibet for geopolitical reasons and their constructs of Tibet as a modern independent nation-state had considerable impact on the Western popular mind (McKay 1997). However, Tibet had a much larger impact at the time in the spiritual realm, leading to, in the words of Buddhist scholar Agehananda Bharati, a form of "pseudo-Orientalia" (Bharati 1974). Sometimes populizers of Tibetan Buddhism, such as Alexandra David-Neel (Foster et al. 1998), were genuinely interested and devoted to the religion but many were outright frauds such as Madame Blavatsky and Lobsang Rampa.[6]

The huge popularity of James Hilton's *Lost Horizon,* the tale of an idyllic Western society utilizing secret Eastern knowledge secreted deep in the Himalayan mountains became a bestselling novel in the midst of the world-wide economic depression and its further popularization as a Frank Capra-directed Hollywood film played no small measure in the fantasization of a mythic place called Tibet. The arrival of Chinese troops on Tibet's borders in May 1950 produced little interest in the West. The British officials had left when India gained independence in 1947 and to the spiritualists, so caught up in their fascination of Tibetan Buddhism, the fate of the land and the people were of little interest. Tibet was obscure and irrelevant and it became even more so when the Korean War broke out only weeks later drawing the world's attention from smaller conflicts.

The government of the Dalai Lama tried to win diplomatic support for his efforts to maintain Tibet's independence through talks with Indian, American and British diplomatic officials but there was no attempt at eliciting public opinion. Tibet, having cut itself off from the ways of the world, had no knowledge of what was required to promote their cause (Goldstein 1989). Little changed in that regard even after the abortive revolt in Lhasa in March 1959 and the flight of

---

5 For a selection of early American views about Tibet from *The New York Times,* see Miller 1988.

6 Rampa, an Irish blue-collar worker named Cyril Hoskins who moved to Toronto and died in 1981, fashioned himself a Tibetan monk although he never set foot in the place and his portrayals of Tibet are figments of his fertile imagination mixed with information from books he must have read. Nevertheless, his *The Third Eye* sold 300,000 copies in the first 18 months after its 1956 publication and went through 9 paperback printings in the UK in just 2 years (Lopez 1998a:97). It not only remains in print today but is an astonishing 10,338 on www.amazon.com as of September 2005. In total, Rampa currently has16 books in print in English as well several in Spanish and French. All told there are about 15 million copies of Rampa's books in print.

the Dalai Lama and tens of thousands of Tibetans into exile to India, Nepal and Bhutan. In the United States, the American Emergency Committee for Tibetan Refugees and, in the UK, the Tibet Society and Relief Fund of the UK, were established and although they had been constituted partly out of public concern for the plight of the Tibetans, in fact both were connected to, and covertly supported by, their respective governments (Grunfeld 1996:195–196).

During the 1960s the lack of interest in the plight of the exiled Tibetans continued and no nation ever recognized the Dalai Lama's exile administration. But at the time these were secondary matters as the Dalai Lama had his hands full settling refugees in their new homes and fighting a guerrilla war inside Tibet; although, officially, the Dalai Lama did not condone violence. Besides, covert support from the American Central Intelligence Agency (CIA) led Tibetans to assume that the world's most powerful country would allow them to achieve their objective of independence. The CIA had no such intention seeing the Tibetans as merely useful allies in their on-going Cold War harassment of the government of the People's Republic of China (PRC) (Grunfeld 2003).

There was so little public interest in Tibet at that time that even appeals on human rights grounds went unheeded. When, in 1977, an American journalist gathered evidence from imprisoned Tibetan guerrillas in Nepal, including 300 pages of notes smuggled out of a Nepali prison, he could not arouse any interest in their plight from Amnesty International, the Jimmy Carter administration in the U.S., Chogyam Trungpa (the most prominent Tibetan Buddhist teacher in the US at the time), nor several anti-Chinese U.S. Senators (Long 1981).

Living in exile with a large number of his countrymen placed the Dalai Lama in a unique and complicated situation. In Lhasa he was the undisputed political leader of the government of central Tibet and the spiritual leader of the Gelugpa sect of Tibetan Buddhism. In exile he was called upon to expand his role as political leader of the entire refugee community, a community that included Tibetans from many regions including areas (Amdo and Kham) which had traditionally not recognized him as their political leader. In addition to having to overcome deep regional differences among the exiles, he also had to overcome religious differences between the various schools of Tibetan Buddhism. Monastic communities brought not only monks and their teachings into exile but also their monastic politics (Singer 2003; Gearing 2003). Today, almost half a century since coming into exile, these regional and religious differences still eat away at the unity of the 130,000–140,000 strong Tibetan exile community. The need for unity is crucial, not only for their marketing strategy, but, more importantly, to show a united opposition to Chinese rule in Tibet.

It's difficult to determine the nature of nationalist feelings among Tibetans prior to 1950. Tibetans had many ways of distinguishing themselves from non-Tibetans of course; a common religion above all else, history, language, dress, jokes, social conventions, and the eating of tsampa (a high altitude barley indigenous to Tibet) – all perceived affinities which created a form of nationalism (Manz 2003). Political loyalties tended to be regional and spiritual loyalties were reserved for the nearest monastery although the Dalai Lama was accepted by all Tibetans as their most important spiritual leader.

Although there were attempts by the 13th Dalai Lama to create a modern conception of nationalism in the early decades of the 20th century, these efforts – a national flag, anthem, modern army, color guard, military bands, postage stamps, etc – did not penetrate very deep into the population (Klieger 1992:72–78).

But now in exile a modern sense of identity had to be created if the Tibetans were to be noticed in a world of nation-states so the Dalai Lama established a Western style "government" replete with a westernized constitution, a governmental bureaucracy, a parliament, "embassies" around the world, a judicial system, a security apparatus and a publications operation. His goal was to "invent [a] tradition of secular nationalism" (Ibid.:65).[7] This effort included the official adoption of a national flag, the creation of a national day, national holidays (such as the Dalai Lama's birthday), having all school children begin their day by singing a prayer song composed by the Dalai Lama, placing his photo in every classroom, teaching children to attribute all successes to the Dalai Lama as well as constructing a history of pre–1950 Tibet as an "idealized […] spiritual Shangri-la." All these activities have, for the first time, created a population of highly nationalistic Tibetans committed to independence (McLagan 1996:216).

One additional, and vital, aspect to the creation of a new form of Tibetan nationalism was the Dalai Lama's commitment to preserve Tibetan culture in the fear that Chinese rule in Tibet would either irrevocably alter, or worse eradicate, it altogether. He rebuilt monasteries in exile, established the Library of Tibetan Works and Archives, the Tibetan Medical Institute and the Tibetan Institute of Performing Arts.

By the late 1960s the inability of the Tibetan rebels to mount an insurgency inside Tibet and the need for CIA personnel in the ever-expanding war in Southeast Asia led to the end of the U.S.-supported covert war. Soon after, President Richard Nixon, and his foreign policy advisor Henry Kissinger, fashioned a new relationship with the PRC terminating hostilities and all remaining covert operations targeted at China.

The Tibetan exiles needed a new plan for dealing with Beijing and this would be decided by events far beyond their control – or even imagination. In China, a

[7] McLagan (1996:109) calls this a "diaspora nationalism".

split in the leadership emerged culminating in the mysterious death of Lin Biao, Mao Zedong's heir apparent. Lin's death led to changes in government policies throughout the mainland, including Tibet. In 1976 Mao Zedong died, followed, soon after, by the arrest of a leadership group dubbed "the gang of four" and government policies were further moderated. A series of events were now set in motion which almost led to a compromise solution to the Tibetan issue.

China publicly admitted past policies to have been harmful, tourism was permitted, Tibetans were appointed to positions with at least a modicum of power and refugees were permitted to visit families in Tibet. In February 1978, the Panchen Lama, second only to the Dalai Lama in the Tibetan Buddhist hierarchy, was released from 14 years of house arrest and prison and in the 1980s became a public political champion of preserving Tibetan culture, especially religious freedom and the promotion of the Tibetan language. In December 1978, through the intervention of one of his older brothers, Gyalo Thondup, the Dalai Lama began a series of indirect negotiations with officials in Beijing. These talks resulted in an agreement to send several Tibetan-exile investigative delegations to Tibet.

The Dalai Lama responded positively to these changes and began to speak less of his hopes for achieving Tibetan independence and more about the economic well-being of Tibetans; "if the six million Tibetans in Tibet are really happy and prosperous as never before," he declared in 1978, "there is no reason for us to argue otherwise" (His Holiness the Dalai Lama 1982:51).

The talks were not universally welcomed in the Tibetan exile community, in fact there were demonstrations against them when they were first revealed. The propagating of Tibetan nationalism among the exiles had created illusions about the Chinese as being so evil that they were only capable of inducing destruction. The idea that they may be reasonable came as quite a shock. In 1980 Chinese Communist Party (CCP) leader Hu Yaobang traveled to Tibet and was stunned by how bad conditions were (allegedly telling CCP officials that Chinese rule was "colonial" in nature) and immediately ordered drastic changes. These changes (only partially implemented) and the acknowledgment that there were serious problems in Tibet, continued to set a climate for compromise.

Disappointingly though, in the second half of the 1980s, the talks began to stall. This presented a dilemma to the Dalai Lama who, until now, had exerted little energy in winning wide public and governmental support around the world calculating that as long as he could be at the table with Beijing there was no need for the intervention of a third force. However, if Beijing walked away from the table, how was the Dalai Lama to get them back? The answer was to promote the Tibetan cause in the hope of getting international (read, American) pressure to cajole the Chinese back to the table. So the decision was made to internationalize the Tibetan struggle.

The Internalization of the Tibetan Struggle

To that end, meetings of Tibet-supporters were held around the world and a plan was hatched to create what, colloquially, came to be known as the Tibet Lobby. Their objectives: internationalize the Tibet issue by recruiting lobbing and public relations firms, get media attention, generate popular support on moral grounds (independence, religious freedom, human rights and environmental issues – a subject never raised in exile publications prior to 1985) and hope that public pressure generated by these activities would force governments to pressure Beijing to negotiate with the Dalai Lama. In other words, to market the struggle internationally.

Unbeknownst to the Tibetan exiles this was an opportune time to launch such a campaign for a number of events occurred, almost simultaneously, in harmony with each other, to produce the most successful marketing of a political movement in history.

The Tibetan diaspora of 1959 had rekindled a wave of interest in all things spiritually Tibetan. As we have seen Lobsang Rampa became a best-selling author. The 1927 edition of W. Y. Evans-Wentz's, *The Tibetan Book of the Dead* was adopted by the proponents of the drug LSD as an essential guide to understanding life while the academic study of Tibetan Buddhism was launched as exiled Tibetan Buddhist monks began arriving on American shores and the Library of Congress began the serious collection of Tibetan religious texts.

So Westerners, especially Americans fueled by their New Age dispositions to the spiritual bazaars of the day, were prepared to accept images of a benign, idyllic society practicing secret rituals based on occult knowledge ruled by multitudes of lamas guaranteeing the purity of the culture. This inclination made weaving an advantageous narrative that was easily understood and emotionally appealing remarkable easy since it fit so neatly into the images of an imaginary "Tibet" which were already figments of the Western imagination. To wit: Tibetans were a singularly happy, non-violent people devoted exclusively to the practice of Buddhism living in peaceful isolation in a remote and ecologically conscious land ruled by a string of enlightened, and always benevolent, god-kings, the Dalai Lamas. This peaceful Shangri-la was shattered with the arrival of the forces of evil, the godless Chinese, who were intent on destroying Tibetan culture and religion while attempting to commit genocide.[8]

So with a concerted effort to forge unity among the Tibetan exiles, the availability of a charismatic, English-speaking leader and an affirmative narrative in

---

[8] "This is a compelling story, an enticing blend of the exotic, the spiritual, and the political. But it is a fantasy, ultimately detrimental to the cause of Tibetan independence." (Lopez 1998b)

place, the Chinese government was about to deliver a fourth component of the marketing strategy, its own demonization.

In June 1989 the Chinese government brutally suppressed demonstrating students and workers in Tian'anmen Square. These shocking events – seen live around the world as foreign journalists in large numbers witnessed them – led to a radical change in the world's view of China.

Having been seen in only the most positive light from the early 1970s when it began to slowly "open" itself to the world, China now came to be portrayed as villainous. The shock at Beijing's actions led directly to the awarding of the Nobel Peace Prize to the Dalai Lama, making him an international celebrity. This attitudinal change towards China made the glorification of Tibet that much easier (Peterson 1997).

Inside Tibet resentment against Chinese rule had been growing but kept hidden for justifiable fears of retaliation. However, in September 1987, while the Dalai Lama was proposing a compromise plan for Tibet in front of the U.S. Congress, demonstrations, the first in almost three decades, broke out in Lhasa leading to bloodshed. There is no proof that these events were instigated from outside of Tibet and Tibetan animosity over Chinese rule was real enough. However, news of the Dalai Lama's appearance in the U.S. Congress was available through the Voice of America and the BBC as well as from Chinese radio's denunciation of his activities. At the same time leaflets with the Dalai Lama's picture were clandestinely distributed in Lhasa. It seems safe to say that the Tibetan demonstrators were emboldened by the knowledge that the Dalai Lama was in Washington DC which to many, if not all, meant U.S. support for the Dalai Lama and, perhaps, even for Tibetan independence.

These demonstrations were not only significant in that they were the first in a long time but more to the point that they were witnessed and documented by foreigners (as were the events in Tian'anmen Square). The significance becomes evident when we look at a similar situation which had a very different outcome. In August 1988, a year before the events in Tian'anmen Square, 200,000 Burmese, mostly student and workers but monks as well, peacefully demonstrated against their dictatorial government. They were met with a barrage of gunfire from army units and deaths were estimated at anywhere from 3 – 10,000. Eight thousand students fled the country into exile. The circumstances surrounding these events are strikingly similar to the events in Beijing a year later except the number of deaths, injuries and exiles is far higher. Nevertheless, because not a single Western journalist was present, these developments were barely noticed outside the very small circle of those interested in Burmese affairs and since the Burmese dissidents lacked international recognition they, consequently, lacked international legitimacy.

In Lhasa, the foreigners' accounts galvanized the exile community and generated support among non-Tibetans. It helped immensely that these foreigners were professionals who had access to media outlets and influential institutions and that they were not only observers (as were the journalists in Tian'anmen Square) but also participants. Some foreigners gave medical assistance to the wounded, some gathered information to be taken out of the country, some banded together to support the demonstrators, etc (McLagan 1998:324). Indeed, some went on to establish NGOs in Washington and London and remain active in the Tibetan independence struggle to this day.

So all the elements for a successful marketing plan were in place: charismatic leader, easily understood narrative, unity among the refugees, international legitimacy and the demonization of the opponent. The plan for internationalization was straightforward: 1. the Dalai Lama would travel more and make the trips openly political, 2. support groups would be established around the world, especially in the United States, to lobby their governments on the Dalai Lama's behalf, 3. members of parliaments of major nations would be recruited with the eventual goal being official support from the governments of these nations, 4. peaceful civil disobedience inside Tibet would be encouraged, and 5. the Dalai Lama would continue to plead for talks offering flexible terms to Beijing.

Meanwhile, continued unrest inside Tibet had revitalized a policy debate in Beijing between moderates who wanted a compromise and the return of the Dalai Lama and hard liners who were just as happy breaking off ties to him and waiting for him to die. This latter group also argued for less freedoms for the traditional Tibetan way of life and greater efforts at assimilation.

Evidence of this political struggle could be read in the Chinese media. "We must deal resolute, accurate and rapid blows against the serious crimes of a small number of separatists," read an editorial in *Xizang Ribao* (Tibet Daily), on 13 March 1988, "[...] [they] are the cause of this earthquake and a cancer cell in society." The head of the Public Security apparatus, Qiao Shi, called for "the government [to] adopt a policy of merciless repression toward all rebels".

"There are people who think it necessary to strike down the lamas and destroy the monasteries," the Panchen Lama said of the hard liners, "We must not fall back to the errors of the past [...] I must seriously warn against people who have the idea of 'dealing merciless blows at the lamas and closing all the temples.'" Premier Zhao Ziyang was quoted as saying that while some of the unrest may be due to "splittists in foreign countries" there is the problem of "long-standing leftist policies in Tibet [...][for example] a serious degree of sectarianism existed among Tibetan leaders. The work of addressing the wrongs was advanced very slowly. The Tibetan people's autonomous rights, the Tibetan language and the customs and habits of this nationality were neglected and such mistakes were not properly and quickly corrected."[9]

The Panchen Lama died suddenly in January 1989 and the Dalai Lama was invited to funerary ceremonies in Beijing even though he had not been in China for 30 years. We believe he was told informally that there would also be the opportunity to discuss political issues with high-level officials. It seemed the opening he was looking for direct talks with the Chinese leadership. But he and his advisors were cautious; the international campaign seemed to be going well, they believed, and would give them greater leverage if he went later when the support was greater. How would the Dalai Lama be treated in Beijing? Would he be permitted to visit Lhasa? So, in the end, he didn't go and some observers believe it was the gravest error of his political life.[10]

The 1980s had seen a sizable increase in the use of the Tibetan language, the rebuilding of religious buildings (in some regions there are now more than there were before 1951) and a general resurgence of Tibetan culture. Nevertheless, the inability of the moderates to produce the Dalai Lama and manage a deal, the continuing public protests in Tibet itself, the escalating China-bashing around the world all strengthened the hand of the hard liners who won the policy battle in Beijing. In March 1989 after yet another demonstration which resulted in more brutal Chinese suppression, martial law was declared in Tibet and was to last until May 1990.

Talks with China had now stopped altogether with both sides blaming each other for the breakdown. The Dalai Lama continued to travel extensively and the Tibet Lobby he created continued to grow expeditiously implementing its marketing and media strategy and utilizing public relations and influential lobbying firms in Washington DC which opened the doors to Congress and opinion makers in the American capital. As one public relations consultant observed: There is "difference between publicity and media strategy. Publicity is insignificant and useful only so far as it sells out events [whereas] a media strategy is meant to help an organization or movement to develop long-term relationships with then press which in turn can be used to further ongoing objectives." (McLagan 1996:508)

---

[9] Quoted from British Broadcasting Corporation, Summary of World Broadcasts [BBC-SWB], Part III, Far East, 16 March 1988 the South China Morning Post, 20 July 1988; Foreign Broadcast Information Service (FBIS)-CHI-88-060, 29 March 1988; FBIS-CHI-88-066, 6 April 1988. The sudden and unexpected death of the Panchen Lama at the age of 50 in Shigatse in January 1989 removed from the scene an important player who could have contributed greatly to the solution of the Tibet problem. See Grunfeld 1988; SWB, Part III, Far East, FE/0169 - B2/1, 4 June 1988 *Ming Pao*, 2 June 1988. For an excellent description of events inside Tibet during the 1980s see Tseten 1992.

[10] For an argument that it was not a major political error see Tashi/Tseten 2004. This is the best, and most thorough, history of the negotiations to date.

The world-wide media – newspapers, magazines, television, radio – have all played their unwitting part in this strategy by allowing only the voices of the Tibetan exile community to be heard. The Chinese voice is quickly dismissed as irrelevant but never does one hear the voices of Tibetans inside Tibet or China itself. There are many Tibetans in Beijing and Shanghai and Qinghai Province where foreign journalists can easily travel to, but the narrative of the exiled community is so deeply ingrained as the only acceptable one that no effort is made to see if there are others.

Most of the support groups were established after 1987. In 1990 the First International Contact Conference of Tibet Supporters – 231 supporters from 26 countries – met. In May 2000 Tibet support groups met in Berlin with 300 delegates from 52 countries and they created the International Tibet Support Network which consisted of 349 groups in 70 countries (McLagan 1996:1).[11]

Meanwhile foreign tourism exploded as the PRC invested millions to promote it; $215 million on tourist facilities in 1984 alone. The number of foreign visitors went from less than 2000 annually in the early 1980s to 4000 in 1984 to 15,000 in 1985 to 30,000 in 1986 (when they spent some $40 million) (Xu 1997:1066) to a little over 100,000 in 1999 to 130,000 in 2002 (O'Callaghan 1985; Xinhua News Agency, 11/16/1984; 12/09/1999; 01/09/ 2003). The Chinese government saw foreign tourism as a source of much needed revenue but also as an antidote to the portrayals of Tibet dominant in the West. When people saw the material gains being made in Tibet and the natural and man-made wonders, Beijing believed, they would be less inclined to support the Dalai Lama's "splittist" activities. But these hopes were divorced from the reality. Prepared to dislike the Chinese, foreigners arrive in Tibet already inclined to favor the Tibetan exile view. Moreover, given their inclinations to view Tibet as a place frozen in the Middle Ages, modernization, the destruction of the monasteries, the destruction of traditional Tibetan buildings and, most importantly, the negative attitude of most Tibetans towards the Chinese, often results in foreigners leaving Tibet even more inclined to hate Chinese rule than when they arrived.

Tourism and the freedom for Tibetan exiles to visit their homeland has also allowed for the free flow of information in the form of pictures of the Dalai Lama and his chosen Panchen Lama who, it is believed, remains under house arrest, cassette and video tapes of the Dalai Lama, pro-independence literature and anti-Chinese propaganda all of which easily make it across the less than secure frontier.

The success of the internationalization of Tibet can be seen in the immense growth of interest in all matters Tibetan. On the religious side, a 1979 survey found that in the United States there were 55 Tibetan Buddhist teachers/mission-

---

[11] See also http://www.tibet.org.itsn/index.html.

aries, 12 universities with Tibetan Buddhist programs and 16 dharma centers. A recent study found 1062 Buddhist teaching centers of one kind or another with an estimated 100,000 American born Buddhists (Kutcher 1982; Van Biema 1997). In 1973, the *Tibet Society Newsletter* listed only 223 members in North America, both academics and others, who were self-identified as having an interest in Tibet. In contrast, Students for Free Tibet began in 1994 with 45 chapters, had grown to 350 chapters by 1997, and to 650 chapters in 35 countries by 2004. Moreover, in recent years they have orchestrated annual Free Tibet! Action Camps to train organizers (Tibet Society 1973; Seager 1999:116–117).[12] The US-Tibet Committee boasts of a membership exceeding 10,000, as does the Tibetan Aid Project, with the International Campaign for Tibet claiming some 40,000.[13] Whether these claims are accurate or fanciful there can be no doubt that the number of people interested in Tibet, as well as activists engaged in Tibetan related political activities, has gone from a few hundred at most to several tens of thousands in the United States alone.

In addition to support groups, various other types of organizations have sprung up such as the Milarepa Fund founded by musician Adam Yauch, Tibet House in New York City, established by Richard Gere and Robert Thurman in 1987, and four publishers who produce a steady flow of religious and lay texts as well as audio and video tapes to keep the market satiated: the general interest Shambala Publications founded in Berkeley in 1969; Dharma Publishing founded also in Berkeley in 1971, Wisdom Publications connected to the Foundation for the Preservation of the Mahayana Tradition and founded in Boston in 1975 and, finally, Snow Lion Publications founded in Ithaca, NY in 1980.

But none of these activities created the stir raised by Hollywood when it discovered Tibet. This relationship began when some movie stars became enamored of the religion, particularly Richard Gere who has taken it upon himself to be the chief promoter of the religion and the Dalai Lama in the United States. Celebrities who have followed Gere into Buddhism, both Tibetan and otherwise include basketball coach Phil Jackson, singers Tina Turner and Melissa Manchester, musical groups such as Nirvana and musician Herbie Hancock, actors Sharon Stone, Goldie Hawn, Harrison Ford, Dennis Quad, and Steven Seagal. Seagal has even been recognized as the reincarnation of a prominent 17th century lama of the Nyingma School raising complaints that he "bought his recognition" (Parker 1997).

This high profile created by the growing American fascination in Buddhism, the political campaigns and the Hollywood spotlight has resulted in Tibet and the

---

[12] See also http://www.studentsforafreetibet.org/.

[13] Gale's Ready Reference Publications, http://galenet.gale.com/. See http://www.savetibet.org/.

Dalai Lama becoming a part of the popular culture. "Tibet is hip and Buddhism is trendy," declared *Newsweek* in 1997, "so Tibetan Buddhism is extra-cool" (Emerson/Power 1997; Fisher 1998). Tibet and Buddhism began popping up all over the popular cultural landscape from American television programs like "The Simpsons" to "Dharma and Greg," to ads for IBM and Apple Computers which incorporated Buddhist themes, to the Lycos search engine which uses Himalayan Sherpas as "guides." There is a makeup called Zen Blush and an Om perfume as well as a fruit juice container which says on its label; "Please recycle this bottle. It deserves to be reincarnated too." And a product called Tibetan Root Beer which purports to contain "gently invigorating cardamom, and coriander in a Tibetan adaptation of Ayurvedic herbs (Van Biema 1997; Lopez 1998a:2).

In 1997 Hollywood released three major motion pictures designed to further the cause of Tibetan independence and further elevate the Dalai Lama to a god-like status in the realm of marketing. "Seven Years in Tibet" was based on the famous book of the same name by Austrian mountaineer and former Nazi Heinrich Harrer. Partially funded by Gere it seemed bound to be a major hit since it starred a current heartthrob, Brad Pitt (Schell 2000; Kennedy 1997). "Kundun", "[…] a beautifully crafted piece of Dalaidolatry" (French 2003:101), was based on the Dalai Lama's autobiography and directed by Martin Scorsese.[14] And "Red Corner," a Richard Gere vehicle, was intended to demonize all Chinese.

There was great hope placed in these films. In conjunction with their release the International Campaign for Tibet launched "Seven Days for Tibet" with 300,000 "action kits" to be handed out at theaters and protests organized in 34 states (Schell 2000:305–306). With all the publicity and all the attention it seemed to excite the imagination of the Tibetan exiles and their supporters. A Tibetan photographer was quoted as saying "Hollywood does have the tools and power and they're really, in Asia and all over the world, they are considered very powerful and Hollywood can really save Tibet." Former Tibetan monk and Buddhist scholar Robert Thurman was also hopeful, "So our hope is that these films and Hollywood will accelerate the process by which they will wake up to this misguided policy" (Kennedy 1997). The International Campaign for Tibet's membership jumped from 2,000 in early 1997 to 16,000 by year's end. Its Web site went from 5,000 hits a month to 50,000 a week at the Hollywood movies' peak, and still got 35,000 weekly hits weeks after the movies finished their run (Said 1998).

As it turned out, all three films were flops. "Kundun" cost \$25– \$35 to produce and made only \$6 million in its four month run, "Seven Years in Tibet" cost \$60–\$70 million and returned only \$35 million to its backers while MGM wrote off a \$30 million loss on "Red Corner" (Schell 2000:314, Collins 1997). And while

[14] For an astonishingly level-headed and thoughtful review see Jaehne (without year).

they may have been responsible for recruiting more members into the various NGOs, they had no discernable effect on U.S. policy or the situation in Tibet.

While the films failed to live up to the expectations of the activists they did further embed Tibet and the Dalai Lama in the popular mind; the Dalai Lama was a household name while at the same time he became a large business. His many books – those written by him and those with his name on the cover – had huge sales. His *The Art of Happiness* alone sold 1.2 million copies. A check of www.amazon.com has over 3000 listings for Dalai Lama (Business & Finance 09/25/2003).[15]

The Dalai Lama was even asked to be the guest editor of the December 1992/January 1993 issue of *Paris Vogue*, a periodical not previously noted for its interest in serious subjects. He was also on the cover. No one else had been so honored in the 23 year history of the publication as an editorial explained: "we can say that it is because in the midst of fanaticisms, [sic] he is a symbol of tolerance." (Paris Vogue 1992)

In a more serious vein the U.S. Congress also became enamored of the Tibetans with several prominent members taking Tibet on as a personal cause. As a result Congress passed a number of legislative measures which had Tibet-related clauses added to them referring to it as an "independent country" and "an occupied sovereign country under international law". It passed legislation granting $500,000 to Tibetan refugees, providing thirty college scholarships (for $1,000,000) in the U.S. for Tibetan exile students, prohibited defense goods being exported to China, urged the imposition of trade sanctions against China and began Tibetan language radio broadcasts on the Voice of America in spring 1991. In 1996 Congress authorized the creation of a federally funded Cold War-era, Radio Free Asia, to broadcast Washington's official version of the news into regions of East Asia where governments were seen as hostile to U.S. interests, including Tibet. In 1997, bowing to public and Congressional pressure, President Bill Clinton created the post of Special Coordinator for Tibetan Affairs. This part-time Department of State position could have no influence over Tibetan affairs and was meant to be nothing more than a political sop to the president's critics. The appointment is symbolic of official U.S. support for the Tibetan exiles which came about as a direct result of the pressure exerted by the Tibet Lobby: feel-good gestures but no serious policy initiatives which could bring about concrete results nor any change in U.S. policy on the issue.

---

[15] It's not only the Dalai Lama who has benefited from this interest in Buddhism. The Paris-based Vietnamese monk, Thich Nhat Hanh, has sold 100,000 hardcover copies of his *Living Buddha, Living Christ* (Van Biema 1997). For a story about financial malfeasance concerning a Dalai Lama extravaganza, see Vanderpool 2005.

Congressional and public pressure led to the Dalai Lama's meetings with members of both houses of Congress and visits to the White House meeting President George H. W. Bush and National Security Advisor Brent Scowcroft, President Bill Clinton and Vice-President Al Gore, as well as President George W. Bush and Vice-President Dick Cheney. Each time, US officials insisted that the visits were "private," that the Dalai Lama was invited as a spiritual leader and to demonstrate that he has never been formally invited to, nor allowed to sit in, rooms where state visitors are received.

Neither the U.S., nor any other government, has ever recognized the Dalai Lama's self-styled "government-in-exile." The official view is that "[...] the United States Government considers Tibet to be a part of China and does not in any way recognize the Tibetan government in exile that the Dalai Lama claims to head." (Department of State Bulletin 87–2129)[16]

The advantages of internationalization are obvious, the risks less so. First, there is Hollywood's famously short attention span. In years past Hollywood personalities have felt as strongly about Marxism, Hinduism, Scientology and Jewish Kabbala as they now do about Buddhism (Parker 1997; Dawson 1998).[17] Tibetans also have to be wary of the uncertainty caused by the "[...] unstable life span of American celebrityhood" (Prothero 1997). As *Newsweek* magazine observed, "in the end, Hollywood's new Tibet chic will tell us more about Hollywood than about Tibet. And when filmdom is done with Tibet, a new season will usher in a new pet cause." (Emerson and Power 1997)

There is also the possibility that the mass marketing of the Dalai Lama could dilute his message and subject him to the same superficiality which is associated with his Hollywood friends. The "exigencies of global politics and celebrity culture" (French 2003:115) could lead to embarrassments such as CNN interviewer Larry King referring to him as a Muslim leader (CNN 12/31/1999). Or an infamous encounter with movie star Sharon Stone at a Hollywood benefit where, barefoot and wearing a feather boa, she introduced the 14th Dalai Lama as "Mr. please, please, please let me back into China" and "the hardest working man in spirituality" (Huffaker 2000).

The messages of the movement can also get confused. In another instance, after a benefit concert in Los Angeles the artists were on the stage with Tibetan monks but all the reporters' questions were for the artists. "Nobody seemed particularly

[16] See also Sciolino 1987. For a more thorough examination of the history of U.S.-Tibet relations see Grunfeld 2005.

[17] Earlier era New Agers, enamored of a different Asian religion, thought the same thing about their newly found faith. In the 1960s and 1970 Shri Guru Maharaji ji was all the rage as his highest official acknowledged, "In the world? About four million spread over 63 countries. It is catching on like wildfire." (Singh 1973)

interested in asking the monks questions about Tibet – and they were the ones most qualified to answer," commented one journalist (Emerson and Power 1997).

A convergence of interest is evident as Western Tibet groupies have developed a "[…] nostalgia for the already lost secrets of Tibetan Buddhism," observes Tibetologist Donald Lopez, "and there is a patronizing contempt for the exiled Tibetans as custodians unequal to the task of preserving their own culture without our help. That they were perceived as inadequate caretakers of that culture derives not so much from the difficult times in which they found themselves as from the fact that the culture they were charged to preserve was not of their making, but of ours." (Lopez 1995:269; see, also, Peter Bishop 2000)

"The Tibetan movement has become a symbol of hope for those promoting a global political culture of non-violence and dialogue," observes one Tibetan exile, "But the cost of remaining a moral example is too great for a growing number of Tibetans who simply want an end to the atrocities inflicted on their land and people. While the world fawns over romanticized images of a gentle Himalayan utopia, frustration simmers among Tibetans as they are forced to watch the real Tibet die before their eyes." (Tsering 2000)

Foreign patronage has a price; loss of some independence over the movement – a not uncommon phenomenon for groups that have successful marketed themselves and find the necessity to conform to the goals of their patrons in order to maintain support. The more dependent they become on wealthy people from the wealthy nations, the more they have to bend to their patron's wishes (Bob 2002). This may explain why the Dalai Lama is more accessible to foreigners than to Tibetans who must overcome bureaucratic obstacles to see him (Klieger 1992:80).

Foreign patronage can also lead to conflicts. While the Milarepa Fund supports a boycott of Chinese goods, as do some exiled Tibetans, the Dalai Lama opposes such a strategy on political grounds (Fisher 1998). And there is conflict over proselytization as the Dalai Lama has said, "[…] in the West, I do not think it is advisable to follow Buddhism. Changing religions is not like changing professions. Excitement lessens over the years, and soon you are not excited, and then where are you? Homeless inside yourself." (French 2003:21) Nevertheless the flow of Westerners into the ranks of Buddhism continues to grow. After all, it is not only the political movements but, also the religious community, which needs patronage from foreign donors, tourists and students (Klieger 1992:86, 99).

No one is exempt from the pressure to conform. For his best selling book, *Ethics for the New Millennium*, the Dalai Lama originally wrote: "I am a Buddhist and, for a Buddhist, a relationship between two men is wrong. Some sexual conduct in marriage is also wrong […] For example using one's mouth and the other hole." However, his U.S. publisher thought this might offend readers and at their urging he removed it (French 2003:218).

Successfully marketing means that message has to be effective for the market at which it is aimed. To that end, "Over the years, the Western media's desire for 'atrocity stories' has not diminished; in fact, the demand has grown exponentially. It is now commonplace to point out how images of mass suffering and atrocities are needed to mobilize governments and others into taking action in case of political disasters." (McLagan 1996:179)[18] In 1988, after a decade of futile attempts, I was finally given permission to visit Tibet and promised freedom to roam at will and the opportunity to interview officials. Prior to leaving the United States I inquired of several publications if they would be interested in any articles I may write based on my trip. *The New York Times Magazine* told me they would be most interested in "Chinese atrocity stories," and only those stories. Anything else about Tibet was of no interest to them.[19]

According to the most prominent Tibetan polemicist, "the national struggle for an independent Tibet has been replaced by a squishy agenda of environmental, pacifistic, spiritual and 'universal' concerns that has little or nothing to do with Tibet's real problems." (Norbu 1998:21)

China's Response

Chinese response has been to publicly declare that its accusers have had no effect on domestic policies towards Tibet; that the West should mind its own business and not interfere with the internal affairs of the PRC. This may not sound plausible to Western ears but resonates inside China with its history of more than a century of foreign exploitation.

Despite its protestations to the contrary, the Tibet Lobby has indeed influenced policies in China. Tibetans and Tibet have a far higher profile than any of the other 55 official designated "ethnic minorities" in China. While there are academic institutions devoted to the study of all the minorities only Tibetans have had think tanks devoted exclusively to them.

Chinese media is satiated with programs concerning Tibet; on television, in movie theaters and frequent articles in the print media. If there is a single theme that ties these media ventures together it is the argument that the lengthy historical record proves Tibet has been a part of China for centuries and the vast majority

[18] "[…] narratives of suffering play an important role in constructing Tibetans as a moral community and as a people." (McLagan 1996:147)

[19] It is in this light that one has to access the claim that 1.2 million Tibetans have lost their lives since 1950. It is a figure created "in response to demands from foreign supporters of the Tibetan cause" and "needed to impress Western legislators." When an outside observer was allowed to see the documents upon which this figure was based, he found them largely implausible yet it continues to be cited universally (French 2003:279–281).

of Tibetans are grateful for the material progress they have made since 1950 and only possible under the leadership of the CCP.

One can only attribute all this attention to the activities of the Tibet Lobby. Tibetans are not very numerous in China; in fact, they rank only ninth in terms of population size behind the Zhuang, Manchu, Hui, Miao, Uygur, Yi, Tujia and Mongol minorities. Other minorities, Uygur, Kazak and Mongols, have expressed displeasure at being part of the Chinese state while terrorist activities such as bombs on buses and theaters have occurred in Xinjiang where they are attributed to separatist Uygurs. Yet Tibetans get all the money, publicity and attention.

Present-day Chinese have no legacy of Shangri-la fantasies about Tibet to build on. Since the 1950s official propaganda has portrayed Tibet as backward and unhealthy for Chinese, a feudal land of harsh realities for the majority of Tibetans who had to endure physical torture and considerable other unspeakable horrors. Officials assigned to work there considered it a punishment and frequently left their families home rather than subject them to the harsh conditions they envisioned. In other words, the Chinese had created a fantasy Tibet of their own; an inhospitable place inhabited by an inferior people.

Nevertheless, the recent considerable media attention has led to a fascination with all things Tibetan. The media spotlight, the attainment of disposable income, and the freedom to travel have led to the development of a Tibetan chic. To be sure many Chinese, particularly of an older generation, continue to view Tibetans as inferior, but there is a discernable change as tens of thousands of Chinese now live in Tibet voluntarily. Young Chinese artists flock to Tibet, reminiscent of an earlier generation of American artists who went to Paris for inspiration. Internal tourism has boomed. In 2002, 720,000 Chinese tourists visited Tibet, a 30% increase above 2001 (Douglas 2003). Tibetan Buddhism has also become popular as have religious pilgrimages by Chinese Buddhists.

As in the West commercial interests are using Tibetan themes to sell products. Tibetan beer is popular as is Tibetan Grass brand ginseng-berry juice, a sorghum liquor called Tibet Fragrant Spring and Tibetan Highland barley wine. Moreover, traditional Tibetan medicine has gained a huge following with 90% of the patients in the Tibetan Traditional Medicine Hospital in Beijing being Chinese. And there is the story of a struggling Chinese pop star named Zhu Zheqin who became famous only when she adopted a Tibetan stage name, Dadawa, and began singing songs like "Ballad of Lhasa". Her video showed her in Tibetan costume herding yaks and clowning with nomads in Tibet.[20]

[20] Her CD was equally popular in Tibet until it was discovered that in the background a female voice could be heard praising the Dalai Lama in Tibetan. It was immediately withdrawn and edited and her videos were subsequently banned in Tibet (Forney 2001). In a book review of

There is no discernable opposition to the official view in China that Tibet has long been a part of China, that the material lives of Tibetans are getting inexorably better, that Tibetans are all happy to be citizens of the PRC and that all problems stem entirely from outside forces dedicated to weakening China or overthrowing it's government. So for the Chinese government the propaganda challenge lays outside its boundaries where the Tibet Lobby has been so successful. In this battle for the hearts and minds of non-Chinese the Beijing authorities have failed miserably. For the PRC this is a long-standing problem with its propaganda organs, since 1949, demonstrating that they have a tin ear for what works in the West.

China's inability to adequately market itself is certainly not for lack of trying. During the Maoist era China's isolation made world opinion of little import. But now that China is an active participant in the world community international opinion can embarrass the Chinese government and they are acutely aware of it.

Beijing has responded to the Dalai Lama's media blitz in a number of ways. They have produced copious printed materials on Tibet in several languages for external consumption, began a magazine devoted specifically to Tibet, *China's Tibet*, and a corresponding website, www.tibetinfor.com. They sent Tibetan cultural troupes and scholars around the world. They arranged group visits to Tibet for foreign journalists and visiting heads of state.

The quantity of materials is impressive (and the Chinese authorities gauge success by the quantity of their work) but the quality is amateurishness (replete with grammatical errors) and lacks credibility. It goes beyond the media. There is not a single diplomat in any Chinese diplomatic mission in the West who understands Tibet nor knows how to effectively access the Western media. On the few occasions that Chinese diplomats have gone on camera to defend their government's position on Tibet they have been ridiculed. And the foreign visits to Tibet don't help either because they are so tightly scripted, limiting the movements of the visitors, that they did more to malign the hosts than to bring them much desired support (Tibetan Information Network 2001).

An excellent example of China's failed efforts can be seen in a 1997 major, big budget, motion picture entitled "Red River Valley," devised to counter Hollywood's efforts. The film received virtually no attention in the West and was, by Hollywood and professional standards, simply dreadful. It depicted the Tibetan attempt to counter the 1904 Anglo-Indian invasion and was intended to show Chi-

---

Sky Burial by Xinran (a "[…] novel by a Beijing journalist [which] plays into the fantasy of the region as a Wild West populated by noble savages with much to teach the cosmopolitan Chinese"), the reviewer observes that "in China these days, Tibet is all the rage: Beijing hipsters lounge in bars festooned with yak horns, pop divas sing ballads about Lhasa, and tourists mob the rooftop of the world" (The New Yorker 08/22/2005:75).

nese and Tibetans fighting heroically side-by-side against foreign aggression as they are, presumably, doing today in a different guise (Tibet Information Network 2001).[21]

Chinese authorities were alarmed enough by the successes of the Tibet Lobby to organize a series of fora in Beijing and Lhasa beginning in 1991 to discuss the nature of the Dalai Lama's internationalization of the Tibet issue and how to further their own propaganda efforts to counter it. From leaked documents it is clear that the Chinese authorities are adequately appraised of the situation they face.[22] It is also clear that they have no idea how to effectively counter it nor do they seem to fully comprehend the nature of their problems in Tibet; blaming everything on external causes.[23]

Conclusion

After the Dalai Lama's refusal to visit Beijing in 1989, the demonstrations in Lhasa and the attacks on China as a result of the Tibet Lobby's efforts, officials who had tried to negotiate a compromise with the Dalai Lama were transferred from doing Tibet work. In their place hard-liners were appointed, men who believed that restrictions on religious activities, Chinese immigration into Tibet, patriotic education campaigns and waiting for the Dalai Lama to die would solve all of Tibet's problems. Each success of the Tibet Lobby was held up as proof of the "imperialist" intentions of the Western nations who are committed to weakening China and preventing it from taking its rightful place in the world community.

In two decades or so the Tibet Lobby has achieved two very contradictory results. On the one hand, outside of Tibet it has made the Dalai Lama and Tibet household words and has monopolized a narrative about them to the exclusion

[21] Also, see http://www.tibetinfor.com/tibetzt/fil_001.htm. See annotation in http://www1.esc.edu/personalfac/tgrunfeld.

[22] International Relations vs. "Tibetan Issue" – China's Tibet, 10 September 2000 Symposium. See http://www.tibetinfor.com.cn/englisch/services/form/for_203.htm (August 25, 2002).

[23] www.caccp.org/conf/doc7.html. "The so-called issue of Tibet is the main pretext for western countries, including the United States, to westernize and split our country. Western countries, including the United States, want to topple our country and further the cause of their own social and value systems and national interests. In order to achieve this, they will never stop using the Tibet issue to westernize and split our country and weaken our power [...]" Zhao Qizheng, minister in charge of the Information Office of the State Council, at the meeting on national research in Tibetology and external propaganda on Tibet. "Tibet-related external propaganda and Tibetology work in the new era" 12 June 2000, International Campaign for Tibet, April 9, 2001. www.tibetinfo.co.uk/news-updates/west.pdf (August 28, 2003).

of all others[24] although it doesn't seem to have produced any tangible benefit to the majority of Tibetans in exile, except for those on Washington's payroll. But on the other hand, for the vast majority of Tibetans – those in China, the Tibet Lobby has done the opposite of what was intended, strengthening the power of hard-line officials whose policies have resulted in a serious long-term threat to Tibetan culture.

Patrick French quotes a Tibetan he spoke to as observing: "The exiled Tibetans in India and Nepal who talk about freedom are wasting their time. I say to them, if you want independence for Tibet, why don't you come here and make a protest and see how far it gets you? It may make them feel good, but for us, it makes life worse. It makes the Chinese create more controls over us." (French 2003:127)

In discussions with knowledgeable Chinese intellectuals in Beijing and Lhasa in 2001, I found them lamenting the demise of the officials who were willing to work with the Dalai Lama after his refusal to visit in 1989. They believed that the Tibet Lobby's efforts in the media, trying to embarrass top Chinese officials on trips overseas and getting foreign leaders to complain personally, had relegated Tibet to such an exalted status that only the top officials could make major decisions leaving almost no political space for officials and scholars to have any input.

It is not only Chinese intellectuals who feel that the activities of the Tibet Lobby have hindered a search for a possible solution rather than aiding it. Some Western scholars also believe that: "[...] The emigre myth is pervasive in the West and is an obstacle to a negotiated settlement of the Tibet question." (Sautman 2001:283)

Since 2002 the Dalai Lama and the Beijing authorities have held talks on four occasions and while Beijing has been publicly silent about these talks, the Dalai Lama's representatives have publicly characterized them in unusually positive terms. Indeed, in summer 2005, the head of the Dalai Lama's administration in Dharamsala referred to the talks as being at a "make or break" (World Tibet Network 2005) point. It is too early to know if the Tibet Lobby influenced these talks or whether it is a result of new leadership in Beijing or, even, if it is nothing more than a public relations ploy on Beijing's part in the run-up to the 2008 Olympics. Indisputably the Dalai Lama's major success has been his ability to create interest and fascination with himself, his cause and his religion around the world. This

[24] When Donald Lopez was asked to appear on National Public Radio's "Talk of the Nation" to discuss his book, Prisoners of Shangri-la, he was told there would also be someone "from the other side." He thought this meant someone from the PRC but it turned out to be someone from the International Campaign for Tibet as any criticism of Tibet had come to be seen as criticizing the whole endeavor (McMillan 2001:247–248, fn. 5).

fascination has led – not for the first time but never so widespread and with such intensity – to an infatuation with a romanticized and idealized Tibet. A highly successful campaign has propelled the Tibet Lobby to heights unimagined by its originators; Hollywood movies, rock concerts, celebrities practicing Buddhism, a compliant international media have all combined to make the Dalai Lama and Tibet household words. Ironically, there is a similar phenomena going on in China where the government's attention to Tibet has resulted in a different sort of a fad; an infatuation with Tibetans as 'noble savages' with their exotic ways.

So for all of its success the Tibet Lobby may have achieved a Pyrrhic victory. Tibetans – real people, with a real history, with a real struggle, have been cartoonized by American (and Chinese) popular culture (Schell 2000; Stewart 2000).[25] As historian Tsering Shakya (1992:13) put it, "Tibet was being recreated and reformed into Western imaginations and enthused with psychedelic experiences." And in the final analysis it may not have done any good for the millions of Tibetans in China.

A. Tom Grunfeld, Department of History, State University of New York Empire State College, New York

References

Bharati, Agehananda (1974): Fictitious Tibet: The Origin and Persistence of Rampaism. In: Tibet Society Bulletin 7, 1–11.

Bishop, Peter (2000): Caught in the Cross-Fire: Tibet, Media and Promotional Culture. In: Media, Culture and Society 2:5, 645–664.

Bob, Clifford (2001): Marketing Rebellion: Insurgent Groups, International Media, and NGO Support. In: International Politics 38 (Sept. 2001), 321–327.

Bob, Clifford (2002): Merchants of Morality. Globalization at Work, how Certain Independence Groups, such as Tibetans in China, Get Positive Publicity for Their Cause. In: Foreign Policy (Mar. 2002).

Business & Finance (09/25/2003): The Business of Being the Dalai Lama. In: Business & Finance (September 25, 2003).

CNN (12/31/1999): Larry King Live.

Collins, L. (1997): 007 is on a Mission to Revive his Ailing Studio's Fortune. In: Courier Mail. Queensland, Australia, 26 December 1997).

Dawson, Jeff (1998): Devout's not out Anymore: Hollywood Gets Religion. In: The Dalles Morning News (04/11/ 1998).

Department of State Bulletin 87–2129 (Dec. 1987): Human Rights Situation of the Tibetan People, 50.

---

[25] For a series of articles critical of the exile Tibetan view of Tibet see: www.members.tripod.com/~journeyeast/Tibet.html (August 28, 2002).

Douglas, Ed (2003): Ring Road Threatens Sacred Slopes of Pilgrims. In: The Observer (09/14/2003).
Emerson, Tony and Carla Power (1997): Tibet Gets Chic. In: Newsweek (05/19/1997).
Fisher, Marc (1998): Great Wall of Sound; Faraway Tibet: Peak of Chic. In: The Washington Post (06/07/1998).
Forney, Matthew (2001): China Falls for Tibet Chic. In: Time (01/ 29 2001).
Foster, Barbara M. et. al. (1998): The Secret Lives of Alexandra David-Neel: a Biography of the Explorer of Tibet and its Forbidden Practices. Woodstock, NY: Overlook Press.
French, Patrick (2003): Tibet, Tibet. A Personal History of a Lost Land. New York: Alfred A. Knopf.
Gearing, Julian (2003): Tibetan Buddhism the Western Way. In: Asia Times (12/ 25/ 2003).
Goldstein, Melvyn C. (1989): History of Modern Tibet, 1913–1951: The Demise of the Lamaist State. Berkeley, CA: University of California Press.
Grunfeld, Tom (1988): Enigmatic Buddha Who Works From Within. In: The Guardian (London) (10/08/1988), 8.
Grunfeld, A. Tom (1996): The Making of Modern Tibet, revised edition. New York and London: M. E. Sharpe, Inc.
Grunfeld, A. Tom (2003):'God We Had Fun:' The CIA in China and Sino-American Relations. In: Critical Asian Studies 35:1 (Mar. 2003), 113–138.
Grunfeld, A. Tom (2006): Tibet and the United States. In: Sautman, Barry and June Teufel Dreyer (eds.): Contemporary Tibet: Politics, Development and Society in a Disputed Region. Armonk: M. E. Sharpe, Inc.
His Holiness the Dalai Lama (1982): Collected Statements, Interviews and Articles: Dharamsala, India: The Information Office of His Holiness the Dalai Lama.
Huffaker, Donna (2000): Blessings for Peace; Dalai Lama Preaches. In: The Daily News of Los Angeles (06/30/ 2000).
Jaehne, Karen (no date): Kundun. http://www.filmscouts.com/scripts/review.cfm?File=kundun (August 23, 2005).
Joan Kutcher (1982): Tibetan Resources in North America. Occasional Paper; updated and expanded in 1982.
Joan Kutcher (ed.) (1979): Tibetan Resources in North America. New York: The Himalayas Council of The Asia Society, 1979).
Karl E. Meyer and Shareen Blair Brysac (1999): Tournament of Shadows. The Great Game and the Race for Empire in Central Asia. Washington, DC: Counterpoint.
Kennedy, Dana (1997): Entertainers Focus on Tibet. In: ABC Good Morning America (10/05/1997).
Klieger, P. Christiaan (1992): Tibetan Nationalism. The Role of Patronage in the Accomplishment of a National Identity. Meerut, India: Archana Publications.
Kluver, Randy (no date): Globalization, Informatization, and Intercultural Communication. In: American Communication Journal. http://www.acjournal.org/holdings/vol3/Iss3/spec1/kluver.htm (March 7, 2005).
Long, Jeff (1981): In Search of a Tibetan Guerrilla, Tibetan Review 16:9 (Sept.1981), 8–14.
Lopez, Donald S., Jr. (1995): Foreigner at the Lama's Feet. In: Lopez, Donald S. Jr. (ed.) (1995): Curators of the Buddha. The Study of Buddhism under Colonialism. Chicago and London: The University of Chicago Press.
Lopez, Donald S. Jr. (1998a): Prisoners of Shangri-la. Tibetan Buddhism and the West. Chicago and London: The University of Chicago Press.

Lopez, Donald Jr. (1998b): No Shangri-la for Tibetans – Romanticizing Tibet Only Obscures the Real Issue. In: MSNBC in World Tibet Network (05/06/1998).
Manz, Beatrice F. (2003): Multi-ethnic Empires and the Formulation of Identity. In: Ethnic and Racial Studies 26:1 (Jan. 2003), 70–101.
McKay, Alex (1997): Tibet and the British Raj. The Frontier Cadre, 1904–1947. London: Curzon Press.
McLagan, Margaret J. (1996): Mobilizing for Tibet: Transnational Politics and Diaspora Culture in the Post-Cold War Era. PhD, New York University.
McMillan, Laurie Hovell (2001): English in Tibet. Tibet in English. New York: Palgrave.
Miller, Beatrice D. (1988): American Popular Perceptions of Tibet from 1858–1938. In: The Tibet Journal 13:3 (Aug. 1988), 3–19.
Norbu, Jamyang (1998): Dances With Yaks. Tibet in Film, Fiction, and Fantasy of the West. In: Tibetan Review 33:1 (January 1998), 21.
O'Callaghan, Mary-Louise (1985): TIBET/China's Backdoor Swings Open, Quietly Ending Years of Tibetan Isolation. In: The Christian Science Monitor (06/10 /1985).
Paris Vogue (1992): Editorial, Paris Vogue 732 (Dec. 1992/Jan. 1993), 127.
Parker, Shafer Jr. (1997): Dalai Mania: Tibetan Leader Now a PC Cause. In: World (09/20/1997).
Peter Bishop (1993): Dreams of Power. Tibetan Buddhism and the Western Imagination. London: Athlone Press.
Peterson, Jonathan (1997): China's President Will Tour U.S.: As Pop Culture Villainizes His Nation. In: Los Angeles Times (10/26/1997).
Prothero, Stephen (1997): Buddha Chic. In: Salon (05/24/1997).
Rabgey, Tashi and Tseten Wangchuk Sharlho (2004): Sino-Tibetan Dialogue in the Post-Mao Era: Lessons and Prospects. In: Policy Studies 12. Washington, DC: East-West Center.
Said, Carolyn (1998): Trying to Save Tibet. From Palo Alto to Pacifica, Activists and Artists Lead Fight for Freedom. In: San Francisco Chronicle (02/20/1998).
Sautman Barry (2001): Tibet: Myths and Realities. In: Current History 100, 647 (Sept.2001).
Schell, Orville (2000): Virtual Tibet. Searching for Shangri-la from the Himalayas to Hollywood. New York: Metropolitan Books.
Sciolino, Elaine (1987). US Official Defends Stance on Turmoil in Tibet. In: New York Times (10/15/1987), A18.
Seager Richard Hughes (1999): Buddhism in America. New York: Columbia University Press.
Singer, Wendy (2003): The Dalai Lama's Many Tibetan Landscapes, In: Kenyon Review 25:3/4 (Summer/Fall 2003), 233–256.
Singh, Khushwant (1973): The Guru Business. In: The New York Times Magazine (04/08/1973), 35.
Stewart, Barbara (2000): Current Films on Tibet, Hold the Shangri-La. In: New York Times (03/19/2000).
Tibet Society (1973): Tibet Society Newsletter (Aug. 1973), 3.
Tibetan Information Network (2001): Propaganda and the West: China's Struggle to Sway International Opinion on the 'Tibet Issue' (16 July 2001). http://www.tibetinfo.co.uk/news-updates/nu160701.htm (April 26, 2002).
Tsering, Shakya (1992): Tibet and the Occident. The Myth of Shangri-la. In: Tibetan Review, 27:1 (Jan. 1992), 13–16.
Tsering, Chokey (2002): Which Way to Freedom. Shambala Sun Online, 2002. http://www.shambhalasun.com/Archives/Features/1998/Nov1998/Tsering.htm (October 24, 2003).

Tseten, Wangchuk Sharlho (1992): China's Reforms in Tibet: Issues and Dilemmas. In: The Journal of Contemporary China 1:1 (Fall 1992), 34–60.

Van Biema, David et al. (1997): Buddhism in America; An Ancient Religion Grows Ever Stronger Roots in a New World, With the Help of the Movies, Pop Culture and the Politics of Repressed Tibet. In: Time (10/13/1997).

Vanderpool, Tim (2005): Dalai Lama Inc. Making Hay from His Holiness, Tuscon (AZ) Weekly (09/15/2005).

World Tibet Network (2005): Tibetans Urged Not to Mar Hu Jintao's America Visit. In: World Tibet Network (09/0 5/2005).

Xinhua News Agency (01/09/ 2003): Tourists to Tibet up 24 percent in 2002.

Xinhua News Agency (11/16/1984): Developing tourism in Tibet. In BBC-SWB, Part 3. The Far East; B. Internal affairs; China II; FE/7806/BII/1.

Xinhua News Agency (12/09/1999): Tourists visit Tibet in Record Numbers.

Xu Guangqiu (1997): The United States and the Tibet Issue. In: Asian Survey 37:11 (Nov. 1997).

Judith Hufnagel

Dangerous Liaisons

Examining the Triangle between Taiwan, the United States, and the People's Republic of China from an International Law Point of View

Among the number of unsolved disputes about questions of sovereignty and territory in Asia today, the problem posed by the island of Taiwan is second to none in complexity and significance. The sovereignty conflict in the Taiwan Strait between the People's Republic of China (PRC) and the Republic of China (ROC)[1] on Taiwan has lasted for more than half a century, and a permanent solution is not yet in sight. This conflict constitutes the most serious contentious point between the United States and the PRC and, in the words of Thomas W. Robinson, "the only one for the foreseeable future with the potential for a direct military clash" (Robinson 1996:1357–1358) between Washington and Beijing.

The PRC, on the brink of becoming an economic as well as a political and perhaps even military big player in Asia, has shown a desire to be part of the world community and has professed to abide by its laws. It has been successful in its integration in international organizations such as the United Nations (UN), the World Trade Organization (WTO), or the Association of Southeast Asian Nations (ASEAN) Regional Forum (see Kang 2003:68). It even initiated the Shanghai Cooperation Organization (SCO) to enhance regional cooperation in Central Asia and has solved most of the territorial conflicts with the 14 nations with which it shares land borders and the seven that share its maritime boundaries. (Shambaugh 2002:285–286, 290). In contrast to this, the PRC government views the Taiwan conflict as part of "the Chinese people's struggle for national reunification and territorial integrity" (TAO 1993) ("中国人民为推护国家统一和领土完整的斗争", ZXB 1993) – in other words: this is not to be regarded as an international

[1] In using ROC as abbreviation of the international legal entity on Taiwan, I follow the Taiwanese authorities; however, I do so merely for the sake of briefness and in a way for the sake of fairness, using the official abbreviations in use on each side of the Taiwan Strait respectively. I do not wish to imply that the Taiwanese standpoint on matters of sovereignty and nomenclature is necessarily my own. For the use of different labels for Taiwan see deLisle 2000:37.

issue but rather as a domestic or internal affair and as such to be dealt with solely under PRC jurisdiction.

The ROC on the other hand is still striving to return to the international community as a fully-fledged member, its plight to be readmitted to the United Nations having lasted for over a decade (Hutchings 2001:416). When taking office in 2000, President Chen Shuibian (陳水扁) pledged that Taiwan would continue to "actively participate in international affairs, expand Taiwan's room for survival in the international arena, and contribute to the welfare of the international community" (Chen 2000a) ("積極參與國際事務， 擴大台灣在國際的生存空間， 並且回饋國際社會", Chen 2000b). Having successfully mastered the transition to democracy, Taiwanese voices on cross-Strait relations have shown a new confidence, demanding to meet with the PRC in "direct dialogue […] under principles of democracy and parity" (Kau 2002:2), a stance which demonstrates the ROC's demand to be treated as a separate state on equal footing with the PRC.

From the Korean War of 1950 onwards, the United States has been the most involved third party in the region. Throughout major changes in the political arena (the changing attitude of the international community towards communist China in the 1970s, economic reform and opening to western investment of the PRC under Deng Xiaoping (鄧小平), the disintegration of the Eastern Bloc and the end of the Cold War, the end of martial law in Taiwan, political reform and the establishment of democracy in the ROC during the 1990s, to name but a few) the U.S. had to find a way of defining and supporting its policies in the area. For the ROC, America constitutes the only, if not openly professed supporter of substantial influence on the international plane. Their relationship, however, is by no means independent of the general sovereignty dilemma in the region, but rather exists in a fairly complex triangle of PRC-U.S.-ROC relations. The very fact that the sovereignty dispute has not been resolved yet makes keeping up a stable relationship with both parties very tricky for the U.S. Were both sides widely acknowledged as independent states (and did the PRC share that estimation), the U.S. could maintain economic and political relations to both without further ado. As it is, however, relations to the PRC are closely tied to the absence of the same to the ROC, a fact that makes upholding the (admittedly unofficial) ties between the U.S. and the ROC a challenge and a difficult balancing act.

For decades now, the three parties have devised and adhered to a framework that functions as a *modus vivendi* for their dealings with each other: the 'one China' policy – or, more accurately, their 'one China' policies. It is the aim of this paper to examine how the three different parties interpret 'one China', what international legal principles they cite to uphold their interpretations, and how they develop their policies regarding cross-Strait issues accordingly. The focus will lie on the respective legal interpretations in order to show how one and the same concept may be motivated and explained in three different ways to effectuate different policies. Of course, as Ted Galen Carpenter puts it, "[w]hen it comes to territorial disputes, [...] international law is a far less important factor than military power" (Carpenter in Carpenter/Dorn 2000:80); however, it is still a factor. Since only very few countries openly admit their unwillingness to comply with international law and because consistency with international legal principles can give argumentative strength to policy positions, having a look at the legal implications can be very helpful in understanding and motivating the actions of countries on an international level.

So how does Taiwan fit into the international legal framework, according to the three parties, and what light does that shed on politics? For a long time, the PRC, the ROC, and the U.S. have 'agreed to disagree', all three using the same terms to outline their general policy but interpreting them in very different ways.

The PRC and the 'one China' policy

The PRC's general stance on 'one China' is fairly simple:

> "There is only one China in the world, Taiwan is an inalienable part of China and the seat of China's central government is in Beijing. This is a universally recognized fact as well as the premise for a peaceful settlement of the Taiwan question. [...] Taiwan's status as an inalienable part of China has been determined and cannot be changed. 'Self-determination' for Taiwan is out of the question." (TAO 1993)

The basic claim that Taiwan is part of China is the fundamental assumption of the so-called 'one China' policy to which the Chinese leadership has adhered since the founding of the PRC. The PRC's legal arguing is based on the differentiation of sovereignty on the one hand and administrative authority and jurisdiction on the other (Shen 2000:1119). In the PRC's opinion, since "[t]he sovereignty of each State is an integral whole which is indivisible and unsharable" (TAO 1993) ("每个国家的主权是完整的， 既不能分割的， 也不能分享", ZXB 1993) and rests with the central government, it follows that there cannot be two separate entities both lawfully claiming sovereignty within the concept of 'one China'. This stems from the notion that "one thing cannot have two owners" ("一物不能二主", Huang/Wang 2002:30). However, numerous formulations in the two government White Papers especially dealing with the Taiwan question suggest that it is conceivable for the administrative authority and jurisdiction to temporarily rest with an authority other than the central government.[2] In consequence, whenever

[2] Such formulations include, e.g., "in 1945, the Chinese government *reinstated* its administrative authority in Taiwan Province" (TAO 1993) ("一九四五年 [...], 中国政府重新恢复了台湾省的行政管理机构", ZXB 1993) and "the Chinese government *recovered* Taiwan and the Penghu Archipelago, *resuming* the exercise of sovereignty over Taiwan" (TAO 2000)

parts of China (as defined by the historic and cultural bond between the Chinese people "of the same flesh and blood" (TAO 2000) (骨肉同胞, ZXB 2000) fall under the control of foreign or internal powers other than the central government, this does not result in a split of sovereignty but merely in a split of jurisdiction and administrative authority. In the PRC's concept, undivided sovereignty thus can never reside with any entity but the Chinese people (Lee 1997:700) represented by the central government. Even if administrative authority and jurisdiction are exercised by a power other than the central government, the PRC denies that this exercising administration also results in the *right* to do so, as that right is tied to the possession of a sovereign title (Lian 2002).

In order to legitimize the concept of an indivisible sovereign title from a historical and legal perspective, the central government argues that in the course of the Civil War of the 1940s "the government of the 'Republic of China' in Nanjing was [...] overthrown by the Chinese people" (TAO 1993) ("中国人民 [...] 推翻了南京 '中华民国' 政府", ZXB 1993) and that with the founding of the PRC the government of the ROC was *replaced*. Following this line of thought, the revolution of 1949 constituted a 'succession of government' that changed the form of government but left the state of China's 'international personality' untouched and thus did not constitute a 'succession of state' (Shen 2000:1118). This estimation is grounded on the view that

> "according to international law, if a country experiences a revolution that leads to the overthrow of the old government and the establishment of a new government, the latter will naturally inherit the whole authority and sovereignty held by the old government [up to that point]".[3]

As a consequence of this full transfer of rights, in the eyes of the PRC the Republic of China ceased to exist in 1949, being replaced by the People's Republic. Thus, the ROC existing on Taiwan today, even though using the same name, cannot claim to be the same legal person (TAO 2000).

According to PRC authorities and scholars, Chinese sovereignty has been united with the retrocession of the island by Japan, and since 1949 it has rested in the hands of the PRC government (Ruan 1994:18). The Taiwanese people are therefore regarded a special group within the bigger whole of the Chinese nation. As such they merely partake in the sovereign title held by the Chinese people, but cannot claim to hold a full, independent sovereign title of their own (Huang/Wang 2002:35). As a result, no separate sovereign title exists for the Taiwanese territory

("中国政府收复台湾, 澎湖列岛, 重新恢复对台湾行使的主权", ZXB 2000). Emphasis added.

[3] Quoted from Chinese: "按照国际法, 一国因发生革命导致旧政府被推翻, 新政府成立, 后者当然继承旧政府行 使的一切权力和主权." (Liu 2002)

and that it is part of Chinese territory, a fact that in the view of the PRC cannot be changed no matter what happens:

> "No matter who takes office in Taiwan, no matter what method is used at what time, nothing can change the fact that Taiwan is part of the Chinese territory."[4]

To resolve all the above-described sovereignty issues within the 'one China' framework, the PRC has found the formula of 'one country, two systems' (一国两制). Already implemented in the Hong Kong and Macao scenarios, this formula finally aims at reuniting the exercise of sovereignty with the sovereign title. The 'one country' part of the concept reflects the indivisibility of sovereign title, while the 'two systems' part takes note of the divisibility of the exercise of sovereignty (Huang/Wang 2002:36). Following this formula, the Taiwanese authorities would go on to administer the island very much as before (including their own military forces). They would have to relinquish their claim of being a separate state, though, and they would ultimately have to accept being a local authority subordinate to the national government in Beijing (the PRC regards this to be the case already, even without the ROC's having accepted it).

The 'one China' principle does imply some far-reaching consequences for the way the PRC applies rules of international law to the Chinese context, or rather how it exempts the Chinese context from the sphere of international law. Since in PRC-Taiwan relations Beijing embodies governmental authority that is placed *above* the local authorities of Taiwan (deLisle 2000:40–41), it follows that all relations between Beijing and Taipei are regarded as a domestic and "purely internal affair of China" (TAO 1993) ("纯属中国的内政", ZXB 1993) neither taking place in the international arena nor being subject to international law. Here the PRC calls upon the protection of her territorial integrity and the principle of non-intervention into domestic affairs of states (Ruan 1994:18).

The PRC's policy of 'one China' and the resulting formula for reunification of 'one country, two systems' form a consistent theoretical framework that follows its inherent logic. The most important foundation of this framework is the concept of indivisible state sovereignty. The PRC argues that this concept is the fundamental principle without which the whole system of international law could not have been established in the first place and without which this system cannot function at all (Yang 2002:43, Zhu 2002:72).

It is true that the formation of the present system of international law is tied to the rise of the nation state and that for its implementation the concept of independently acting sovereign states is indispensable, since "the preservation of states in

[4] Quoted from Chinese: "在台湾，无论谁上台，无论在什么时间采取什么方法，都改变不了台湾是中国领土一部 分的事实." (Lian 2002)

their found territorial existence simply is a constitutive element of international law" ("[d]ie Erhaltung der Staaten in ihrem vorgefundenen territorialen Bestand […] ein schlechthin konstituierendes Element der Völkerrechtsordnung [ist]", Herdegen 2002:39). Nevertheless, the PRC's use of the concept seems excessively formalistic, and especially the notion of the territorial extent of sovereignty being exempt from change, ensuring that no part of the territory once belonging to 'China' can *ever* lawfully be transferred to another state's sovereignty, appears antiquated and obsolete.

What the PRC fails to take into account most of all is that in present practice of international law sovereignty only exists if a state is able to demonstrate actual exercise of sovereignty (Austin 1998:340). Even if one assumes that the exercise of sovereignty is not lawful unless it is tied to and legitimized by a sovereign title (as the PRC does), the effectiveness of the control of territory is an important part in determining the possession of sovereignty (principle of effectiveness, *Effektivitätsprinzip*). Because international law strives to be based on a realistic evaluation of facts, accepting the present allocation of power is often preferred to taking the theoretical legality of this *status quo* into account (Herdegen 2002:40). Accepting the "normative power of the factual" ("*normative* […] *Kraft des Faktischen*", Seidl-Hohenveldern/Stein 2000:326), the international community often yields to the practical need of dealing with the authorities actually in control. In some cases (e.g., when recognizing legally formed governments in exile who do not effectively control any territory at all), states try to deny that legally binding rules can arise from unlawfully committed acts (*ex iniuria ius non oritur*). Generally speaking, though, facts that do not change over an extended period of time create legally binding rules, even if these facts were brought about by unlawful actions (*ex factis ius oritur*) (Seidl-Hohenveldern/Stein 2000:326). Following such an application of the principle of effectiveness, even if one postulates that the administrative control over Taiwan by ROC authorities was unlawfully established, it is hard to deny the ROC's claims of sovereignty over its territory, since the actual effective control of said territory by Taiwanese authorities is not doubted at all, not even by the PRC.

Another trend in modern international law which is not reflected in the PRC's evaluation of the sovereignty issues in the Taiwan Strait is the fact that democracy is by now the form of government preferred by international law (Kokott/Doehring/Buergenthal 2003:18). The legitimacy of a government claiming to be in charge of a territory enters at least to some extent into the evaluation of that claim (principle of legitimacy *Legitimitätsprinzip*) (Herdegen 2002:40) – and with the ROC's having successfully mastered the transition to democracy within the last two decades, again its claim of an independent sovereign identity on the international plane has been bolstered.

The arguing of the PRC's concept of 'one China' is free of inner contradictions, yet at times it appears simplistic: Sovereign title is reserved for states; Taiwan is not a state, because it belongs to Chinese territory and is subject to the sovereign title held by the whole of the Chinese people; therefore it cannot be sovereign itself (Liu 2002). Taiwan's existence as a state is denied because of the absence of a sovereign title, and its non-existence as a state again results in the denial of its sovereignty. Such argumentation essentially amounts to the scheme of 'Taiwan cannot be sovereign because it is not', a stance that hardly meets common standards of argumentative power. Moreover, this position's foundation crumbles if one assumes that it might be conceivable for the Chinese people to be divided up into the population of two separate states, or even more drastically, if one assumes that the decades of divided development have already given rise to a separate 'Taiwanese nation' entitled to its own national sovereignty.

As so often with the PRC's international policies, domestic problems seem to play quite a strong role in determining the rigid position Beijing takes on cross-Strait issues. Allowing Taiwan to inch away from the concept of an indivisible Chinese whole is equal, at least in the heads of many PRC decision makers, to weakening the position of the central government in relation to local separatist forces on China's periphery in general. The PRC leadership is clearly concerned that budging on the Taiwan issue might well mean opening the floodgates to the acknowledgement of regional identities and the following disintegration of the multi-nation state the PRC is at present. Tibet and Xinjiang are the two examples of such strong regional identities on China's periphery that immediately come to mind.

The ROC and the 'one China' policy

Compared to the arguing of the PRC, the ROC bases her views far less explicitly on principles of international law. In the Mainland Affairs Council's (大陸委員會, MAC) White Paper *Relations Across The Taiwan Straits* (臺海兩岸關係說明書) of 1994 which answered the PRC's 1993 White Paper, no interpretations of the various post-war treaties nor any explicit statements on the *exact* legal status of Taiwan are to be found. Nevertheless, the official statements of the MAC and other government officials clarify the ROC's point of view sufficiently.

Basically, the ROC authorities also adhere to a 'one China' policy.[5] Their concept of what exactly this 'one China' implies, however, differs greatly from

5 Even though ROC officials of both the Democratic Progressive Party (DPP) and the Guomindang (國民党, Kuomintang, KMT) have recently altered their stance on cross-Strait issues, the Taiwanese interpretation of 'one China' has so long been consistently implemented that

the PRC's, encompassing "China as a historical, geographical, cultural, and racial entity" (MAC 1994) ("歷史上，地理上，文化上，血緣上的中國", XDW 1994) but mentioning no legal or political dimensions. Accommodating this notion of 'one China' while at the same time underpinning the ROC's separate stance on the international stage, the ROC government develops the model of "one China, two equal political entities" (MAC 1994) ("一個中國，兩個對等政治實體", XDW 1994). It sees China as a "divided country" ("分裂國家") with two "political entities with de facto authority" (MAC 1994) ("擁有統治權的政治實體", XDW 1994). These formulations together with the frequent use of the word 'parity' (對等) imply that the ROC authorities view Taiwan as *equal* partner in cross-Strait relations and that they wish to disassociate themselves from Beijing's interpretation of the relationship as one between central and local government or super- and subordinate. It follows that, contradictory to PRC interpretations of sovereignty, the Taiwanese authorities believe that not merely the administrative control of the Chinese territory is divided but also sovereignty itself. Their concept of sovereignty thus is not indivisible and or sharable in the case of China.

In the view of the MAC "the Republic of China has been an independent sovereign state since its foundation in 1912" (MAC 1994) ("中華民國 [...] 一九一二年創立以來, [...] 是一個具獨立主權的國家", XDW 1994), that merely "transferred" (MAC 1994) ("播遷", XDW 1994) its government from Nanjing to Taipei. In the MAC's response to the PRC's second White Paper on the Taiwan issue of 2000, it again claims that the ROC "never for a moment vanish[ed]" (MAC 2000) ("非僅不曾消滅", XDW 2000). By giving this interpretation of historical events, the MAC opposes Beijing's view of a complete 'succession of government' that resulted in the replacement of the Republic by the People's Republic. Rather, the ROC devises numerous ways of saying – without officially declaring independence – that Taiwan is an independent country that holds sovereignty over its territory and is not subject to Beijing's sovereignty. This stance is summed up by President Chen Shuibian in his concept of "one country on each side" (Chen 2002) of the Taiwan Strait (一邊一國). Notwithstanding, the MAC proclaims China's division to be a mere "temporary, transitional phenomenon" (MAC 1994) ("暫時的，過渡時期的現象", XDW 1994), thus manifesting the intention to keep Chinese reunification as the ultimate aim. The MAC also states in its 1994 White Paper that the relationship between the two sides of the Taiwan

---

a description and an interpretation of the concept in its conventional form is required first. In how far the new policies will be durable is difficult to assess at present. In any case they are developments which are based on some aspects of the long-standing policy and are thus tied to the same principles of international law.

Strait can, in a way, be regarded "'domestic' or 'Chinese' in nature" (MAC 1994) (“屬於　‘一國内部’ 或　’中國内部’ 的性質”, XDW 1994), because both sides belong to the above-defined Chinese whole. By doing so, they disassociate themselves from Taiwanese secession and official independence.

Nevertheless, with much of the controversy so far appearing to be a struggle for the right wording rather than the tow of two incompatible interpretations, the fundamental clash of opinions becomes clear when taking a look at the constitutional reforms implemented in the ROC during the 1990s. The first step towards change was the 1991 abolishment of the Temporary Provisions that superseded the Constitution as long as the 'period of Communist rebellion' lasted, i.e. from 1948 until then (Office of the President 2003). This meant that the Beijing government was no longer regarded as an unlawful rebel organization (MAC 1994). In the course of six revisions the National Assembly redefined the Constitution as applicable to the present area of the ROC only (Office of the President 2003). By doing so, the ROC took a major step away from her official policy up to that point which had been to claim representation of the whole of China on the international stage (deLisle 2000:44).

Defining the Communists as a 'rebel government' had been a vital part of the Guomindang's (國民党, Kuomintang, KMT) legitimization during the period of rule by martial law on Taiwan, and the claim to represent all of China had been its logical consequence (deLisle 2000:36). Now, however, after democratization, the Taiwanese electorate is so clearly confined to the present borders of the ROC that dropping the claim to represent the whole of China appears to be the inevitable consequence of the process.

As mentioned earlier, there are a few principles of international law that bolster the claim of a separate and independent state on Taiwan such as the principles of effectiveness and legitimacy. The ROC authorities do not appeal to any of these explicitly, but in their arguing for a separate Taiwanese state they put the emphasis on their *de facto* control of the Taiwanese territory and the democratic legitimacy of their government and thus indirectly call upon the said principles.

The ROC's view of China as a 'divided state' appeals to aspects of international law which are rather unconventional and have not taken root very firmly as of yet. A set of rules emerged during the Cold War that gave the international community a way of dealing with the cases of, e.g., a divided Germany and a divided Korea by granting them dual recognition in international organizations. However, most of the circumstances that applied to those two countries then do not apply to the Chinese situation today (e.g., a more or less equal share of territory, population, and international recognition), making it difficult to apply the rules one-to-one. Moreover, it does not appear desirable for the Taiwanese government to 'translate' especially the German context to their situation, since the German reunification scenario was that of the smaller state joining the bigger while giving up its own political system completely (deLisle 2000:53–55).

Much in the ROC's publications on the matter of 'one China' implies that for Taiwan upholding the 'one China' principle means pragmatism more than anything else. The ROC's interpretation of the concept is very different from the PRC's, and subscribing to it at all appears to be lip service more than conviction – the recent changes in the ROC authorities' position on the subject also suggest that this has been the case for some time.

Recent developments

Starting in 2003, ROC authorities and President Chen in particular have stepped up the rhetoric in cross-Strait relations, creating some doubts in the PRC, the U.S., and the international community as a whole whether the long-standing Taiwanese policy of not declaring formal independence will hold true for much longer.

When first taking office in 2000, Chen Shuibian was anxious to play down differences across the Strait and alleviate PRC fears of formal Taiwanese independence under a DPP president. His stance on the 'one China' issue in 2000 – "I hope that everyone can show wisdom and creativity in trying to define 'one China' in a way that's acceptable to people on both sides of the strait" (Chen as cited in Baum/Pao 2000) – stands in stark contrast to his more recent statements:

> We don't want Taiwan to be a second Hong Kong. We reject "one country, two systems". We oppose "one China". […] We have our own national sovereignty, dignity, and safety. (Chen as cited in Dean/Kaufman/Vatikiotis 2003)

Chen openly renounces the 'one China' policy as applied by the PRC, especially the 'one country, two systems' approach to reunification. What appears at first to be quite a shocking new take on cross-Strait issues, upon closer scrutiny reveals to be a more drastic way of saying what had been said many times before. As has been described above, for a long time Taiwanese authorities had subscribed to a 'one China' policy similar to that of the PRC in name only but not in content. What exactly is meant by 'one China' has been defined differently by both sides for years, and openly stating that the PRC's 'one China' policy does not match the ROC's notion of 'one China' accurately describes the *status quo*. ROC authorities have avoided such frankness for years, so as not to provoke the PRC and to pay at least lip service to Beijing's demand that the 'one China' policy be adhered to; therefore, an open rejection does constitute a certain realignment in cross-Strait diplomacy. It has to be remembered, though, that Chen Shuibian cannot singlehandedly shape the Taiwanese stance on cross-Strait relations. Similar to his American colleague, the Taiwanese President is to some extent dependent on the lawmaking body (the Legislative Yuan (立法院) in the Taiwanese case, Congress in the U.S.) in shaping his policies. Majorities in this body have for quite some time not been in his favor; therefore, Chen's statements can be regarded as moves in the tug and tow of politics rather than a fundamental new take on policies in the Taiwan Strait. With Chen's having faced presidential election in March 2004, the renewal of his aggressive stance on cross-Strait issues can be viewed as a predictable attempt to mobilize the pro-independence faction of his voters. Also, it places the PRC authorities in a tight spot: They have to object to Chen's statements, and yet as soon as they do, they nurture Taiwanese national sentiment and help in mobilizing Chen's voters as they did in 2000 (Dean 2004). Chen was in the advantageous position (a position Taiwanese authorities can seldom call their own) of commanding a win-win situation: He could take a firm stand on cross-Strait issues and impress voters; he could probe and possibly expand the scope of his options in the Strait, because Beijing's hands were, if not quite tied, at least constricted; and even if Beijing had chosen to take strong measures against his statements, Chen would have profited from an expected surge in national sentiment.

Much more than by Chen's statements, doubts have been fostered regarding the ROC's sober-mindedness and prudence in cross-Strait relations by the move to add the word 'Taiwan' to newly issued passports in June 2003, by Chen's announcement in September of the same year to aim at a new constitution for Taiwan (not the ROC) by the year 2006, and most of all by the passing of controversial referendum legislation in November 2003. The passport issue has led to the first threat of a PRC military strike in the Taiwan Strait in two years, because the PRC views a change in name of her 'renegade province' a step away from the *status quo* towards independence. The plan of a new constitution and in particular the referendum law (公民投票法) that opens the possibility of holding plebiscites on major national policies as well as on constitutional amendments[6] have met with opposition and suspicion in Beijing and in the international community alike.

Beijing's reaction, however, has been rather moderate, in part, as has been argued above, because strong rhetoric and saber-rattling on the part of the PRC would only help to grow support for Chen Shuibian. Beijing sometimes calls on Washington to take a stand and restrain Chen's moves towards formal indepen-

---

[6] There are many restrictions on the possible content of referenda, excluding independence and changes of the island's flag and name. The government is banned from proposing or endorsing referenda with the only exception of a 'defensive referendum' called by the president in case of a military attack on Taiwan (see Lu 2003). Chen circumvented this ban by arguing that the PRC missile buildup opposite Taiwan was constantly posing a threat to the ROC's national security, he called a referendum for March 20, 2004 on whether the PRC should its ballistic missiles. The low turnout of voters, however, shows that the Taiwanese electorate sees through such dubious moves and handles cross-Strait issues with extreme care.

dence. But PRC authorities cannot depend on the U.S. too much, because this would undermine their claim that the Taiwan issue is a strictly domestic and not an international concern (Kuhn 2004).

It is not easy for the authorities in Beijing to weigh different options of action against each other, particularly not so since some of their assumptions of the past have proven wrong. Lately, e.g., PRC authorities had to admit that their long-standing belief in the integrative power of economic ties between the two sides had been misguided and that economic benefits from cross-Strait trade and investment had nurtured Taiwanese self-confidence rather than drawn the 'lost' province closer to the motherland (Dean 2004). For the development of mutual prosperity, further economic integration seems sensible, even if this would again result in stronger Taiwanese self-esteem. At the moment, PRC authorities seem not too much interested in escalating cross-Strait differences, and they mostly confine themselves to reiterating their long-standing policies of 'one China' and 'one country, two systems', as Premier Wen Jiabao (溫家寶) did, for example, in a December 2003 interview with the *Washington Post*:

> "Our policy toward Taiwan is a clear-cut one. It is peaceful reunification and 'one country, two systems'. We will not give up our efforts for a peaceful settlement of the question of Taiwan because a peaceful settlement is in the fundamental interests of all Chinese people, our Taiwan compatriots included. […] China's sovereignty and territorial integrity brook no division and the position of the Chinese government on upholding the one-China principle is rock firm and defies all challenges." (Wen as cited in Bennett et al. 2003)

Because at present the new leadership around Hu Jintao (胡錦濤) and Wen Jiabao is still preoccupied with consolidating their own power, they have no interest in a serious clash over the Taiwan issues neither with Washington nor Taipei (Kuhn 2004). Therefore, the PRC leaders are mostly willing to play down differences in order to alleviate domestic and international fears of an impending conflict in the Taiwan Strait. They appear to adopt a rather sober-minded approach to these expressions of Taiwan's new self-confidence, seeing them in the context of the Taiwanese election campaign. This is reflected in an article in *Current Events Report* of January 2004:

> "Our opinion is that the basic pattern of cross-strait relations that have developed over a long time has been gravely challenged, but not basically changed. […] we have basically contained the overt threat of Taiwanese independence since Chen took office, avoiding a worst-case scenario and maintaining the status of Taiwan as part of China." (*Current Events Report*[7] cited after Kuhn 2004)

---

[7] *Current Events Report*, according to Kuhn, is "a Communist Party Propaganda Department magazine that analyzes current events for the bureaucratic rank and file" (Kuhn 2004).

Sometimes, however, the PRC itself does not shy away from using the Taiwan Strait conflict in its domestic power play, either. In the spring of 2005, for example, Premier Wen Jiabao started out the annual sessions of the National People's Congress by rallying the delegates support for anti-secession legislation that would legalize the use of force should Taiwan choose to declare independence. This move created some anxieties on Taiwan and in the international community about growing tensions in the Strait; however, many analysts immediately saw it as Wen's attempt to start out the session on a note of unanimous approval to smooth the way for more controversial issues later (CNN 2005). Beijing's overall policy at present speaks for the fact that for now the PRC is content to endorse the *status quo* up to a point and to focus on economic development and integration. In recent years, it seems that both parties have become accustomed to the way the issue is dealt with by the other side and at times exploited for domestic reasons.

But does the present *status quo*, Beijing's being content for the present with Taipei's *de facto* independence as long as it does not alter its status *de jure*, and Taipei's plea not to declare formal independence as long as Beijing does not force reunification, still accurately reflect the will of the population? A look at Taiwanese opinion polls concerning the question of national identity suggests that the recently changed positions of the ROC leadership might be in step with the Taiwanese *zeitgeist* – a fact that is quite alarming for the authorities in Beijing who until recently could claim that Chen and his DPP were taking radical positions not backed by the majority of Taiwan's population. When comparing the numbers on national identity of June 1992 to the most recent numbers of June 2003 (as collected by the Election Study Center at Taipei's National Chengchi University), the sharp increase in respondents who identify themselves as Taiwanese only (from 17.3% in 1992 to 41.5% eleven years later) bears witness to a new self-confidence in the ROC and the rise of a separate identity (taken from Dean 2004). This sense of a separate Taiwanese identity that is no longer primarily Chinese in nature is likely to trigger some changes in the way cross-Strait issues are dealt with. Nonetheless, people who identify themselves as Taiwanese do not necessarily endorse rash action in cross-Strait issues. The overwhelming majority of the people questioned by the MAC in November 2003 (aged 20–69) favored the *status quo* for the present. Roughly 80% of respondents opted for a present prolongation of the *status quo*, differing merely in their favored course of action in the future.

Preserving the *status quo* for now also reflects the opinion of a majority of PRC citizens. According to a poll conducted by Horizon Research in Beijing in January 2004, 15% of the 4000 people questioned favored immediate military action, but a majority of 58% deemed military force to be unnecessary and opted for economic integration instead (taken from Kuhn 2004).

The U.S. and the 'one China' policy

The United States has in general a strong interest in the Pacific Rim region, partly due to its rapid economic development and partly because of American strategic considerations of its military presence in Asia (Lin in Chang 1988:44). But how exactly does the United States see its role in the cross-Strait conflict? As a third party that is only indirectly involved in the conflict, the need to comprehensively argue its point of view is not as strong for the U.S. as it is for the PRC and ROC respectively. There are three basic pillars to the United States policy in the region: adherence to a 'one China', the call for a peaceful settlement of the conflict, and the insistence that the Chinese themselves should resolve the issue (Lee 2000:185). Again, 'One China' is cited as the main framework, this time interpreted by the U.S. State Department as follows:

> "The U.S. 'one-China' policy acknowledges that both Taiwan and the Mainland are part of China. The U.S. insists on the peaceful resolution of cross-Strait differences and encourages dialogue to help advance such a resolution. The U.S. does not support Taiwanese independence. […] The United States is opposed to any attempt by either side to unilaterally alter the status quo in the Taiwan Strait. The United States has endorsed dialogue and exchanges between the two sides and has encouraged the P.R.C. to engage the democratically elected leadership of Taiwan." (BEAPA 2005)

The wording of the statement already implies that more than one 'one China' policy exists, and that this is the version adhered to by the United States. The U.S. does not go into any legal detail of how its interpretation was reached. However, the wording clarifies that this interpretation of facts is quite different from that of the PRC: The U.S. calls both Taiwan and the Mainland part of China, clearly equating 'the Mainland' and not 'China' with the PRC.

This interpretation of 'one China', that might look at first like a bending of the knee to Beijing's wishes but upon closer scrutiny reveals to be aimed at establishing a balance in cross-Strait forces, is emblematic of U.S. policies in the region. Winston Lord, United States Assistant Secretary of State for East Asian and Pacific Affairs during the 1990s and former Ambassador to the PRC, sums up the U.S. strategies in dealing with cross-Strait issues quite nicely when talking about the 1996 missile crisis:

> "It is prudent generally that you don't state in advance what you will do in specific situations. […] If the PRC thinks that we won't come to the defense of Taiwan in a crunch, they're going to be aggressive and they're going to press Taiwan. […] If Taiwan thinks that we're going to come to their defense, no matter what happens, they're going to be provocative, knowing that they're going to have a free ride, no matter how angry Beijing gets. Therefore, we can't be precise." (Lord as quoted in Bernkopf-Tucker 2001:489–490)

The U.S. has, in general, pursued a policy of 'strategic ambiguity' towards both sides of the Strait, i.e., Washington backs Beijing's claim of 'one China' and at the same time ensures – via weapons sales and military assistance – that Taiwan can effectively defend itself against a PRC military attack (Lampton 2001:99–100). This policy is designed to strengthen the *status quo* in the region, making sure that the PRC is never too confident that it can take Taiwan by force and that the ROC never feels too sure of U.S. support and thus becomes reckless.[8] This ambiguity has ensured stability and to some extent predictability in cross-Strait relations and has thus been crucial in establishing a favorable environment for economic growth on both sides of the Strait (Lin in Chang 1988:40). However, ambiguity continually runs the risk of misinterpretation by one side or the other (Lee 2000:187).

Every once in a while, therefore, the need for clearer words arises. Triggered, for example, by the scheduling of a Taiwanese referendum on the PRC missile buildup opposite Taiwan for March 20, 2004 (the same day as the Presidential elections on Taiwan), U.S. officials felt compelled to find clearer words and to abandon their former ambiguity. In December 2003, they spelled out the U.S. vision for the region, namely: no unilateral alteration of the *status quo* by either side. Even though part of the warning was directed at the PRC, the bulk of Washington's admonitions were aimed at ROC authorities whom they perceived to be stretching the limits of U.S. patience and PRC goodwill too far (Allen/Kessler 2003). The warnings directed at the ROC have been met with skepticism in some parts of the international community, because they can be seen as hampering democratic consolidation on Taiwan and can be interpreted as the Americans deferring to the authorities in Beijing (Wieser 2003). Looking at the U.S. actions in the region over a longer period of time, however, the continued arms sales to Taiwan over decades in spite of Beijing's complaints, the sending of two aircraft carriers to waters close to Taiwan in the 1996 missile crisis (marshaling the biggest fighting force in the Western Pacific since the Vietnam War) (Lord cited in Bernkopf-Tucker 2001:486) – bear witness to the fact that the U.S. is strongly committed to safeguarding peace and stability in the region, deterring aggression or provocation by either side, and in general maintaining the fragile equilibrium of forces in the triangle of relations. Thus, the basic goals of the general policy of ambiguity and the incidents of clarity are the same. The U.S., just like the international community as a whole, is mainly interested in ensuring economic and

[8] This policy was interrupted only shortly when President George W. Bush assured Taiwan in a TV interview in April 2001 that the U.S. would do "whatever it takes" to defend Taiwan – a blunder that was followed quickly by backpedaling and the administration's retreat to its reliable policy of ambiguity (see Allen/Kessler 2003).

political stability in the Taiwan Strait, and it sees the best chance of achieving this by preserving the *status quo.*

It has been argued above that the U.S. does not motivate its position in cross-Strait issues by international legal principles, but that it merely follows pragmatic considerations and its interest of stability in the region. Quite intriguingly, however, the fact, that U.S. policy in the region has been as consistent as it is in the long term, to a large extent owes its existence to American *domestic* law-making. In American international politics, the White House and the State Department are usually the main decision makers who generally operate independently of the law-making body, Congress. The Chinese context, however, constitutes the first exemption to this rule: When the U.S. withdrew its official support for the ROC in the late 1970s and established official diplomatic ties with the PRC, Congress, in passing the Taiwan Relations Act (TRA) in 1979, made sure that there was a legal basis for upholding unofficial ties with the island's authorities and that consistency in policies towards Taiwan was ensured. For the first time in history, Congress built a legal framework for 'foreign' relations, as the provisions of the TRA (among them an indefinite security commitment of the U.S. in the region and arms sales to Taiwan that ensure self-defense) are "not a structure of discretionary administrative regulations and loose practice [but] a binding set of national commitments and policies enforceable in a court of law" (Emerson in Chang 1988:53). Some analysts argue that the TRA constitutes a quasi-official *de facto* recognition of Taiwan by the United States (Emerson in Chang 1988:53–65) because the TRA treats Taiwan as a foreign country and functions as a defense treaty; however, it seems more appropriate, given the above-described U.S. interest in maintaining a balance of forces in the region, that the TRA is not so much a guarantee towards Taiwan as it is the legal basis for an option to act. Since it is not in the U.S. interest to definitely take sides in the cross-Strait conflict, the TRA gives a legal foundation for a military presence of the U.S. in the Western Pacific, and East Asia, but it does not stand in the way of trying to achieve 'comprehensive engagement' of the PRC as well (which includes treating the PRC as a strategic partner in the region while working towards her integration into the international economy, military transparency and cooperation, and her acceptance of international law) (Lee 2000:195–196). Also, the State Department is again very careful not to anger Beijing too much by going out on a limb and supporting Taiwan as if it were a sovereign state:

> "In keeping with its one-China policy, while the U.S. does not support Taiwan independence, it does support Taiwan's membership in appropriate international organizations, such as the WTO, APEC forum, and the Asian Development Bank, where statehood is not a requirement for membership. In addition, the U.S. supports appropriate opportunities for Taiwan's voice to be heard in organizations where its membership is not possible." (BEAPA 2005)

For the ROC the fact that Congress is involved so directly in U.S. decision making in the Chinese arena is good news. The TRA has ensured that in the course of five administrations, both Republican and Democrat, the U.S. policy of offering the ROC help whenever it is needed has been quite consistent.[9] Obviously, however, the general policy of strategic ambiguity takes precedence.

The American position in cross-Strait relations illustrates how important it is to analyze both legal considerations as well as politics when trying to understand the actions of countries on the international plane. As argued above, the U.S. keeps up the fragile equilibrium of forces in the South China Sea and thus ensures stable conditions for prosperous economic relations by continuously sending signals to both sides of the conflict, supporting the ROC with such measures as ensured by the TRA and at the same time adhering to Beijing's requirement of not entertaining official diplomatic ties to the island or recognizing it as a sovereign state. Did the United States only consider international legal principles in crafting its policies in the region, it could quite easily decide to fully acknowledge the ROC as an independent state. International law as practiced today is rather clear on what an entity needs to be regarded a state. Following Georg Jellinek's *Lehre von den Staatenverbindungen* (1882), present legal practice as defined by the Montevideo Convention on the Rights and Duties of States demands that the following four criteria for statehood be met: "*(a)* a permanent population; *(b)* a defined territory; *(c)* government; and *(d)* capacity to enter into relations with the other States" (League of Nations 1936:25). The ROC fulfills all these criteria for statehood, and since modern international law perceives statehood to exist prior to and independent of recognition, the fact that the ROC is not recognized by the majority of the international community does not stand in the way of her being an independent state *de jure* (deLisle 2000, Shen 2000). However, since the PRC still upholds that whoever wants to have diplomatic ties with her may not recognize the ROC, the members of the international community have to decide with which Chinese government they want to have dealings. The vast majority – and with them the ROC's most important international contact, the U.S. – chooses the PRC over the ROC. Thus, although the ROC might well be a state *de jure*, it certainly is not treated as one *de facto*.

9 One might argue that the sheer bulk of weapons the U.S. is selling to Taiwan explains the United States' unaltered interest in keeping the relationships in the area stable. Taiwan is the U.S.' second best customer for defense equipment and has perhaps the world's most advanced semiconductor fabrication infrastructure, important for the production of weapon sensitive electronic components. Both facts strongly argue for a U.S. interest in maintaining the *status quo* (see Tkacik 2003).

Closing remarks

Much of the controversy about the correct interpretation of the legal facts in cross-Strait issues circles around questions of the ROC's *de jure* possession or non-possession of sovereignty and her *de jure* existence or non-existence as a state. The first question is hard to answer conclusively due to the two rather diametrically opposed interpretations of state sovereignty put forth by the contesting sides and the U.S.' unwillingness to lead the way in making a definite decision one way or the other. Who holds sovereignty in the Chinese context will ultimately have to be decided by future developments within the international framework, either pointing towards a strengthening of nation-state concepts of integrity or towards a fortification of territorial communities and their rights. The second question regarding statehood is a little simpler. Not only are the criteria for statehood comparatively clear and universally accepted, but they can also be put to the test quite easily. Modern concepts of international law as well as some aspects of international life strongly argue for Taiwan's *de jure* existence as an independent state despite the PRC's as well as the U.S. reservations on this issue and even in lack of universal recognition on the international plane.

De facto it can hardly be doubted that the ROC, regulating her affairs as it sees fit and conforming to international standards of law and human rights, acts as a sovereign and independent state, as far as it is permitted to do so, in the international community. That this does not result in her *de facto* treatment as a sovereign state by that community is due to multiple factors of politics and national sentiment and the fact that there are no ready-made solutions for such complex relationships as the one between the two sides of the Taiwan Strait. The international community's attitude towards the Taiwan Strait conflict is far from univocal, many countries being torn between their natural sympathy for the Taiwanese society that has been awarded a "democratic stamp of approval" (Henckaerts 1996b:242) and the attraction of the allegedly huge future market on the Mainland. What exactly the future of the conflict will be is therefore hard to predict, much speaks in favor of a continuation of the present "creative ambiguity" (Charney/Prescott 2000:277) by all parties concerned.

In recent years, the ROC is increasingly unhappy with its isolation on the international plane and has stepped up her rhetoric in cross-Strait diplomacy. What is regarded as reckless agitation by some, is plausible and to some extent even necessary when viewed from the vantage point of international law. It is one innate characteristic of international law that it is created by the same entities which are to be bound by it, i.e., by states in the international arena. As long as the ROC is kept out of this arena almost completely, it is extremely difficult for it to actively shape the future of the international legal systems in a similar way as the internationally recognized states are allowed to do (and with them the PRC). For the ROC, the question of participation in the international arena may well prove to be a question of survival in the long term. For quite some time, therefore, the government on Taiwan has employed all means at its disposal to alter its state of "diplomatic orphanage" (Van Vranken Hickey 1996:65), resorting to the so-called 'pragmatic' or 'informal diplomacy' of establishing unofficial ties wherever official ones are beyond its reach. This may ensure a stable relationship with many states worldwide, including the ROC's most important strategic partner, the U.S., who has been very receptive to Taiwanese lobbying over the years.[10] In the relations with Beijing, however, this unusual approach to international diplomacy is viewed as promoting Taiwanese independence (Wu 1996:51–52). Taiwanese ties to other states are thus 'inversely proportional' to a good climate between Taipei and Beijing. And since the PRC is as yet the major stumbling block in ROC relations to the international community, and since the ROC is the most important contentious point between the PRC, arguably the most important rising force in Asia, and the only superpower, the United States, strange as it may appear, in the ROC's way to a firmly established position in the international arena seems to lead through a phase of inner-Chinese rapprochement.

Judith Hufnagel, Institute of Chinese Studies, University of Heidelberg

References

Allen, Mike; Kessler, Glenn (2003): "Taiwan Warned by U.S.: Island Asked Not To Provoke China." in: The Washington Post (12/09/2003), A01.http://www.washingtonpost.com/ac2/wp-dyn/A46623-2003Dec8 (March 7, 2004).

Austin, Greg (1998): China's Ocean Frontier: International Law, Military Force and National Development. Studies in World Affairs, 17. St. Leonards, NSW, Australia: Allen & Unwin in association with the Dept. of International Relations and the Northeast Asia Program, Research School of Pacific and Asian Studies, Australian National Univ., Canberra, ACT.

Baum, Julian and Maureen Pao (2000): Interview: Chen Shui-bian: Taking the Lead. In: Far Eastern Economic Review (10/26/2000). Hong Kong: Review Publishing Company Ltd. http://www.feer.com/articles/2000/010_26/p18region.html (March 1, 2004).

Bennett, Philip et al. (2003): Interview with Wen Jiabao: A Complete Transcript from Chinese Premier's Meeting. In: The Washington Post (12/22/2003). http://www.washingtonpost.com/wp-dyn/articles/A6641-2003Nov22.html (March 7, 2004).

---

[10] Thomas W. Robinson argues that, even in the absence of exact numbers, it is beyond doubt that Taiwan has spent at least hundreds of millions of dollars on the targeted lobbying of Congress, numbers only paralleled by Israel's spending. For this information and a more detailed account of Taiwanese influencing of American policies, see Robinson 1996:1343–1356.

Bernkopf-Tucker, Nancy (2001): China Confidential: American Diplomats and Sino-American Relations, 1945–1996. New York: Columbia University Press.

BEAPA 2005: Bureau of East Asian and Pacific Affairs (2005): Background note: Taiwan. July, 2005. Washington, DC: Bureau of Public Affairs, U.S. Department of State. http://www.state.gov/r/pa/ei/rls/dos/413.htm (August 8, 2005).

Carpenter, Ted Galen (2000): Confusion and Stereotypes: U.S. Policy toward the PRC at the Dawn of the 21st Century. In: Carpenter, Ted Galen and James A. Dorn (eds.) (2000): China's Future: Constructive Partner or Emerging Threat? Washington, DC: Cato Institute, 69–94.

Charney, Jonathan I. and J.R.V. Prescott (2000): Resolving Cross-Strait Relations between China and Taiwan. In: American Journal of International Law 94:3 (Jul. 2000), 453–477.

Chen Shuibian (2000a): Taiwan Stands Up: Toward the Dawn of a Rising Era. Inauguration Address (05/20/2000). New York: Information Division, Taipei Economic and Cultural Office. http://www.taipei.org/chen/chen0520.htm (July 13, 2003).

Chen Shuibian (陈水扁) (2000b): 台湾站起来： 迎接向上提升的新时代： 宣誓就职演说 (Taiwan Stands up: Toward the Dawn of a Rising Era Inauguration Address) (05/20/2000). New York: Information Division, Taipei Economic and Cultural Office, 2000. http://www.taipei.org/chen/chen0520c.htm (July 13, 2003).

CNN (2005): China: No Independence for Taiwan. (03/05/2005). http://www.cnn.com/2005/WORLD/asiapcf/03/05/china.npc/ (August 08, 2005).

Dean, Jason; Kaufman, Jonathan and Michael Vatikiotis, Michael (2003): Interview: Chen Shui-bian: Political Pugilist. In: Far Eastern Economic Review. Issue cover-dated July 31, 2003. http://www.feer.com/ articles/2003/0307_31/p016region.html (March 1, 2004).

Dean, Jason (2004): The Strait Grows Wider. In: Far Eastern Economic Review. Issue cover-dated March 04, 2004. http://www.feer.com/articles/2004/0403_04/p024china.html (March 1, 2004).

deLisle, Jacques (2000): The Chinese Puzzle of Taiwan's Status. In: Orbis 44:1 (Winter 2000), 42–44.

Emerson, J. Terry (1988): The Taiwan Relations Act: Legislative Recognition of the Republic of China. In: Chang, King-yuh (ed.) (1988): ROC-US Relations under the Taiwan Relations Act: Practice and Prospects. English Monograph Series No. 33. Taipei: Institute of International Relations.

Henckaerts, Jean-Marie (1996a): The International Status of Taiwan in the New World Order: Legal and Political Considerations. London: Kluwer Law International.

Henckaerts, Jean-Marie (1996b): Self-Determination in Action for the People of Taiwan. In: Henckaerts 1996a, 241–256.

Herdegen, Matthias (2002): Völkerrecht. (International Law) 2. edition. München: C. H. Beck.

Huang Jiashu (黄嘉树) and Wang Yingjin (王英津) (2002): 主权构成研究及其在台湾问题上的应用. (Research on the Structure of Sovereignty and its Use for the Taiwan Question). In: 台湾研究集刊 (Taiwan Studies Quarterly) 76:2, 29–31.

Hutchings, Graham (2001): Modern China: A Companion to a Rising Power. London: Penguin Books.

Kang, David C. (2003): Getting Asia Wrong: The Need for New Analytical Frameworks. In: International Security 27:4 (Spring 2003), 57–85.

Kau, Michael Y. M. (2002): The Impact of WTO Accession on Political and Economic Relations between the Two Sides of the Taiwan Strait. Washington, DC: Center for National

Policy. http://www.cnponline.org/Press_Releases/Transcripts/Michael_Kau_Remarks.pdf (July 3, 2003).
Kokott, Juliane, Doehring, Karl and Tomas Buergenthal (2003): Grundzüge des Völkerrechts (Introduction to International Law). 3., neu bearbeitete Auflage. Heidelberg: C.F. Müller.
Kuhn, Anthony (2004): The View from Beijing: A Sliver of Hope Would Be Welcome. In: Far Eastern Economic Review. Issue cover-dated March 04, 2004. http://www.feer.com/articles/2004/0403_04/p027china.html (March 1, 2004).
Lampton, David M. (2001): Same Bed, Different Dreams: Managing U.S.-China Relations 1989–2000. Berkeley and Los Angeles, CA: University of California Press.
League of Nations (1936): Convention on the Rights and Duties of States adopted by the Seventh International Conference of American States: Signed at Montevideo, December 26th, 1933. In: Recueil des traités et des engagements internationaux enregistrés par le Secrétariat de la Société des Nations 165: 3802.
Lee Che-Fu (1997): China's Perception of the Taiwan Issue. In: New England Law Review 32:1 (Fall 1997). Boston, MA: New England School of Law.
Lee, David Ta-wei (2000): The Making of the Taiwan Relations Act: Twenty Years in Retrospect. New York: Oxford University Press.
Lian Xisheng (廉希圣) (2002): '主权对等' = 国家分裂. ("Sovereign Equality" = Division of the Country). In:两岸关系 (Relations across the Taiwan Straits) 64:10, 10.
Lin Bih-jaw (1988): Taipei-Washington Relations: Moving Toward Institutionalization. In: Chang King-yuh (ed.). (1988): ROC-US Relations under the Taiwan Relations Act: Practice and Prospects. English Monograph Series No. 33. Taipei: Institute of International Relations.
Liu Guanghua (刘光华) (2002): '主权对等' 的要害是分裂中国主权. (The Crux of "Sovereign Equality" is the Division of Chinese Sovereignty). In:两岸关系 (Relations across the Taiwan Straits) 64:10, 10–11.
Lu, Fiona (2003): Legislature Passes Referendum Law. In: The Taipei Times. (11/23/2003). Taipei: The Taipei Times. http://www.taipeitimes.com/News/front/archives/2003/11/28/2003077523 (March 8, 2004).
MAC 2000: Mainland Affairs Council; Executive Yuan (2000): How We View Beijing's White Paper 'One China Principle and the Taiwan Issue'. Taipei: Mainland Affairs Council (02/22/2000). Taipei: Mainland Affairs Council. http://www.mac.gov.tw/english/english/macpolicy/890222e.htm (August 19, 2003).
MAC 1994: Mainland Affairs Council; Executive Yuan (1994): Relations Across The Taiwan Straits. Taipei: Mainland Affairs Council. http://www.mac.gov.tw/english/english/macpolicy/policy5/mlp1_1.htm – …/mlp1_5.htm (August 19, 2003).
Office of the President (2003): Constitution. Republic of China: 2003. Taipei: Office of the President. http://www.president.gov.tw/1_roc_intro/e_law_intro.html (August 21, 2003).
Robinson, Thomas W. (1996): America in Taiwan's Post Cold-War Foreign Relations. In: The China Quarterly 148 (Dec. 1996), 1340–1361.
Ruan Guoying (阮国英) (1994): Guojia zhuquan de wanzhengxing yu Taiwan wenti (国家主权的完整性与台湾问题). (The Integrity of State Sovereignty and the Taiwan Question). In: Political Science and Law 10, 18–20.
Seidl-Hohenveldern, Ignaz und Torsten Stein (2000): Völkerrecht (International Law). 10. neubearbeitete Auflage. Köln/Berlin/Bonn/München: Heymanns.
Shambaugh, David L. (2002): Modernizing China's Military. Berkeley and Los Angeles, CA: University of California Press.

Shen Jianming (2000): Sovereignty, Statehood, Self-determination, and the Issue of Taiwan. In: American University International Law Review15:4, 1101–1161.

TAO 2000: Taiwan Affairs Office; Information Office of the State Council (2000). The One-China Principle and the Taiwan Issue. (02/21/2000). Washington, DC: Embassy of the People's Republic of China in the United States of America. http://www.china-embassy.org/eng/7128.html (August 20, 2003).

TAO 1993: Taiwan Affairs Office; Information Office of the State Council (1993): The Taiwan Question and Reunification of China. (08/1993). Beijing: China Internet Information Center. http://www.china.org.cn/e-white/taiwan/10-1.htm – .../10-7.htm (July 12, 2003).

Tkacik, John (2003). Taiwan's Presidential Countdown: What Does It Mean for the United States? In: China Brief 3:9 (05/6/2003). Washington, DC: Jamestown Foundation. http://china.jamestown.org/pubs/view/cwe_003_009_001.htm (June 6, 2003).

Van Vranken Hickey, Dennis (1996): Taiwan's Return to International Organizations: Policies, Problems and Perspectives. In: Henckaerts 1996a, 65–77.

Wieser, Beat U. (2003): Bush auf Clintons Spuren in Taiwan (Bush on the line of Clinton in Taiwan). In: Neue Zürcher Zeitung (12/11/2003). http://www.nzz.ch/2003/12/11/al/page-kommentar9A9QO.html (March 10, 2004).

Wu Linjun (1996). Limitations and Prospects of Taiwan's Informal Diplomacy. In: Henckaerts 1996a, 35–52.

XDW 2000: Xingzhengyuan dalu weiyuanhui (行政院大陸委員會) (2000): 對中共一個中國的原則與台灣問題白皮書之看法 (How We View Beijing's White Paper "One China Principle and the Taiwan Issue") (02/22/2000). Taipei: Mainland Affairs Council. http://www.mac.gov.tw/big5/mlpolicy/890222.htm (August 21, 2003).

XDW 1994: Xingzhengyuan dalu weiyuanhui (行政院大陸委員會) (1994): 臺海兩岸關係說明書. (Relations Across The Taiwan Straits). Taipei: Mainland Affairs Council. http://www.mac.gov.tw/big5/mlpolicy/mlp2_1.htm – …/mlp2_5.htm (August 19, 2003).

Yang Zewei 杨泽伟 (2002): 论国际法上的民族自决与国家主权 (On Self-Determination of Peoples and State Sovereignty in International Law). In: 法律科学 (Law Sciences) 3 [General No. 118].

ZXB 1993: Zhonghua renmin gongheguo guowuyuan xinwen bangongshi (中华人民共和国国务院新闻办公室) (1993): 台湾问题与中国统一 (The Taiwan Question and Reunification of China) (8/1993). Beijing: China Internet Information Center. http://www.china.org.cn/ch-book/tongyi/tongyi.htm – .../tongyi6.htm (July 13, 2003).

ZXB 2000: Zhonghua renmin gongheguo guowuyuan xinwen bangongshi (中华人民共和国国务院新闻办公室) (2000):一个中国的原则与台湾问题 (The One-China Principle and the Taiwan Issue). Beijing: China Internet Information Center. http://www.china.org.cn/ch-sbook/taiwan/taiwan.htm – .../taiwan6.htm (August 20, 2003).

Zhu Shuli (朱淑丽) (2002): 国际法和国际组织对国家主权的冲击 (The Assault of International Law and International Organizations on State Sovereignty). In: 南通职业大学学报 (Journal of Vocational University of Nantong16:1 (Mar. 2002).

Margareta Grieszler

Imperial Death Ritual and International Relations

The Unprecedented Participation of the Diplomatic Corps at Mourning Services in Late Imperial China

Introduction

If anything is essential to describe Chinese culture, it is the ritual, and if anything is central to the maintenance of a unified Chinese culture, it is the standardization of ritual, the correct way to perform rites. In Confucian state ideology, ritual, the performance of rites and roles, was conceived of as essential background of order and unity. Rituals explicitly differentiated the social relations. The correct performance of the prescribed rites functioned as a means to order the family structure, to stabilize the social hierarchy, to consolidate the state, and thus to prevent all these organizations from disorder.[1]

Death ritual, in particular, was an elaboration of filial piety the central Confucian value within family relations, preventing disorder after the death of a family member had struck the hierarchical order of the family. This is also true for the imperial death ritual, which had a similar stabilizing function and – during Ming and Qing times – was of significant importance for the legitimacy of the chief mourner, the heir to the throne, and the ruling family, consolidating the power of the successors. The new emperor had to perform the death rites in filial respect for his predecessor and thus served as an ideal model affirming the basic value of filial piety within family and state. Through the performance of the death ritual he simultaneously reinforced the legitimacy of his reign and symbolically strengthened his own position. Thus, an imperial funeral with all the political threats it brought along for the dynasty was actually transformed into an imperial accession rite.[2] In this sense, imperial death rituals turn out to be fascinating keys to the biography of some personalities and their background.[3]

---

1 For a wide-ranging examination of Chinese state and court ritual from 1000 BC to AD 1750, see McDermott 1999.

2 For an impressive case study of medival China, see McMullen 1999.

3 For a more detailed account on (death) ritual within Confucianism, see Rawski 1988a, for the conception of kingship and its ties to ritual, see also Rawski 1988b.

This is especially the case with the funerary rites at the demise of the Empress Dowager Cixi in the year 1908. This was an unprecedented and unique death ritual in Chinese history for several reasons. Firstly, the coincidence in time: Never during Qing times had there been two imperial deaths so close together. Emperor Guangxu died a few hours earlier than the Empress Dowager, so that the officials in charge had to memorialize simultaneous ceremonies. Secondly, the alteration of the ritual prescriptions: on the one hand, the Empress Dowager's dominant position in life was reflected very clearly in her death rites; on the other hand, her successors wanted to affirm the legitimacy of their reign in the way they had Cixi's death rites arranged and modified from common imperial ritual.

Thirdly, the most striking and since then unparalleled event: the participation of the diplomatic body.

It was the first time in Chinese history that foreign representatives participated in a ritual of specific importance within Chinese culture. A close look into the deaths of Mao Zedong and more recently, Deng Xiaoping will show that this really was an event of singularity. Never before and never again in Chinese history until today, had foreigners participated officially in the ceremonies at an imperial/state leader's funeral. Thus, the last two imperial deaths in China, at the gradual waning of the dynasty, gain special significance by the outstanding participation of foreigners.

The Death of the Imperial Majesties and the Unprecedented Visit of Condolence of the Diplomatic Corps, November 1908

According to the official announcements, the last two imperial deaths of the Qing dynasty occurred within the space of a single day: The Emperor Guangxu died on November 14, 1908, the Empress Dowager Cixi died a few hours later on November 15. As two imperial deaths had occurred so close together, the Board of Rites, *li bu*, in charge of the entire organization and preparation of the ceremonies had to submit two sets of memorials with the prescriptions for the ceremonies both for the late Emperor as well as for the late Empress Dowager.

It is conspicuous enough that the authority of the late Empress Dowager in her death rites was elevated to a status equal (or almost superior) to the Emperor. The basic mourning regulations for an empress dowager laid down in the dynastic statutes were deliberately altered. In no aspect did the modified mourning prescriptions differ from those for the late emperor: The use of blue ink, the ban on ancestor worship, the suspension of transmitting memorials to the Throne, the rigorous ban on marriages for high- and low-ranking officials were entirely according to the ritual prescriptions for a late emperor, which were even surpassed by the regulation of the three-times-a-day assembly for libation during the whole period of primary mourning. Another fact made Cixi's death ritual an unprecedented one: Her coffin remained within the Forbidden City until the final entombment, though imperial coffins were usually transferred to a hall on Coal Hill.[4]

But there were no regulations found in the statutes dealing with western foreigners who were urging to participate in an imperial funeral for the first time in the history of China's international relations.[5] This time, not only the Board of Rites, the most prestigious of the government's ministries was kept busy, but also the Board of Foreign Affairs, *waiwu bu*, had a difficult and unprecedented job to do: the handling of the interests of the diplomatic corps, the representatives of the imperialistic nations.

On the afternoon of November 15, 1908, the accredited representatives of the various nations were singly informed by an official note of the Foreign Ministry about the death of the Emperor the day before. There had been lots of rumors earlier, since an official announcement on November 14 stated that the Prince Regent would take over the agenda. At about noon of November 16, 1908, the death of the Empress Dowager was confirmed.

The members of the diplomatic body gathered the same day in the Spanish mission and decided to adopt the court's mourning period, and that the whole staff of the legations had to wear mourning for twenty-seven days. During this period the flags of all the legations were hoisted at half mast; all the consulates had to follow suite. During this meeting the chief of the American mission, William Woodville Rockhill, suggested to ask for a date to officially present the messages of condolence to the Court. The Doyen of the Diplomatic Body, the Spanish minister, Manuel de Carcer y Salamanca, was thus authorized to submit an official note to the Foreign Ministry, expressing condolences, informing the ministry about the mourning regulations within the legation quarter — and asking for a date for the visit of condolence.

The written answer of the Foreign Ministry to the Doyen – setting the date for November 21 – was received about two days later, together with a very precise description of the ceremonious program for the visit. The letter was circulated by the Doyen on November 19 within the Diplomatic Corps.

> "On entrera par Tonghuamen et on descendra de chaises devant le Changsseyuan. Les Ministres monteront sur de petites chaises à porteurs; ils passeront les portes Sitchingmen et Houangtchimen. A la sortie de cette dernière porte, ils descendront de chaises et iront à pied. Ils passeront la porte Ningcheoumen et se réuniront sous la tente dressée en dehors de cette porte."

---

[4] For a detailed study on the death rites at the demise of the Empress Dowager Cixi, see Grieszler 1991a, b.

[5] The most important state rites of imperial China were witnessed by hardly anyone; see Laidlaw 1991.

"A dix heures les ministres du Waiwupu conduiront le Corps Diplomatique jusque devant la porte du Houangtchitien. Ils feront une révérence, entreront dans le pavillon (2ième révérence) et s'approcheront de la table des sacrifices dressée devant le cercueil de Sa Majestè l'Impératrice Douairière (3ième révérence), ils se tourneront de côté vers le Prince Régent (4ième révérence). Le discours funètre sera prononcé puis traduit. Le Prince rendra le salut et répondra au discours qui sera traduit. La lecture et la traduction terminées, les Ministres feront une révérence en avant (devant la table des sacrifices), ils s'écarteront de quelques pas (2ième révérence), arrivé à la porte du pavillon (3ième révérence). De là ils regagneront la tente dressée en dehors de Ningcheoumen où ils se reposeront un instant. […]" (Circulaire no. 112, November 19, 1908 in BA 5760/08)

On November 21, 1908, thirty-nine representatives of fourteen nations – Spain, USA, Austria-Hungary, France, Great Britain, Belgium, Germany, Russia, Japan, Italy, Mexico, Netherlands, Portugal, Sweden – headed by the Doyen entered the Imperial Palace from the side of Donghua Men to offer condolences. According to the strict protocol the foreign delegates gathered at Ningshou Men; at 10 o'clock in the morning, they were led by high officials of the Foreign Ministry to the Huangji Dian first, which might be another significant aspect reflecting the Empress Dowager's dominant position. In front of the coffin of the late Empress Dowager, the Doyen bowed to the imperial remains, then to the Prince Regent, read an address of sympathy, and this address having been translated, the Prince Regent expressed his thanks. Carefully holding to the prescribed ritual program, the foreign representatives left the hall to advance to the Qianqing Gong, where the ceremony was repeated in front of the coffin of the late Emperor Guangxu.

Though since former times, tributary states had sent emissaries or special envoys to offer condolences at an emperor's death, this was definitely the first time that all the accredited diplomats were permitted to be present at an official ceremony of condolence at the biers of the late Empress Dowager and the late Emperor Guangxu. It was for the first time that representatives of foreign western countries were officially invited to proceed to the Forbidden City for a personal visit of condolence.

Not only had the Court to accept the visit of condolence but it also was confronted with persistent and obstinate notes by the foreigners to obtain permission for participation at the imperial funeral procession. Finally the diplomats succeeded in getting consent, albeit reluctantly, from the authorities and took part in the funeral procession for the late Emperor in May 1909. The foreign diplomats apparently were less interested in insisting upon another troublesome participation in the funeral procession for Cixi, in November 1909.

THE FUNERAL PROCESSION FOR THE LATE EMPEROR GUANGXU, MAY 1909

The participation of the diplomatic body in the funeral rites was an important affair and involved much negotiation. At the end of January 1909, an imperial decree was issued stating that the funeral procession with the remains of the late Emperor to his temporary resting place at Liangge Zhuang would start at May 1st. Intense negotiations were carried out between the diplomatic body and their governments on the one hand, and the Chinese government on the other. According to rumors the Japanese would send a prince as special envoy for the event. Thus the diplomats tried to find out "whether the Chinese government really would be pleased if foreign countries were represented at the ceremony by special delegates" as the German minister wrote, stating at the same time, that he himself "had not the least idea as to the intentions of my own Government", and that he did not know at all, "whether they will eventually appoint a delegate or not" (Note of February 1, 1909, to the Foreign Ministry in BA 444/09).

The answer was clear:

> "Dear Count Rex: The Chinese Government would be pleased if foreign countries sent special delegates at the removal of the coffin of His Majesty the late Emperor. But if it is done on that occasion, we would also expect delegates sent on the occasion of the removal of the coffin of Her Majesty the late Empress Dowager which comes some times in the 9th moon." (Note from the Foreign Ministry to Graf von Rex, February 1, 1909 in BA 532/09)

Was this an elegant attempt to make a foreign participation impossible, being aware that sending a special envoy two times within half a year for a funeral would hardly be acceptable for the foreign governments? But a few days later, the Doyen informed his colleagues of the official communiqué of the Foreign Ministry inviting the foreign governments to send special envoys:

> "[…] le Gouvernement Chinois compte inviter aux funerailles […] tous les Représentants étrangers qui se trouvent actuellement à Pékin et qu'en outre il sera très honoré si les chefs d'Etat veulent bien envoyer des Ambassadeurs spéciaux […]".(Circulaire no 17, February 6, 1909 in BA 580/09)

For the period of days around the funeral, between April 26 and May 4, a whole program with entertainment, banquets and visits of places of interest (like the Palace Gardens, the Zoological Garden, the Summer Palace etc) would be arranged, additionally (ibid.).

On April 15, the diplomats gathered at the American mission to further discuss their participation.

To minimize the risk of possible disturbances the Chinese Foreign Ministry had issued a very detailed program and order for the participants. It conveyed a totally professional arrangement: The special envoys would be picked up upon their arrival into the country, official carriages would be provided for the foreign delegations and official interpreters would be at their disposal for the duration of their stay.

> "[…] 6. The Special Envoys will be received in a body on April 26th for the presentation of their letters of credence. Each Envoy will present his letter of credence separately. The usual ceremony for the presentation of letters of credence will be observed.
>
> 7. On the day after the presentation of the letters decorations will be conferred.
>
> 8. A Minister of the Imperial Household will call out the name of the Regent to all the Special Envoys on the 27th of April.
>
> 9. On the 27th and 28th the Summer Palace and other places of interest will be visited.
>
> 10. On the 29th of April the Special Envoys with their suites will pay their respects to the remains of the late Emperor and Empress Dowager. A pavilion will be set up outside the Hsi Ch'ing Gate (in the Palace) where the foreign representatives may assemble. After all are assembled, each Envoy accompanied by his suite will advance separately and pay his respects to the Imperial Remains.
>
> 11. On the 1st of May the funeral procession of the late Emperor will take place. The Special Envoys and their suites will first gather in the pavilion outside of the east gate of the Coal hill and await the arrival of the Imperial Coffin. They will stand in rank and bow. They will then escort the Coffin on foot as far as the pavilion inside Hou Men. The order of Procession will be as follows:
>
> a. The Wai Wu Pu and members of staff of foreign Envoys.
>
> b. Grand Council.
>
> c. Imperial Princes.
>
> d. Special Envoys in order as decided upon by the Diplomatic Body, i.e., in reverse alphabetical order of the names of their respective countries (Z-A) in the French language.
>
> e. Dean of the Special Envoys and one official of his staff.
>
> f. Japanese Prince.
>
> g. Prince Regent.
>
> h. Imperial Coffin.
>
> On arrival of the cortège at this latter pavilion the Foreign Envoys will retire from the procession taking position in front of the Pavilion. The Prince Regent will bow to the Special Envoys and depart. The Special Envoys will enter the pavilion and the cortège will proceed on its way.
>
> 12. A pavilion will be erected beside the pavilion mentioned above (inside the Hou Men), where the ladies of the Diplomatic Corps and the officials of the Legations not in the cortège will witness the funeral procession; admission by ticket only.
>
> 13. A pavilion will be erected on the street of the Hsi Ssu P'ai Lou (Western Four P'ai-lous) where foreign guests may gather to await the funeral cortège. They shall stand at the side

of the road and bow as the Coffin passes. Admission to the pavilion will be by ticket only […].” (Note of April 15, 1909 in BA 1879/09)

On the morning of April 26 at 10:30 the special envoys were received by the Prince Regent to present their credentials in the Throne Hall, the Qianqing Gong, in the following order: USA, Brazil, Spain, France, Mexico, Russia, Austria-Hungary, Great Britain, Belgium, Germany, Italy, Sweden, Portugal, Netherlands (Circular of the American Legation, April 24, 1909 in BA 2039/09).

Later that day the American minister sent out a notification to his colleagues:

> “In view of the fact that it has been informally agreed today to issue tickets to the Diplomatic Pavilion (for the ceremonies on May 1st) to Consuls-General and Consuls and their wives, and to army officers above the rank of captain and their wives, and to naval officers above the rank of lieutenants and their wives, the American Minister has the honor to request his honourable colleagues who desire, in view of this to revise their requests for tickets to do so as soon as possible, stating the number required for the Diplomatic Pavilion, and also the number required for the Distinguished Guests Pavilion at the Four Western Pailous. All tickets will be issued on Thursday, April 29th in accordance with the requests […].” Circular of April 26, 1909 in BA 2060/09)

Thus it was not only the special envoys but also an enormous crowd of curious foreigners eager to watch this outstanding ritual intervening for tickets. For the German mission 14 tickets for the Diplomatic Pavilion were issued and 60 tickets for the Foreigners’ Pavilion at Xisi (Note of April 29, 1909 in BA 2124/09). This means, taking only the Germans into consideration, there were about 75 people watching the procession; if we assume that every nation would be represented by an average of about 50 people, there were about 500 to 600 foreigners intruding at this core event of Chinese ritual. This must have cost the Chinese a great deal of self-discipline.

The only thing the Foreign Ministry could do was to advise the Diplomats that “there must be solemn silence on all the streets through which the cortege passes. Neither Chinese nor foreigners, military or civilian, are to be allowed on the streets. If there are foreigners who wish to witness the ceremonies they may gather at a place selected by the Board of the Interior, outside the Fu Ch’eng Men to the west of the temporary bridge and the Chiu T’ien Temple.” (Note from the Foreign Office to Mr Rockhill, April 28, 1909 in BA sine)

On April 29, the special envoys went to the Forbidden City to pay respect to the late Majesties; on May 1, the special envoys gathered in the pavilion outside of the east gate at Coal Hill and awaited the arrival of the imperial coffin, there. They joined the cortège and accompanied the catafalque to the pavilion inside the Hou Men where they bid the remains of the late Emperor farewell and retired from the procession.

The Funeral Procession of the Late Empress Dowager, November 1909

As to the funeral procession for the late Empress Dowager in November 1909, the foreign diplomats apparently were less interested to accompany the catafalque. This time they did not lay much effort into the negotiations: In their meeting of October 18, 1909, at the Austro-Hungarian mission, the diplomats deliberated upon their participation in the forthcoming funeral procession. The Doyen, Mr Kuczynski, reported the strict regulations of the ceremonies: November 6, at 10.00 a.m., they were invited to pay respect to the late Empress Dowager, whose sarcophagus had been placed until then in the Huangji Dian. November 9, they were to gather at 05.00 a.m. at Donghua Men to join the cortège coming out of the Forbidden City and accompany the procession. They emphatically opposed the early hour, 5 o'clock in the morning. It would be too dark then, they argued, for maintaining order, forming the cortège, even for recognizing each other:

> "On aborde ensuite la question de l'heure à laquelle le Corps Diplomatique est convié. Le Doyen déclare qu'il a déjà fait tout son possible pour obtenir un changement d'heure, en faisant valoir toutes les objections à un rendezvous si matinal, l'obscurité complète, l'impossibilité de se reconnaître, de former le cortège, d'assurer le service d'ordre, mais aucune de ces objections n'a suffis pour changer la décision du Gouvernement chinois, qui, de son côté, déclare que cette heure est fixée par la nécessité qui s'impose de faire une certaine étape avant la tombée de la nuit. Le Doyen prie, donc, ses honorables collègues de prendre une décision et de lui indiquer si, dans le cas où ses démarches ultérieures devaient rester infructueuses, il faut accepter l'invitation purement et simplement. Il s'ensuit une discussion générale. De l'avis de tous les Ministres l'heure de convocation n'est pas raisonnable et plusieurs déclarent qu'il leur serait bien difficile de se rendre la nuit en grand uniforme à une cérémonie dans les conditions existantes ici. D'un autre côté il serait également difficile de s'abstenir, si le Gouvernement chinois insiste, puisque, en règle générale il faut se conformer, autant que possible, aux coutumes du pays. [...]"(Séance du Corps Diplomatique du 18 Octobre 1909 in BA 5856/09)

Finally, the Foreign Ministry informed the Doyen on October 21, that to accommodate the foreigners the hour for their participation had been changed. The question arises whether the Chinese had scheduled the foreigners' participation at that early hour being aware of the fact that the foreigners might oppose; while changing the time of participation to 07:30 a.m. they might have appeased the diplomats and simultaneously minimized their own dislike of the foreign participation.

Accordingly, the place of gathering was changed, as well: they were to await the catafalque at Beixin Qiao and accompany it for a short distance to Yuewang Miao, at Dongzhi Men. Another two pavilions were installed there for the staff of the missions and the rest of the foreigners (Circular no 136 in BA 5180/09).

In another note the Foreign Ministry announced that the diplomats were invited to pay their respects in front of the coffin of the late Empress Dowager, on November 6, at 10.00 a.m., in the order of their seniority. Again even the way they had to go was described in every single detail. A few days before the funeral procession left the Imperial Palace, ninety-eight representatives of thirteen nations proceeded to the Huangji Dian to perform a ritual resembling that of November 21, one year before.

For the day of the funeral procession, it was decreed again, that each chief of mission may be accompanied by one person of his choice to join the procession; all the other foreigners were advised to assemble at the pavilions specially installed for that occasion. But the tickets issued were not sufficient: Only 354 tickets instead of 594 were made available by the Chinese (Circulaire no 145 in BA 5432/09).

In those difficult days of the declining empire and of the growing threat from outside even ritual – for centuries the basics of Chineseness – has lost its stabilizing power. China was not able to keep the foreigners out of its ritualized demonstration of cultural identity which was actually a means of political strategy for internal use. The traditional correct performance of (imperial) death ritual, practiced through hundreds of years, was all of a sudden blurred by the intrusion of foreign participants.

The Mourning Services for Mao Zedong, September 1976

The Communists tried to change the funeral practices in order to get rid off the "superstitious" traditional rituals, which rather strengthen kinship ties and the individual's family than foster loyalty towards the party and the nation. The procedure was to be simplified, the waste of expenditure reduced, cremation should be adopted instead of burial, and one memorial meeting should replace the elaborated traditional funeral rites. The leaders of the revolutionary movement were to be cremated so that only their ashes remained. They were usually buried apart from their historical monument, i.e. no grave or mausoleum should function as public a shrine. The cremation policy of the communist party was aimed at discouraging any form of a personality cult.[6] Mao Zedong himself declared in 1944:

> "From now on, when anyone in our ranks who has done some useful work dies, be he soldier or cook, we should have a funeral ceremony and a memorial meeting in his honor. This should become the rule. And it should be introduced among the people as well. When someone dies in a village, let a memorial meeting be held. In this way we express our mourning for the dead and unite all the people." (Whyte 1988:297)

---

6 Zhou Enlai was the first leader to be cremated at Babaoshan Revolutionary Crematorium, his ashes scattered thereafter.

But the great Chairman's mourning services went against all the attempts to simplify death ritual. It turned out that death ritual still was the meaningful political instrument that it had been during imperial days. The strong symbolism of death ritual as a means to demonstrate authority and legitimateness to (Chinese) society was still alive and important as ever.

Some 60 years after the last two imperial deaths, communist China held mourning services at the demise of Chairman Mao Zedong who died on September 9, 1976. It was no longer the Board of Rites issuing the mourning decrees.[7] This time, the Central Committee and the Military Commission of the Chinese Communist Party, the Standing Committee of the National People's Congress and the State Council formed a funeral committee headed by Hua Guofeng, the political heir of Mao Zedong. In order to coordinate the mourning services and to stabilize society two announcements were issued: The first one highlighted the role of Mao Zedong as founder of the Communist Party, praising his achievements and reminding the public to continuously follow his thoughts. The second one declared all the relevant details for the mourning services.

> "For seven days Mao Zedong would be laid in state in the Great Hall of the People, mourning services would be held during this period from September 11 to 17. A big memorial rally was to be held in the afternoon of September 18, on Tian'anmen-Square. From September 9 to 18, flags should be lowered all over the country as well as at all the Chinese institutions abroad, embassies etc. A three minute-mourning silence should be the beginning of the culmination of mourning services, of the big rally on September 18. All over the country, sirens would sound in mourning for three minutes. Foreign governments, fraternal parties or friendly personages are not invited to take part in the official mourning ceremonies. Chinese diplomats should inform about this decision." (Xinhua News Agency 09/09/1976)

Mourning services began on September 11. Mao's corpse[8] was put on public view in the Great Hall of the People, while the leaders of the new government in hierarchical order paid tribute before Mao's bier. "The chief mourners remained the carefully listed state and party leaders, and more important than Mao's relatives were the representatives sent to the services from the areas where Mao had undertaken great revolutionary activities: Shaoshan, the Anyuan Colliery, Ruijin County, and so on. Mao as a person, with family and friends, was displaced by Mao as a transcendent revolutionary leader without a private domain of his own." (Wakeman 1988:263)

---

7 For a detailed study on the mourning services for Chairman Mao, see Wakeman 1988.

8 When preparing the funeral arrangements for the late Dr Sun Yatsen, Republican China was already inspired by the embalment and public display of Lenin. Communist China followed the example – a team of specialists worked for about ten months on the preservation of Mao's remains.

During the next seven days more than 300,000 people came in a perfectly mobilized arrangement to pay respect to the remains of Mao Zedong. On September 18, at 3.00 p.m., about one million people gathered at Tian'anmen-Square to hold a mass memorial rally. After a three minutes' silence with sirens sounding in mourning, after the national anthem and the "Internationale", Hua Guofeng as political heir of Mao Zedong and his appointed successor delivered the memorial speech. At 3.30 p.m. the rally came to a close.

Again, death ritual was practiced in the traditional Chinese way, the observance of mourning being mainly a means of claiming legitimateness, of stabilizing a society which was threatened to be deteriorated by death, by chaos. Even the ongoing struggle between Hua Guofeng and Mao's widow, Jiang Qing, came to centre upon the Chairman's funeral rites and, at the end, was won by the Chairman's political heir. Mao's physical remains could be used as "a source of charismatic authority" (Wakeman 1988:276); thus Hua was very much in favor for a public memorial enshrining the remains of the Chairman against those who rather would have the tomb and the monument kept apart. But Hua Guofeng managed to get his idea through; on the same day, when the plan for a memorial hall was officially announced, the publication-project of a new selection of Mao's works was started by the editor Hua Guofeng. Thus, Hua Guofeng appears as the legitimized heir of the physical and ideological remains of the late Chairman. On November 24, 1976, construction work on Mao's memorial hall was initiated by Hua Guofeng personally, one year later, at the first anniversary of Mao's death the Memorial Hall was officially opened.

In this account, there was no place left for foreigners. For centuries in practice the death ritual was a political message towards the interior, towards society. The traditional choreography of mourning communicated that the struggle for power had been won, already, and showed in a very precise way who was going to be the leader for the years to come.

The Mourning Services for Deng Xiaoping, February 1997

The most recent "imperial death" occurred when Deng Xiaoping died on February 19, 1997. Though the funeral of Deng Xiaoping was the largest after Mao's in Communist China – and probably also the last great funeral along the line of ancient imperial tradition, the authorities were quite aware of the high risk of public mourning: The emotional public outpouring of grief at Mao's death had brought the country to a standstill; the thousands of people mourning the late Premier Zhou Enlai and placing countless wreaths in Tian'anmen Square in 1976, on grave-sweeping-day while protesting against the growing power of the "Gang of Four" – clashed with militia members and police; the memorial service for General Secretary Hu Yaobang in 1989 – giving way to pro-democracy protest – ended up in a bloody military intervention and a huge setback in the development of modern China. Thus they tried to prevent public emotion: "The Party Central Committee calls on the whole party, the whole army and the people of various ethnic groups to turn grief into strength, carry forward Comrade Deng Xiaoping's behest and express our mourning with our concrete actions in redoubling our efforts to do work well in various aspects"(Mufson 1997a), Xinhua stated. On the other hand, the political strategy behind the arrangements of mourning services still followed the important symbolism of highlighting the role of the (legitimate) successor.

The late Deng Xiaoping had insisted on a simple funeral with his corneas being donated to an eye-bank and his ashes cast into the sea. Deng Xiaoping said in 1989, "in assessing me, don't exaggerate. Some put me above Chairman Mao; this isn't good. I'm afraid of this sort of thing; too much prestige is a burden. I want to retire simply and after I die I want a simple funeral, I beg you all" (Associated Press Worldstream 02/20/1997).

Against the backdrop of the profound meaning of death ritual, the authorities tried to keep mourning services for the late Deng Xiaoping as simple as possible – to minimize the threatening potential of public mourning, to maximize the political outcome for a stronger position of the successor. The funeral committee was made up out of members of the Communist Party's Central Committee, the National People's Congress, the State Council and the Central Military Commission, altogether 459 officials – more than twice the number of the Central Committee's members were appointed to this committee. As usual an obituary was released, praising the achievements of the late party leader, and again, the committee declared that no foreign dignitaries and no foreign media would be allowed to attend the funeral and mourning ceremonies. The relevant statement carried by Xinhua on February 20, said that in accordance with China's practice, foreign governments, political parties and friendly personages would not be invited to send delegations or representatives to attend the mourning activities. Instead, Chinese embassies were being asked to prepare to receive condolences. Foreign journalists were notified that they would not be allowed to cover the event; this media ban also included reporters from Hong Kong, Macao and Taiwan. A six-day mourning period was ordered. The only event open to the carefully supervised public was the transfer of Deng's body from the hospital to the crematory prior to the final official memorial service. The memorial service at the Great Hall was broadcast on all eight Chinese Television channels and on radio live across the country; the committee stated that officials and the masses should be organized to listen to or to watch the live transmission of the memorial meeting at the Great Hall in their working units. After the funeral, Deng's ashes were to be scattered at sea according to his last wish.

On February 25, at 10 o'clock in the morning, the funeral service for the last eminent figure of the 20th century was held in the Great Hall of the People, at Tian'anmen Square, where an urn with Deng's ashes was displayed. The ceremony was led by President Jiang Zemin. And again – as in former times – the ritual aimed at highlighting the role of the successor, legitimizing the rightful heir to the throne.

The ceremony began with a three minutes' silence while throughout the country sirens were sounding as a sign of respect. After the national anthem, Jiang Zemin delivered a 50-minute eulogy to the late party leader. 10,000 carefully invited mourners attended the ceremonies, all former and current top officials with no international dignitaries or international press witnessing. Thus Jiang Zemin followed the path of Deng Xiaoping. There was no need to have foreigners there, the ritual still being a sign strongly demonstrating the stabilization of the Chinese society and the claim of power within the country. The message was clear:

> "The funeral will not only be the closing political act for Deng, who entered politics in mid-teens, but it will also be the opening act in a highly political year that will climax in a major Communist Party congress in the fall that is expected to reshuffle several of the top government and party posts. For President and party chief Jiang, Deng's funeral offers an opportunity to further cement his position as the country's top leader. Jiang will be seen on national television inheriting the mantle of leadership from the man who handpicked him in 1989, and leading the Communist Party's call to rally around flag, party and leadership." (Mufson 1997b)

Conclusion

The "Treaty Century" after 1842 in China has brought along an era of foreign participation in the life of the Chinese people and is considered an era of international history as well as of Chinese history. It is a "high point of cultural interchange in world history" (Fairbank/Goldman 1998: 205).

With the establishment of diplomatic missions in China, the foreigners could not be neglected any longer. The empire was weakened and in decline. When the diplomatic body requested its participation at the imperial funeral rites at the death of the Emperor Guangxu and of the Empress Dowager Cixi, the Chinese Court did not dare to refuse. But the first official participation of representatives of western countries at the last two imperial funerals in China stayed singular and outstanding until today.

A close view on the death rituals for the last two important figures of imperial China and the last two eminent personalities of modern China shows that, despite the changing position and the active role of China within the international world of today, China still sticks to her own cultural roots, to the tradition of strong symbols. […] "mourning itself enabled a new emperor to affirm simultaneously the cardinality of filial piety and, by taking the role of chief mourner, his right to the throne" (Rawski 1988b: 253). In imperial China, ritual clearly was "both subject to, and also a central instrument of, bureaucratic administration […]. Ritual appears to have been distinguished from other branches of government only in being its highest form" (Laidlaw 1999:404–405). Death ritual traditionally was and still is a key in the question of authority, of legitimateness. It is a means to show the rightful succession in power within the remaining community.

While today, it is international common practice that heads of states show respect and solidarity in mourning by their personal presence at the funeral ceremonies of another late state leader, China still keeps the Chineseness of this ritual – despite the increasing openness to foreign contacts during the last years of the recent century.

Margareta Grieszler, Department of East Asian Studies, University of Vienna

References

Associated Press Worldstream 02/20/1997: All of China to Stop for 3 Minutes of Mourning for Deng.

BA: Bundesarchiv (German Federal Archives). Different files.

Fairbank, John K. & Goldman, Merle (1992): China. A New History. Cambridge, Mass.: Cambridge University Press.

First Historical Archives of China (Beijing).

Grieszler, Margareta (1991a): Das letzte dynastische Begängnis. Chinesisches Trauerzeremoniell zum Tod der Kaiserinwitwe Cixi. (The last Imperial Funeral: Mourning Ritual for the Late Empress Dowager Cixi). Münchner Ostasiatische Studien Bd. 57. Stuttgart: Franz Steiner Verlag.

Grieszler, Margareta (1991b): The last Dynastic Funeral. Ritual Sequence at the Demise of the Empress Dowager Cixi. In: Oriens Extremus 34, 7–36.

Laidlaw, James (1999): On Theatre and Theory: Reflections on Ritual in Imperial Chinese politics. In: McDermott 1999, 399–416.

McDermott, Joseph P. (ed.) (1999): State and Court Ritual in China. Cambridge University Press.

McMullen, David L. (1999): The Death Rites of Tang Daizong. In: McDermott 1999, 150–196.

Mufson, Steven (1997a): China's Deng Xiaoping is Dead at 92. In: Washington Post (02/20/1997), A01.

Mufson, Steven (1997b): Deng's Successor to Lead Memorial Rites Tuesday. In: Washington Post (02/21/1997), A01.

National Archives in Austria
Rawski, Evelyn S. (1988a): A Historian's Approach to Chinese Death Ritual. In: Watson/Rawski, 1988, 20–34.
Rawski, Evelyn S. (1988b): The Imperial Way of Death: Ming and Ch'ing Emperors and Death Ritual. In: Watson/Rawski 1988, 228–253.
Wakeman, Frederic Jr. (1988): Mao's Remains. In: Watson/Rawski 1988, 254–288.
Watson, James L. and Rawski, Evelyn S. (eds.) (1988): Death Ritual in Late Imperial and Modern China. Berkeley: University of California Press.
Whyte, Martin K. (1988): Death in the People's Republic of China. In: Watson/Rawski 1988, 289–316.

Xu Xiaoqun

Negotiating Western Models and Chinese Practices

Judicial Reform in the Late Qing "New Policy", 1901–1911[1]

We have now received Her Majesty's decree to devote ourselves fully to China's revitalization, to suppress vigorously the use of the terms "new" and "old," and to blend together the best of what is Chinese and what is foreign. ...But China has neglected such deeper dimensions of the West, and contents itself with learning a word here and a phrase there, a skill here and a craft there, meanwhile hanging on to old corrupt practices of currying favor to benefit oneself. If China disregards the essentials of Western leaning and merely confines its studies to surface elements which themselves are not even mastered, how can it possibly achieve wealth and power?

Imperial edict, January 29, 1901[2]

China's judicial reform that was to transform Chinese laws and judicial practices into modern institutions and processes began with the reform initiatives known as the New Policy in 1901–1911, the final years of the Qing dynasty.[3] While the New Policy involved promoting industry, commerce, and Western-style education, the centerpiece was a program for gradual establishment of a constitutional monarchy. That a complete overhaul of the judicial system was part and parcel of the constitutional project was an understanding widely shared among Qing high officials, even though they differed on the details of such a reform. The tentative judicial reform initiatives in 1901–1902 in turn were encouraged by foreign powers. In the commercial treaties with China of 1902 and 1903, Great Britain, the United States, and Japan promised that given the Chinese government's desire

---

1 The research for this study was supported by a fellowship from the National Endowment for the Humanities.

2 This translated passage is from Reynolds 1993:202–203.

3 The English language literature on various aspects of the New Policy includes Cameron 1963; Reynolds 1993; Bastid 1988; Borthwick 1983 and Thompson 1995. The judicial reform that was part of the New Policy has not been fully studied. Cameron treated it in four pages (1963:171–175). Reynolds touched on it briefly in two short chapters (1993:161–92). Frank Dikotter's recent book (2002) has a chapter on the beginning of prison reform in the New Policy decade. Marinus Meijer's (1950) classic remains an important work on the reform of Chinese criminal law in late Qing, but it did not cover other aspects of the judicial reform.

to reform the judicial system "to bring it in accord with that of Western Nations," they would relinquish extraterritoriality "when the state of the Chinese laws, the arrangement for their administration, and other considerations" warranted such actions (MacMurray 1973: 351, 414, 431). From that point onward, to end extraterritoriality was the most frequently cited rationale in official discourse (official communications) and public discourse (the print media) about judicial reform: A modernized Chinese judiciary tailored after Western models would deprive foreign powers of their justification for maintaining extraterritoriality (Meijer 1950:13, 64–65; Cameron 1963:171, 173; Reynolds 1993:181; CWR 08/19/1922:450).

Although borrowing from Western models to build a Chinese judiciary came to be accepted as conventional wisdom, whether and to what degree traditional Chinese laws and judicial practices should be retained as "the best of what is Chinese" was by no means a settled issue. The decade of 1901–1911 saw debates, negotiations, maneuvers, and compromises on reform agendas among Qing high officials, who should not be easily categorized as conservatives or reformers, and the complexity and difficulty of the reform project, a daunting task in its own right under any circumstances, could be glimpsed at that early stage. This paper examines those developments to reveal how the political, institutional, and ideological issues were identified and approached, what progress was made, and in what false starts, delays, and detours they resulted. Ultimately, whatever was envisioned, proposed, and partially achieved in fashioning a modern Chinese judiciary during the New Policy decade would have far-reaching influences on the continuing judicial reform in the Republican era.

Institutional and Intellectual Context

In June 1901, after the Qing imperial court dominated by Empress Dowager Cixi announced the intention to start the New Policy, Zhang Zhidong, Governor-general of Hunan and Hubei, and Liu Kunyi, Governor-general of Jiangxi, Jiangsu and Anhui, jointly submitted their three memorials on comprehensive reforms. One section of their second memorial dealt with "Moderation in Judicial and Penal Practices" (*xu xingyu*, 恤刑狱). The topic covered nine issues, including alleviating litigation burden on the people, minimizing torture in trial, moderating punishments, and reforming prisons. These constituted a larger part of the judicial reform agenda at the time. The reform initiatives in the subsequent years essentially addressed, and expanded beyond, the issues first raised by Zhang and Liu.

In May 1902, at the recommendation of Zhang Zhidong, Liu Kunyi, and Yuan Shikai, Governor of Zhili and Commissioner of Training the Army, Shen Jiaben and Wu Tingfang were appointed Commissioners of Law Codification and charged with the task of revising existing Chinese laws in favor of foreign models

(Yang Honglie 1930:886; Meijer 1950:10). They were authorized to form and head the Law Compilation Commission (*falü bianzhuan guan,* 法律编撰馆), which was formally established in 1904 and renamed the Law Codification Commission (LCC) (*xiuding falü guan*, 修订法律馆) in 1907.

Versed in Chinese traditional laws and informed by Western and Japanese models, Shen Jiaben was one of the most important individuals who contributed enormously to the development of a modern Chinese judiciary. A native of Gui'an, Zhejiang, and a *jinshi* degree holder, Shen became a deputy chairman of the Board of Punishment (*xingbu youshilang*, 刑部右侍郎) in 1901 and then the president of the Supreme Court (*daliyuan zhengqing*,大理院正卿) in 1906 while concurrently serving as commissioner of law codification. He would serve only on the Law Codification Commission from 1907 onward and leave the Commission in 1910, when much of the drafting of laws was done, to become the deputy chairman of the Government Advisory Council (*zizheng yuan,* 资政院), and the deputy Minister of Law in 1911 (ZLD, QS, Vol.2:384). Wu Tingfang too played an important role in the judicial reform. After receiving legal training in England and practicing law in Hong Kong, Wu served as Minister of Foreign Affairs and in other capacities while working with Shen Jiaben till 1907. He was to become the Minister of Justice in the first Republican government – the Provisional Government of Sun Yat-sen in Nanjing – during January–April 1912, helping to carry over the agenda of the late Qing judicial reform into the Republican era (ZLD, QS, Vol.2:246; Pomerantz-Zhang 1992; Xu 1997).

Besides the LCC, a few other institutions were instrumental as well. In 1906 the Ministry of Law was changed from the Board of Punishment, and the Supreme Court was changed from the Court of Judicial Review (*dalisi*, 大理寺). The first Minister of Law was Dai Hongci, who was succeeded by Ting Jie in 1909. The first president of the Supreme Court was Shen Jiaben, who was succeeded by Zhang Renfu in 1907. In spite of some friction with regard to the demarcation of the responsibilities between them, the Ministry and the Court would often consult with each other and jointly present reform proposals and opinions to the imperial court in 1907–1911.

The Commission for Studying Constitutional Government (CSCG) (*xianzheng biancha guan*, 宪政编查馆), established in August 1907 and headed by Prince Yi Kuang, served as the gatekeeper of all reform proposals and counter-proposals regarding the New Policy. It is the CSCG that proposed in 1907 to reorganize the Law Codification Commission and make it the independent body in charge of drafting laws (QCLDS:849–51; Meijer 1950:42–43). The CSCG would review and make comments on all the proposals and opinions presented to the imperial court, including the laws and regulations drafted by the LCC, the Ministry of Law, and the Supreme Court. During the years of its existence the CSCG proved to be generally supportive of reform initiatives coming from the three other institutions.

Beyond those institutions, many Qing high officials appeared to have understood rather well how constitutional government and judicial system in the West and Japan worked and how the systems might be adopted in China. The fact that Zhang Zhidong and Liu Kunyi initiated the judicial and penal reform suggests that even though considered more conservative than Shen Jiaben and Wu Tingfang, those officials were informed of judicial and penal practices in the West (and Japan) and were capable of introducing judicial reform in light of Western models, at least to a degree. Zhang Zhidong's tenure as Governor-general of Guangdong and Guangxi in 1884–1889 and his efforts at "self-strengthening" projects there had exposed him to a host of ideas borrowed from Western examples, mediated through some of his Western-educated staff members and Western experts hired for the various projects (Bays 1970). According to one study, during his tenure as Governor-general of Guangdong and Guangxi, and then of Hunan and Hubei, Zhang's staff included 398 Chinese and 239 foreigners, and the latter were from Japan, Germany, Britain, the U.S. and other countries (Li Renkai 2005:121–166). Although it remains to be documented, Zhang may very well have learned of Western legal practices during and after that period.

Zhang and Liu were not alone in being knowledgeable about Western practices. In 1907, Ze Gong, Commissioner of Reorganizing Governmental System (*bianzhuan guanzhi dachen*, 编撰官制大臣), submitted a memorial to offer suggestions on establishing an independent judicial system. He once again drove home the issue of abolishing extra-territoriality by pointing out the difference between Chinese and foreign judicial systems. Echoing similar utterances in some radical journals of the time (Svensson 2002:98–100), the concept and language of "protecting human rights (*baohu renquan*, 保护人权)" were articulated in official discourse probably for the first time:

> "Revolutionary storms in various countries all stemmed from miscarriage of justice. That is why all constitutional countries took as their priority the revision of laws to protect human rights. In order to use laws to protect human rights, they all established separate judicial institutions to gain the trust of the people, because only judicial institutions could follow the law and only the law could protect human rights" (DZ 1907, No.8).

Here Ze did not fail to show the purpose of constitutional and judicial reform was to avoid revolution, but he did speak of protecting human rights as positive moral values. He essentially raised the issue of judicial independence to the level of protecting human rights to emphasize its importance and thus introduced the concept of human rights into official discourse where it would stay into the Republican era.

The nationalistic objective remained as strong as that of avoiding revolution in Ze's argument. If China did not lay down the foundation of judicial independence in preparing for constitutional government, said Ze, the repeal of the treaties regarding extraterritoriality would never happen. Refuting the argument that separating administration and justice would allow judicial officers to abuse power, he argued that under the law on disciplining and punishing judicial officers, if there were abuses, judicial personnel would become persons breaking the law and be punished accordingly.

> "The point is that judicial independence is not to respect judicial officers, but respect the law. No matter what governmental system, [the goal of] respecting the law of the country was same in all countries. Whether it can be achieved depends on whether judicial organs are independent. This is the key to preparation for constitutional government and cannot be compromised even if other things might be" (DZ 1907, No.8).

Thus the rule of law and the independence of judicial institutions were forcefully presented as desirable goals for China to reach.

Official discourses from 1907 onward, including those from more conservative elements, would routinely invoke the principles of separation of powers and judicial independence and even the notion of "the people's rights" or "human rights," though opinions differed on the details of how to achieve them. For instance, in the words of Dai Hongci, the first Minister of Law, the essence of constitutional government was to divide the state power into legislature, executive, and judicial branches to protect the people's public and private rights. Only then could the country's territory, the people, and government be connected together and solidified forever (QCLDS:840). The idea of connecting together and solidifying the country's territory, the people, and the government was a political formulation that reform-minded intellectuals such as Liang Qichao, Yan Fu, and others were advocating around the turn of the twentieth century and have been identified as a version of statist nationalism (Goldman and Lee 2002:17–29; Duara 1995:170–174; Karl 2003:33–38, 119–120). Here it was appropriated with ease by the Qing high official to justify judicial reform. Similarly, the notion of protecting the people's public and private rights was also refreshing and even revolutionary to appear in the official discourse.

Some of the memorials from Qing high officials showed their familiarity with Western origins of the idea about judicial independence. Li Jiaju, Commissioner of Studying Constitutional Government (*kaocha xianzheng dachen,* 考察宪政大臣), placed the origins of judicial independence in France. According to him, the nature of judicial independence was that adjudication was left to judges, and that Minister of Justice could not interfere with trial but should supervise judicial administration (QCLDS:879). Zeng Wen, Governor of Zhejiang, traced judicial independence to the theories by John Locke and Charles Montesquieu on the one hand, and on the other hand, argued that separation of administration and judiciary had existed in ancient Zhou times before it was corrupted in the Qin-Han times (QCLDS:876). The attempt to find an equivalency in Chinese tradition to the principle of judicial independence indicated the positive valuation of the principle among Qing high officials at the time.

One may surmise that at least part of the knowledge about the West and Western-derived ideas came to Qing high officials through print media, since such discourse was carried on in various contemporary newspapers and journals. For one thing, the initiatives resulting from the Zhang-Liu memorial caught the attention of the Chinese press. Commentaries in the press responded to the proposals on moderating punishment and reducing abuses in judicial process. On May 9, 1904, the Chinese and Foreign Daily News (*Zhongwai shibao*, 中外时报) carried an editorial on Shen Jiaben and Wu Tingfang's response to the Zhang-Liu memorial (discussed in the following section). It maintained that the judicial system and political system should be reformed first before any new laws could have an effect. All the problems in judicial process resulted from the fact that administrative officials, who were overwhelmed by responsibilities, exercised judicial powers. The solution was to establish independent and separate courts for criminal and civil litigations. New laws should be drafted in light of Chinese and foreign laws and in view of the current conditions in the country (DZ, 1904, No.6).

Another newspaper, the Warning Bell (*Jingzhong bao*, 警钟报), carried an editorial on August 13, 1904. In its view, what needed to be reformed first were not the law, but the punishments outside the law, such as abuses in the hands of yamen runners, sufferings in jails, non-existence of judicial officers (as opposed to administrative officials), and dearth of people with legal knowledge. An even more significant point was made as follows. More than ten years earlier Xue Fucheng had already proposed to follow the Western laws, but he had been motivated not by recognition of the cruelty of Chinese laws but by a desire to please Westerners to end extraterritoriality. That was why Xue had proposed that treaty ports follow Western laws and the interior continue to apply Chinese laws. The current government was not above this state of mind, which was worrisome. Finally, said the editorial, what was good about Western laws included 1) judicial independence, 2) the law was followed by all people from the monarch down, 3) the law was based on rights, and 4) public law and private law were separate – these were the essence of Western laws. In choosing from Western laws for China, the particulars could vary according to the changing conditions in China, but the key was to base the reform on a love for the people. If the Chinese government treated the people's lives callously, it would be difficult to expect it to reform judicial and penal practices (DZ, 1904, No.8). It was a profoundly important observation that judicial reform informed by Western laws had its intrinsic value rather than just to please Westerners and end extraterritoriality. Reformers like Shen Jiaben might have shared such a view, but to push ahead the reform agenda in the face of opposition, citing the nationalistic goal – the need to end extraterritoriality – proved to be the most effective discursive strategy.

The opinions sampled above provide a sense of the wider intellectual-political atmosphere conducive to judicial reform. They indicate that at the time of the New Policy reform, an understanding of how justice and legal systems worked in Western countries and Japan was not limited to Shen Jiaben and Wu Tingfang, but was widely shared among Qing high officials and other Chinese elites. The background to this increasing, albeit haphazard, understanding was a growing body of translations by missionaries and Chinese scholars of Western and Japanese legal works and legal histories that created new vocabularies to express Western legal concepts. And the new vocabularies almost all came from Japanese Kanji, a convenient way for the Chinese to learn and use Western-derived legal concepts (Reynolds 1993:111–27). The word "public law (*gongfa*, 公法)" has been traced to the work on international law written by American missionary William Alexander Parsons Martin in the 1860s. Other words such as "sovereignty (*zhuquan*, 主权)," "civil rights (*minquan*, 民权)," "the people's rights (*renmin zhi quanli*, 人民的之权利)" also came into use. Huang Zunxian's annotated translation of the Japanese criminal code, published as part of *A History Japanese State* (*Riben guozhi*, 日本国志) in 1887, provided a whole set of terminology that was to be used in Chinese new criminal law and litigation law in the early twentieth century (Li Guilian 1998:9–36; Svensson 2002:78).

Such was the institutional and intellectual, as well as political, context in which the late Qing judicial reform was set in motion and pushed forward at a relatively speedy pace. At the same time, a significant amount of conceptual rationalization among high officials and of institutional construction within the state system remained to be realized, even if only at the national level. It is the necessity and difficulty of making those conceptual and institutional adjustments that created the confusion and controversy in the reform process, to say nothing of financial constraints and other unfavorable factors.

Drafting a New Criminal Code

Prompted by the memorial of 1902 from Zhao Erxun, the Governor of Shanxi, and under the leadership of Shen Jiaben and Wu Tingfang, a number of reform measures in penal practices were undertaken in 1902–1905. The cruel punishments such as slicing to death (*lingchi*, 凌迟), displaying the head of the executed (*xiaoshou*, 枭首), and mutilating the corpse (*lushi*, 戮尸) (to punish a guilty person who was already dead) were abolished.[4] So were corporal punishment (flogging) and torture in trial, at least in principle. Another development was the unification of legal and penal treatment of different ethnic groups in the country. Par Cassel has argued that the "legal pluralism" of the Qing provided the immediate precedents for extraterritoriality that was established in the mid-nineteenth century to accommodate Westerners' demands (Cassel 2003). It would be logical in legal reformers' thinking that since extraterritoriality was to be abolished, the differential legal and penal treatment of ethnic groups within China should also be abolished and the principle of legal equality be established.

These developments prepared for a systematic overhaul of the criminal code in light of foreign models, which was the charge of the Law Codification Commission. Under the direction of Shen and Wu, the LCC engaged in extensive work of translating foreign law codes in preparation for revising Chinese laws. By 1907 a total of twenty-six laws and legal works of foreign countries had been translated and ten more items were being completed (QCLDS:839).

What came out of the efforts to compare and choose between foreign models and Chinese laws was a draft new criminal code, completed in October 1907, with the help of Okada Asataro, a Japanese legal expert. The draft code marked a radical departure from the existing Qing law. Under the code, punishment for crimes was limited to four types: death penalty (by strangulation), imprisonment (term or life) (*tuxing*, 徒刑), detention (*juliu*, 拘留) (under two months), and fine, and all other forms of punishment were abolished. Thus, starting with the proposals for moderating punishments, the reform had reached a point where exile and corporal punishment as penal categories were to be totally abolished and incarceration to become the primary form of punishment for crimes. At the same time, under the law, the number of capital offenses was greatly reduced, and strangulation in private would be the only form of capital punishment. Application of the law by analogy was abolished, thus establishing an important legal principle – any act that was not prescribed by the law constituted no offense. The age of criminal liability was set at sixteen, while corrective education was defined as appropriate for adult criminals as well as juvenile offenders (*Qingshi Gao*, "Xingfa Zhi"; QCLDS:845–849; DFD, juan 11; also see Meijer 1950:66–76 for a more detailed explanation of the changes).

---

4 Historian Jerome Bourgon has argued that the move to abolish those cruel punishments was not entirely Western-inspired, but had been pushed by Chinese reformers for a long time (Bourgon 2003). He is right on this particular issue, but the judicial and legal reform as a whole, beyond the abolition of the three cruel punishments, was largely informed by Western models. Moreover, invoking historical precedents to argue against the cruel punishments was exactly the strategy that Shen Jiaben would use repeatedly to advance the reform agenda, as shown in this paper.

Although most Qing high officials were subscribed to judicial and legal reform in principle, many were not ideologically prepared for the sweeping changes in the criminal law. The draft criminal code caused quite a controversy among high officials, especially over the issue of whether the traditionally harsher punishments for offenses against the imperial house, familial ascendants, and men (by women) should be maintained, to which the code spelled out the negative (Matsuda Emiko 1995; Meijer 1950:79–96). Zhang Zhidong, the initiator of penal reform and now a grand secretary (daxue shi, 大学士), Lao Naixuan, a member of the CSCG, and other high officials submitted memorials, vehemently criticizing Shen's notion of separating judicial process from the role of traditional moral code (*lijiao*, 礼教) and his "disregard" of the Confucian five relationships in the draft criminal code (QCLDS:854–57, 858–62, 867–72, 887–89; ZGB, No.284, 8/11/1908; Meijer 1950:43–44, 79–93; Yang Honglie 1930:894). Although such oppositions might have indicated a conservative attitude towards the existing Chinese law and judicial practices, it is important to note that few officials questioned the general thrust of the reform in simplifying and civilizing punishments and making incarceration the primary form of punishment. And most memorials did not fail to mention the necessity of judicial and penal reform in order to cope with the changing world.

The throne was also uneasy about the radical nature of the draft criminal law. On February 16, 1909 the imperial court issued an edict asking all provincial officials in charge of judicial affairs to respond to the draft criminal code. Another imperial edict the following day ordered that Shen Jiaben should revise the draft criminal code in light of the criticisms offered by Zhang Zhidong and others. It read in part: "Nowadays the whole world is connected and there are many international negotiations, so we cannot stick to the old ways and fail to make changes to benefit the people. But we can only take [from foreign countries] what was good to remedy our shortcomings. All articles in our old law regarding social relationships must not be lightly changed so that heavenly ways and the peoples' rules may be preserved. The Commissioner of Law Codification must base the spirit of revising the law on this principle" (QCLDS:857–58).

As might be expected, since the imperial court had expressed its preference, the memorials from provincial officials in response to the February 16 edict continued to criticize the draft code along the lines of Zhang Zhidong's opinion (ZGB, No.284, 8/11/1908; No.345, 10/11/1908). Other objections were directed at issues such as setting the age of criminal liability higher than the old law, abolishing analogy in applying the criminal code, and reducing harsher punishments including death penalty in general. Wu Chongxi, governor of Henan, for one, argued that exile should not be abolished, analogy should be maintained, and fine should continue to be used as redemption for light punishments, not a category of punishment (QCLDS:870–72). Interestingly, at least two officials, Zhang Renjun, Governor-general of Guangdong and Guangxi, and Chen Qitai, Governor of Jiangsu, objected, among other things, to the adoption in the draft criminal code of Japanese terminology which they thought was difficult to understand (QCLDS:860; ZGB, No.284, 8/11/1908). Of course, Shen and his colleagues chose to use vocabulary based on Japanese kanji precisely because they believed it was the best way to translate Western legal concepts and make them intelligible to the Chinese, the role of Okada Asataro aside.

On the other hand, however, at least one high official, Yuan Shuxun, Governor of Shangdong, voiced his support for the draft criminal code as it was. China's criminal law would have to change, said Yuan, whether one wanted it to change or not. The evolution of the principle of criminal codes in various countries from harshness to compassion and science was the heavenly way (*tiandao*, 天道) as well as human efforts. "If we initiate the change, we may reap some benefits in the end; if we are forced to make the change, we may face a catastrophe endangering the whole Chinese people." Yuan brushed aside the criticisms against reduction of capital offenses and abolition of analogy as discussions of the superficial, not the fundamental. If China did not revise its laws, it could not survive the world where great powers competed, nor could it regulate its own people who lived on the land – this was the fundamental issue. In Yuan's view, to make the new criminal code work, what needed to be done first was to have an established police force and a reformed prison system, which was the only reason why the new code should not be put in force just yet (QCLDS:865–866).[5] This opinion should by no means be regarded as among those opposing the draft code, which Meijer seemed to believe (Meijer 1950:96).

At this juncture (probably in early 1910), Ting Jie, the newly appointed Minister of Law, presented to the throne five "Provisional Regulations" to supplement the new criminal code, thus satisfying conservatives and bypassing the matter of rewriting or abandoning the code as a whole. The provisions revived most of what Shen Jiaben had removed from the old law – the harsher punishments for offences against the state, the imperial house, and familial ascendants, for offences of robbery and kidnapping, and for offence of illicit sexual intercourse with a woman without a husband (Meijer 1950:109–112).

On January 25, 1911, three actions took place. The newly-formed Governmental Advisory Council (GAC) informed the throne that during the session that just ended it had discussed and adopted the general articles (*zongze*, 总则) of the new criminal code but not the specific articles (fenze, 分则). In response to those

[5] The training of police force was actually under way in Zhili Province under Yuan Shikai at the time, though it was not done elsewhere in the country (see Reynolds 1993:161–172; MacKinnon 1980:151–162).

delaying tactics, the Commission for Studying Constitutional Government immediately requested the throne, that in spite of the delay at the GAC, the entire code be issued to provinces so that officials could familiarize with the law and prepare for its enactment in the near future (ZGB, No.1182, 2/16/1911). At that request, an imperial edict ordered that with a change of the age of criminal liability to twelve, the new criminal code along with the provisional regulations be printed and issued to provinces, which was done by April 1911, and the enactment of the new criminal code was scheduled for 1915 (QCLDS:890–891).

While the controversy over the draft criminal code was raging, to offer a compromise with conservatives and a transition to the new criminal code, with the imperial court's approval, Shen Jiaben and his colleagues had begun revising the Great Qing Law and Sub-Statutes in 1907. On February 29, 1908, Shen was able to present to the imperial court the revised law as the Current Criminal Law of Great Qing (*Daqing xianxing xinglü*, 大清先行刑律). Not as radical as the draft criminal code in breaking with the past, the Current Criminal Law still incorporated some of the changes proposed over the previous years, such as abolishing exile, substituting fine for flogging, subjecting Manchu and Han to the same law, etc. Shen noted that when the new criminal code was enacted (projected for 1915), the Current Criminal Law would be voided (QCLDS:851–854). The law was referred to the CSCG, and the latter supported the revised law with minor additions (keeping exile and military servitude as punishments, per the former Board of Punishment's opinion in 1902) (ZGB, No.242, 6/30/1908). Under an imperial edict, the Current Criminal Law was printed and issued to provinces in October 1909 (QCLDS:879–80). In other words, toward the end of the Qing dynasty there were two alternative criminal codes to the Great Qing Law and Sub-statutes. It was the more radical version – the draft new criminal code that was adopted as the Provisional New Criminal Code (*Zanxing xinxinglü*, 暂行新刑律) after the founding of the Republic in 1912.

Institutionalizing Judicial Independence

The official discourse during those years already made it a foregone conclusion that a modern judiciary should be separate from administrative bureaucracy, and that an independent court system should be established as an essential condition for a constitutional government and a central part of the judicial reform, even only to satisfy the demands of foreign powers. Shen Jiaben, Wu Tingfang, and their colleagues on the Law Codification Commission were aware that only with an institutional foundation for judicial independence could the new laws be applied as designed in a due process.

The institution-building for judicial independence began when the imperial court decided in November 1906 to rationalize governmental system (*liding guanzhi*, 釐定官制) that included separating the functions of the Court of Judicial Review (*dali si*, 大理寺) and the Board of Punishment. By an imperial edict, the Board of Punishment was changed into the Ministry of Law (*fabu*, 法部), which no longer had trial function and was only in charge of judicial administration. The former Court of Judicial Review became the Supreme Court (*dali yuan*, 大理院) as the final appellate court in the country. Along with the Supreme Court, the General Procuracy (*zong jiancha ting*, 总检察厅) was established, which would function independently while under the supervision of the Ministry of Law. Following the initial separation, the Supreme Court, under Shen Jiaben, quickly requested and obtained from the imperial court an increase in its annual operating budget from six hundred taels, which the former Court of Judicial Review had received annually, to twenty thousand taels (DZ, 1907, No.3).

Most government officials praised the imperial edict that separated judiciary from administration, but apparently veiled criticisms also emerged. In February 1907, Wu Fang, an Imperial Censor, submitted a memorial refuting the criticisms and urging the imperial court not to be swayed by opposition. Wu identified three objections against judicial independence: 1) the educational level of citizens was too low, 2) judicial personnel were too few, and 3) power of administrative officials would be weakened. Wu called those arguments illogical. Firstly, when foreign consular jurisdiction was established in treaty ports and concessions, no objection was raised against it on the ground of low-level education of the Chinese. "It pains me deeply that while foreigners can try the Chinese people, someone is saying our people should not be tried by independent [Chinese] courts." Secondly, county magistrates came to their positions through civil service examination or merit or purchase, never having learned any skills in adjudication, but once in their positions they would try criminal and civil cases with no one questioning their qualifications. Thirdly, the power of administrative officials was granted by the state and need not be augmented by attending judicial affairs. If the power of adjudication was used to increase personal authority and benefit, that was what should not be tolerated. Separating administration and judiciary would allow administrative officials to govern better without abusing power, and judicial officers to protect the people with law. Wu asked the imperial court to stay the course of separating judiciary from administration for the sake of dealing with foreign powers and governing the country better (QCLDS:822–824).

The imperial court did indeed stay the course, and the change made in November 1906 was only the beginning. In a memorial of December 1906 that won imperial approval, the Supreme Court under Shen Jiaben argued for establishing a system of four levels of courts and three levels of trials based on foreign models. The court system would consist of township trial bureaus (*xiang yanju*, 乡谳局), district courts (*difang shenpanting*, 地方审判厅), provincial high courts (*gaodeng shenpanting*, 高等审判厅), and the Supreme Court (*dali yuan*, 大理院). In September 1907 the LCC presented to the imperial court the Law on Organizing Courts (*Fayuan bianzhi fa*, 法院编制法) that was based on the model of "four level courts and three trials", but the lowest court was now called the court of first instance (*chuji shenpan ting*, 初级审判厅) instead of "trial bureau". After the CSCG made a few minor revisions, the imperial court approved the Law on Organizing Courts on February 7, 1910. Probably out of the consideration that the country was not ready to establish what the law prescribed, the law and the related regulations were never officially enacted, though they were frequently invoked as guidelines when matters of the court system and jurisdictions were discussed during 1907–1911, and eventually became the functioning law under the Republic.

While separating judiciary from administration was relatively straightforward, to separate adjudication from judicial administration was more complicated. Although the Supreme Court and the Ministry of Law became independent of each other and of the rest of the central government bureaucracy after the November 1906 imperial edict, it was not immediately clear which institution should handle certain judicial matters formerly under the purview of both. On May 14, 1907, Dai Hongci, the new Minister of Law (*fabu shangshu*, 法部尚书), submitted a memorial proposing a division of responsibilities between the Ministry of Law and the Supreme Court in twelve judicial matters (QCLDS:824–827).

Six days later, Shen Jiaben, who had been concurrently appointed the president of the Supreme Court in November 1906, submitted a counter-proposal. Shen complained that the twelve items submitted by the Ministry of Law had not been fully discussed and agreed to between the two institutions as they should have been. Shen expressed agreement with most of the items, but proposed to change three matters involving two issues. According to Dai, 1) capital cases coming from high courts should be reviewed by the Supreme Court and forwarded to the Ministry of Law for final decision and the Ministry should draft the decision co-signed by the Supreme Court to be presented to the throne. Cases of exile or lesser punishments and emergency cases from high courts should be reviewed and presented to the throne by the Ministry, and the Supreme Court should be notified. 2) The Ministry of Law and the Supreme Court should jointly request for imperial approval of the appointment of officers to the General Procuracy and judges to the Supreme Court. First, in Shen's view, the Supreme Court should have an exclusive authority on reviewing and deciding cases, as independent adjudication was the essence of constitutional government theory. In view of the fact that judicial personnel were not trained, and separation of judiciary and administration in provinces uncertain, however, the Supreme Court was willing to compromise – to continue the old practice where the Board of Punishment and the Court of Judicial Review had jointly presented cases for the Autumn Assizes (*qiushen*, 秋审). But to be consistent, the Ministry and the Supreme Court should also jointly present cases of exile or lesser punishments and emergency cases, just like capital cases. Second, the Ministry of Law was responsible for judicial administration, to which the appointment of judicial officers belonged. But such practice would have to wait until the day when schools of law have trained a large number of judicial personnel from whom the Ministry would appoint all judicial officers. As a stopgap measure for the time being, the Supreme Court and the General Procuracy should be allowed to appoint their own officials without interference from the Ministry of Law (QCLDS:827–29).

The situation was not completely satisfactory thereafter, partly because no relevant laws existed yet. According to Xu Dingchao, an Imperial Censor, as of March 1909 the two institutions continued to assert their conflicting authorities. 1) Claiming the authority on judicial administration and interpreting it as supervising all courts and procuracies in the whole country, the Ministry of Law asked that cases from provinces to be sent to it for review. At the same time, the Supreme Court claimed the authority to draft rejections of appeal cases within Zhili province. 2) The General Procuracy was supposed to have the power to supervise the Supreme Court. But since the General Procurator was recommended by the Supreme Court to be appointed to the position, he was no more than a subordinate of the Supreme Court and not in a position to carry out his duty. 3) The Ministry of Law and the Supreme Court would compile statistics of disposed cases separately, but the Supreme Court's statistics would also include reviewed cases that would appear in the Ministry's statistics, which was like having two Ministries of Law (QCLDS:862–64).

In February 1910 in presenting the Law on Organizing Courts to the throne, the CSCG argued that as the Law demarcated the responsibilities of the Ministry of Law and the Supreme Court, the two institutions should henceforth strictly adhere to their respective duties and not to interfere with each other. All the matters of judicial administration should go to the Ministry, not to be handled jointly by the Supreme Court. All cases tried and reviewed at the Court should not be sent to the Ministry for review. The only exception was that before the new criminal code came into effect in 1915, the Autumn Assizes would continue to be processed by the Ministry (ZGB, No.826, 2/18/1910).

The problem of separating the jurisdictions of the Supreme Court and the Ministry of Law was part of the functional confusion, resulting from fashioning a modern judiciary out of the old institutions, a confusion that had to be sorted out for the new judiciary to function as it should. As the Law on Organizing Courts and the new criminal law were not in effect before the end of the Qing dynasty, the trial function of the Ministry of Law was not entirely and officially abolished because the Autumn Assizes continued. The final separation of judicial administration and adjudication at the national level would be eventually realized after the founding of the Republic.

Introducing Due Process

Drafting criminal and civil codes and building an independent court system were necessary but not sufficient to silence foreign criticisms of Chinese judicial practices for lack of justice. A key element in the judicial reform was to institute a due process in which law was strictly applied and nothing outside law was practiced. Nowhere the issue was more acutely pressed home than in the two notorious practices that affected the fate of criminal defendants – first, torture in trial, and the second, summary execution of robbers and bandits guilty of homicide without a review process.

In their 1901 memorial Zhang Zhidong and Liu Kunyi had pointed a finger at the practice of using torture in trial and called it a violation of the spirit of governing the people. In foreign countries, they noted, conviction was based on testimonies of witnesses, not confessions of the accused, because 1) judicial officers were in charge of trials, 2) few offenses called for capital punishment, and 3) prison life was not harsh. In China, because the punishment was so harsh that being guilty or not would make a huge difference, witnesses would not want to testify and the accused would try anything to escape the punishment. The law provided that if there were unambiguous testimonies, conviction could be rendered without getting a confession from the accused. But in such cases the convicted would always deny guilt on appeals by accusing the trying official or the witnesses of taking bribery to do him in. Officials therefore would not want to close a case without getting a confession from the accused. That was why torture was used to a cruel degree in order to get a confession, many people died in the process, and the convicted would still deny guilt on appeals for being tortured to confess. To solve the problem, proposed Zhang and Liu, except for capital cases that had to have confessions, in cases of lesser punishments, if witnesses were fair and trustworthy, testimonies to guilt were able to stand scrutiny, and questioning of the convicted by superior officials left no doubt, then conviction should stand as such and any appeal to the central government should be rejected. This way torture need not be used and the innocent would not be burdened. In their 1904 response to Zhang-Liu's point, Shen and Wu fully concurred with the opinion expressed, and further proposed that police be gradually established in provinces to reduce criminal and civil cases and help with evidence when such cases did arise (DZ, 1904, No.6). This issue was essentially about the rights of the accused and a due process. The proposal from Zhang and Liu did not address in a fundamental way the problem that was inherent in the traditional institutional and legal framework. They did not, and probably could not, spell out how one would determine such conditions for conviction as they defined had been met, essentially leaving that to the discretion of the trying officials who did not have a procedural law to follow.

Precisely on the ground that a procedural law was not available, some high officials opposed the proposal for prohibiting torture in most trials. In May 1905 Liu Pengnian, an imperial censor, argued that one should not just admire foreign countries that did not use torture without studying the reasons. In foreign countries there were litigation procedural laws. Before the defendant was arrested, police and detectives investigated. When the defendant was tried, there were lawyers and jury. From preliminary hearing to public sentence, trial was based on testimonies, not confessions of the defendant. In China the revision of criminal laws was just beginning, and litigation procedural laws did not exist. If torture was allowed, but not routinely used, the accused would confess out of fear. If torture was suddenly prohibited, the accused would have nothing to fear and refuse to confess, and trying officials would have great difficulty to get confession, which would cause cases to drag out and pile up. Liu maintained that prohibition of torture in trial should not be effected before procedural laws were prepared. The imperial court referred the memorial to Shen Jiaben and Wu Tingfang for comments (DZ, 1905, No.8). Obviously, the key premise of Liu Pengnian's argument was that confession was necessary for conviction in all cases, which Zhang Zhidong and Liu Kunyi had already abandoned.

The response from Shen and Wu was a forceful refutation of Liu's argument. First, the judicial reform was being carried on for the purpose of ending extraterritoriality. To make Chinese laws on a par with foreign laws and to take the merit of foreign laws to remedy the shortcomings of Chinese laws were the first priority of the undertaking. And nothing set Chinese laws more apart from foreign laws than torture in trial. That is why they (Shen and Wu) agreed with the Zhang-Liu memorial that torture not be used in cases entailing penal servitude, exile, and lesser punishments. As expediency torture was still allowed in cases entailing capital punishment, precisely because ordinary people were not morally nurtured and trying officials were not highly skilled. Second, as the existing statute stated clearly, officials trying cases "must obtain willing confession (*wude shufu gongci*, 务得输服供词)," and if the accused did not confess and the offense entailed penal servitude or more severe punishment, the case could be reported, "on the basis of testimonies," to the emperor who would make the final decision. Shen and Wu held that "willing confession" meant confession that was not obtained through torture and "on the basis of testimonies" meant no need for forcing confessions from the defendant by torture (DZ, 1905, No.8:125). What they proposed earlier, therefore, was simply reiterating the existing statute with slight flexibility, really having nothing to do with copying foreign laws. Third, if prohibiting torture would cause cases to drag out and pile up, the use of torture did not prevent that in the past, as provinces had cases backlogged for several years to more than ten years. Fourth, Shen and Wu characterized Liu's argument as being concerned about ordinary people's lack of morals, but not about trying officials' cruelty, which was contrary to the universal truth (*gongli*, 公理). Moreover, normally the meek would fear torture and the tough would rather stand torture than confess, so that the use of torture inevitably led to decisions that erred in either direction (the guilty got away and the innocent wrongly convicted). Using Wu Tingfang's experience as a judicial officer in Hong Kong where British laws were applied to Chinese residents, Shen and Wu denied that there was much difference between foreigners and the Chinese in temperament and psychology to warrant torture. Finally, Shen and Wu pointed out that prohibition of torture in trial was only the beginning, not the end, of the judicial reform, and that procedural laws, among others, would be drafted in light of similar laws of other countries. Their response won the approval from the imperial court (DZ, 1905, No.8:123–27).

The debate between Liu Pengnian and Shen and Wu was noteworthy. In essence, Liu's memorial argued against the prohibition of torture on the ground that foreign practices should not be adopted in China before relevant laws were enacted, as conditions in China were different from foreign countries. At least on the surface it was not so much a traditionalist argument as a practical one, thus having some force of persuasion. But Shen and Wu's argument was even more skillful and persuasive. On the one hand, they emphasized the importance of making Chinese judicial practice consistent with Western norms in order to end extraterritoriality, something both the imperial court and Chinese elite groups desired. On the other hand, they undercut Liu's argument by asserting that 1) they were proposing better enforcement of the existing Chinese law, not really borrowing from foreign laws, and that 2) the Chinese and foreigners did not have much difference in temperament and psychology, besides that 3) torture was no use to serve justice. Their point about enforcing existing statute based on semantics seemed to be quite a stretch in interpreting the Qing law. The Great Qing Law and Sub-Statutes did not contain what Shen and Wu said, and they probably were quoting from the Collection of Criminal Cases for Reference (*Xing'an huilan*, 刑案汇览) compiled by the Board of Punishment in 1834, 1840, and 1886. Such an isolated phrase as "must obtain willing confession (*wude shufu gongci*, 务得输服供词)" that may be found in one of thousands of model cases in the collection could not gainsay the overwhelming thrust in the Qing law that sanctioned torture in trial (see Harrison 1964; Connor 2000 for the confession requirement under the Qing law). But for Shen and Wu, to cite the phrase to make their argument was a necessary strategy to deflect the accusation that they were blindly following Western models.

The end result of Shen-Wu proposal on prohibiting torture in trial was that in theory torture in trial was banned in most criminal cases, but that in reality it continued to be practiced by officials of different levels in charge of judicial process in the country, as noted by reform-minded officials as late as 1911 (ZGB, No.1194, 2/28/1911), and in the Republican era as well. But at least the problem was identified at an early stage of the reform and the practice was rendered illegitimate in principle.

Another controversial issue with regard to due process was how to deal with death sentence of robbers and bandits. Under the Qing law, capital cases should go through an elaborate review process at the levels of prefecture, province, and the central government. Death sentences had to be approved by the Board of Punishment along with the Court of Judicial Review (*dali si*, 大理寺) and the Censorate (*ducha yuan*, 督察院) and finally confirmed by the Emperor. Those condemned to death at the end of the procedures were classified into two categories – 1) to be executed immediately (*lijue*, 立决), which usually applied to those who committed treason or other unpardonable crimes, and 2) to be reviewed again at Autumn Assizes (*jianhou*, 监候), which usually applied to other kinds of crimes. Of the latter category, about ten percent would be judged to be worthy of execution and the rest would be assigned to non-capital punishments or left for next Autumn Assizes the following year. Even those assigned to be executed immediately actually had three days of reprieve before the execution could be carried out (Budde/Morris 1973:131–143; Zhang Jinfan 1994:549–564; Shen Zhiqi 1715:1049).

During the Taiping Rebellion, however, the imperial court allowed the practice of summary execution (*jiudi zhengfa*, 就地正法, lit. execution on the spot) of rebels and bandits, which actually meant execution after the death sentence was approved by provincial authorities. The practice continued long after the Taiping Rebellion was over, and local and provincial authorities often bent the rule to apply the practice to offenders other than rebels and bandits. In 1908 Ling Shaonian, Governor of Henan, asked the imperial court to allow immediate execution even without the advance approval of provincial authorities in order to suppress bandits and secret societies more effectively (ZGB, No. 172, 4/21/1908). It may be assumed that such "quick justice" had actually been happening across the country.

As early as 1898 Wu Weibin, an Imperial Censor, proposed that except in Eastern Provinces (Manchuria) and except in cases of real bandits who resisted government forces like rebels where immediate execution could be temporarily applied, normal robbery cases should be sent to superior authorities for review according to the statute. The memorial was buried for over ten years. Not until

February 1909 when the judicial reform was unfolding, did the imperial court refer it to the Ministry of Law for opinion. The Ministry fully supported Wu's proposal and the opinion was issued to provinces with the imperial approval (ZGB, No.802, 1/18/1910).

Yet, Shen Bingkun, Governor-general of Yunnan and Guizhou, and Yuan Shuxun, Governor-general of Guangdong and Guangxi, requested imperial permission for continuation of summary execution, both citing rampant bandit activities in their provinces. When instructed to respond to the two memorials, the Ministry of Law refuted Shen and Yuan's argument and rejected their requests. First, the judicial process must be uniform in the country, or the future of constitutional government would be endangered. Second, ruthless execution was no answer to banditry, and an effort to get at the source of banditry was. If robbers were everywhere as Shen Bingkun claimed, asked the Ministry, was it not in spite of summary execution practiced heretofore (ZGB, No.802, 1/18/1910)?

Notably, the CSCG under Prince Yi-kuang fully supported the position of the Ministry of Law on this issue. Responding to a memorial from Xi Liang, Governor-general of Eastern Provinces, in April 1911, the CSCG insisted on the Ministry of Law's order that summary execution should not be applied except in cases of real bandits (rebels). The Commission further noted pointedly that even a criminal who resisted arrest was different from open resistance against government forces and should be dealt with according to normal trial procedures (QCLDS:902). Once again, the progressive position taken by the CSCG cannot be overemphasized to contextualize the reform efforts spearheaded by Shen Jiaben and Wu Tingfang.

Clearly, a key to solving such issues in a fundamental way was to have comprehensive procedural laws to safeguard the rights of criminal defendants as well as civil litigants. In their argument against Liu Pengning in 1905, Shen Jiaben and Wu Tingfang indicated that litigation procedural laws would be drafted in light of foreign models. By April 1906 the draft criminal and civil litigation law was completed. Drawing upon European and Japanese models and containing five chapters and 260 articles, the draft litigation law laid down concrete procedures for criminal and civil litigations, including legal representation by lawyers and jury trial. Shen believed that jury trial would avoid either letting the guilty off or punishing the innocent. He held that legal representation was most important for the purpose of recovering the nation's judicial rights since it was the practice in the West (DFD, juan 11:1–15).

When an imperial edict of May 11, 1907, asked provincial governors and governors-general to comment on the draft procedural law, however, the latter all cited inconvenience of implementing the law and requested further study of the matter. Most provincial officials seemed to be uncomfortable with the law that would give offenders more legal protection than before. But Zhang Zhidong, Governor of Hunan and Hubei, was particularly critical of the law for the principle of equality before the law, denying the precedence of father over son, husband over wife. This criticism foretold the central point of the conservative attack on the draft criminal code later that year. When the imperial court ordered the Ministry of Law to respond to the criticisms, the latter asked for eight months to consider the matter. Then in late September 1908, when the new criminal code itself came under attack, the Ministry decided not to proceed with the procedural law until the new criminal code was approved (ZGB, No.338, 10/4/1908; Meijer 1950:43–44; Zhang Jinfan 1994:714). Apparently, the Ministry and the LCC did not want to get entangled in debating the procedural law before the substantive law was accepted.

After the debate on the new criminal code abated and the Current Criminal Code was issued, the LCC had the criminal procedural law and the civil procedural law drafted separately, based on Japanese models. By January 1911 both the Criminal Procedural Law (*Xingshi susong lü*, 刑事诉讼律) and the Civil Procedural Law (*Minshi susong lü*, 民事诉讼律) were completed but were not enacted (Zhang Jinfan, 1994:714–715). The CSCG proposed that before the criminal and civil procedural laws were put into effect, Shen Jiaben should select the most important elements from the laws to draft a set of Provisional Litigation Procedures (*Zanxing shusong chengxu,* 暂行诉讼程序) that could be used in tandem with the Law on Organizing Courts (ZGB, No.826, 2/18/1910). The regulations were never produced, as Shen left the LCC in 1910. In the meantime the Ministry of Law finished drafting the separate sets of provisional regulations on criminal and civil litigation fees in January 1911 (ZGB, No.1182, 2/16/1911). Those procedural laws and regulations would be readily appropriated by the Republican government after 1912.

Conclusion

The judicial reform in the late Qing New Policy left a lasting legacy. In its broad outline, the judicial reform was designed to bring about, after Western models, a set of substantive and procedural laws, a court system independent of administrative bureaucracy, a fair judicial process presided over by trained and disciplined judicial officers and checked by a regulated legal profession, and a reformed prison system. The guiding principles underpinning all the above were the rule of law, judicial independence, and due process. Although most of those goals had not been achieved when the Qing dynasty fell, what was started in the ten years of the New Policy era broke the path, along which the Republican judicial reform would continue, and thus profoundly shaped its course.

In retrospect it seems almost astonishing, and ironic, that the whole project of the judicial reform was triggered by and grew from a memorial from Zhang Zhidong and Liu Kunyi and that the project enjoyed general support among many Qing high officials, besides the well-known reformers Shen Jiaben and Wu Tingfang. It is instructive to see that Shen Jiaben, and many high officials, did not have direct exposure to Western laws and institutions but nonetheless were knowledgeable about Western legal and judicial practices, suggesting a deep level and wide reach of transnational circulation of ideas through translation projects by Chinese and foreigners alike. Even more instructive is that some Qing high officials, as well as Shen and Wu, understood the importance of judicial independence, such as Ze Gong, and others supported the principle of legal equality embodied in the draft criminal code, such as Yuan Shuxun. The facile divide between conservatives and reformers among high officials in late Qing does not stand close scrutiny, and a more complex understanding of the New Policy era is in order.

On the other hand, the willingness on the part of many Qing high officials to follow Western models to change Chinese law and judicial practices had a limit, not surprisingly. Opposition to the new criminal code was one example, and another was the reluctance to abolish torture in trial and summary execution. Yuan Shuxun could support the new criminal code under the imperative of competing with foreign powers in a modern world, but as a provincial governor, he would insist on using summary execution as a necessary tool to deal with banditry. To his mind, it seems, modernizing the Chinese criminal law to meet Western norms did not have to include extending legal protection for the rights of accused bandits and rebels, which was probably a very alien notion indeed to many administrative officials from provincial governors to county magistrates.

In those instances of resistance to reform, Shen Jiaben and Wu Tingfang skillfully argued their case by asserting that they were not copying Western examples but trying to better enforce the intention of Chinese law or Chinese tradition. Where they encountered the fiercest resistance, they were willing to take a step back, such as on the issue of the draft new criminal code, in order not to jeopardize the entire protect of judicial reform. Such strategies, along with accommodation to them on the part of the imperial court and support from such high officials as Prince Yi-kuang, which proved crucial, ensured the progress that was made in transforming Chinese judiciary in a short span of ten years, which laid the foundation for the continuation of judicial reform in the Republican era.

Xu Xiaoqun, Department of History, Christopher Newport University, Virginia

References

Bastid, Marianne (1988): Educational Reform in Early-Twentieth-Century China. Ann Arbor: Center for Chinese Studies, the University of Michigan.

Bays, Daniel (1970): The Nature of Provincial Political Authority in Late Ch'ing Times: Chang Chih-Tung in Canton, 1884–1889. In: Modern Asian Studies 4:4, 325–347.

Bodde, Derk and Clarence Morris (1973): Law in Imperial China. Philadelphia: University of Pennsylvania Press.

Borthwick, Sally (1983): Education and Social Change in China. Stanford: Hoover Institute Press.

Bourgon, Jerome (2003): Abolishing 'Cruel Punishments': A Reappraisal of the Chinese Roots and Long-term Efficiency of the Xingzheng Legal Reform. In: Modern Asian Studies 37:3, 851–862.

Cameron, Meribeth E. (1963): The Reform Movement in China, 1898–1912. Stanford: Stanford University Press.

Cassel, Par (2003): Excavating Extraterritoriality: The 'Judicial Sub-perfect' as a Prototype for the Mixed Court in Shanghai: In: Late Imperial China 24:2 (December), 156–182.

Connor, Alison W (2000): True Confession? Chinese Confessions Then and Now. In: Turner, Karen G. et al. (eds): (2000): The Limits of the Rule of Law in China. Seattle: University of Washington Press.

CWR: China Weekly Review. Shanghai (different editions).

DFD: 大清法规大全 (A Complete Collection of Laws and Ordinances of the Great Qing) (1909). No place: Zhengxueshe.

Dikötter, Frank (2002): Crime, Punishment, and the Prison in Modern China. New York: Columbia University Press.

Duara, Prasenjit (1995): Rescuing History from the Nation: Questioning Narratives of Modern China. Chicago: University of Chicago Press.

DZ: 东方杂志 (The Eastern Miscellany). Shanghai (1904–1911, different editions).

Goldman, Merle, and Leo Ou-fan Lee. (2002): An Intellectual History of Modern China. Cambridge: Cambridge University Press.

Harrison, Judy Feldman (1964): Wrongful Treatment of Prisoners: A Case of Ch'ing Legal Practice. In: Journal of Asian Studies 23:2 (Feb.), 227–244.

Karl, Rebecca (2003): Staging the World: Chinese Nationalism at the Turn of the Twentieth Century. Durham: Duke University Press.

Li Guilian (李贵连) (1998): 二十世纪的中国法学 (Chinese Legal Studies in the Twentieth Century). Beijing: Beijing daxue chubanshe.

Li Renkai (黎仁凯) (2005): 张之洞幕府 (Zhang Zhidong's Staff). Beijing: Zhongguo guangbo dianshi chubanshe.

MacKinnon, Stephen R. (1980): Power and Politics in Late Imperial China: Yuan Shi-kai in Beijing and Tianjin, 1901–1908. Berkeley: University of California Press.

MacMurray, John V. A. (ed.) (1973): Treaties and Agreements with and Concerning China, 1894–1919. New York: Howard Fertig.

Matsuda Emiko (1995): Shinmatsu reihou sogi shoko" (A Brief Examination of the Debate on Propriety and Law in Late Qing), Hougaku Ronsou (Treatises on Legal Study) 137:2, 48–67; 137:5, 113–124.

Meijer, Marinus J. (1950): The Introduction of Modern Criminal Law in China. Batavia: De Unie.

Pan Nianzhi (潘念之) et al. (1992): 中国近代法律思想史 (A History of Legal Theories in Modern China). Shanghai: Shehui kexue chubanshe.

Pomerantz-Zhang, Linda. (1992): Wu Tingfang (1842-1922): Reform and Modernization in Modern Chinese History. Hong Kong: Hong Kong University Press.

QCLDS: 清末筹备立宪档案史料 (Sources on the Preparation for Constitutional Government in Late Qing) (1979). Beijing: Zhonghua shuju.

Qing Shigao (清史稿）(A Draft History of Qing). 刑法志 (Book on Punishment and Law) (1942). No publication place: Lianhe shudian.

Reynolds, Douglas R. (1993): China, 1898–1912: The Xinzheng Revolution and Japan Cambridge, MA: Harvard University Press.

Shen Zhiqi (沈之奇) (1715): 大清律辑註 (Collected Notes to the Great Qing Law). [Reprint 2000]. Beijing: Falü chuban she.

Svensson, Marina (2002): Debating Human Rights in China: A Conceptual and Political History. Lanham, MD: Rowman and Littlefield Publishers, Inc.

Thompson, Roger R. (1995): China's Local Councils in the Age of Constitutional Reform, 1898–1911. Cambridge, MA: Council on East Asian Studies, Harvard University.

Xu, Xiaoqun (1997): The Fate of Judicial Independence in Republican China, 1912–1937. In: The China Quarterly 149, 1–28.

Yang Honglie（杨鸿烈) (1930): 中国法律发达史 (A History of the Development of Chinese Law). Shanghai: Shangwu yinshuguan. Reprint, Shanghai: Shanghai shudian, 1990.

ZGB: 政治官报 (Official Gazette of Political Affairs). Beijing (1906–1911, different editions).

ZLD, QS: 中国历史大辞典 (A Complete Dictionary of Chinese History), 清史 (History of Qing) (1992). Shanghai: Shanghai cishu chubanshe.

Zhang Jinfan (张晋藩) (1994): 清朝法制史 (A History of Qing Legal System). Beijing: Falü chuban she.

Donald A. Jordan

China's National Economic Council and the League of Nations Experts, 1929–1937

Introduction

The topic of the changing position of China in the world seems to be exemplified by the experience of China's National Economic Council interacting with the pre-WW II League of Nations. From 1919 to the end of the Northern Expedition the world view among the Guomindang (GMD) leadership had been that of strident anti-imperialism, and occasionally xenophobic rhetoric. Most of the GMD elites, except for Chiang Kai-shek, himself, were products of Western education, yet they felt ambivalent toward the West because of its imperialism. The Guomindang had begun with the unilateral approach of Revolutionary Diplomacy, and after Versailles, became resentful of Western acceptance of Japanese in Shandong at the opening of the League. With the victory of the Northern Expedition, the outlook among the GMD leadership swung back toward re-engagement with the Western World. In working to reconstruct China, there was among the GMD members a growing consensus that the May Fourth banner of science and greater transfer of technology from the West could end China's backwardness. Furthermore, as soon as Nationalist China began to seek recognition from other countries, pragmatic concerns began to weaken its unilateral isolation.

T.V. Soong was but one of many GMD progressives who wanted China to become a nation-state and to modernize as quickly as her finances would allow. Modernization would necessarily depend on economic development. Soong became aware of the technocratic experts that traveled to East Asia on missions from the League of Nations in which China was a member nation. The focus of this study – the role of League experts in reforming China's miserable state of sanitation and poor health – is but one of the many areas where League expertise fit China's needs. Chinese desire for health reform reached out for the science readily available from the League of Nations.

The League Approaches the New China

One of the major figures among the League experts who influenced Nationalist China during its first decade was the bacteriologist and epidemiologist, Ludwik Rajchman. An extremely cosmopolitan Polish Jew, Rajchman had been active in combating epidemic cholera and typhus in post-World War I Central Europe. His work in medical research in London from 1910 through the war years had provided him with the expertise to be not only on the cutting edge of his science but also with English language skills that would prove invaluable to him as a great communicator with China's modernizers.

Rajchman's first mission to East Asia and China had been in 1925 when he listened to Japanese public health officials voicing concern that nearby China was a source of periodic epidemics that were spreading outward from its trading ports. Japan had quickly modernized its public health system. However, it could not isolate itself from the cholera, typhus, and malaria that periodically spread outward from the backward interior of China, Japan's leading trade partner. Rajchman, an enthusiastic idealist on international cooperation, immediately went to Beijing to spread his message of public health reforms and sanitation for China by means of a quarantine service at Chinese ports. However, like later League technical experts, he knew but little of the local political situation in warlord China that impeded reforms. It is possible that Rajchman met T.V. Soong in Canton in early 1926 as the Guomindang prepared for its military campaign to reunite a China weakened by such warlord regimes as the one he had just won over in Beijing.[1]

In 1928, once the Guomindang (GMD) had at least created the semblance of a national government, it created a Ministry of Health at Nanjing which initiated communication with Rajchman, who headed the League's Health Section and various medical committees in Geneva. Within the highest circle of the GMD, T.V. Soong, committed to centralized economic reconstruction for China and to obtaining the modern technology that was necessary, was busily engaged in creating a financial foundation for the new regime and working as a key diplomat to gain recognition and tariff autonomy for China. His heart was committed to centralized economic reconstruction for China and obtaining the modern technology that would entail. The official opening of contact from the League came with the visit of the Deputy Secretary Joseph Avenal of the League Council who visited the new Chinese government in December 1928 and explained the availability of public health expertise through the League's Health Organization and its founding director, Rajchman. Following this lead, the Minister of Health gained approval

[1] See Balinska 1998: first chapters, 78–79 on trip to China in 1925–26; Hsia 1928:111–12 on Rajchman's initial naiveté in China.

in Nanjing to request that the League send a health commission that could advise Nanjing on creating a new public health system based on the most advanced practices in the West. Since the Finance Ministry initially supervised ports and quarantines through the customs system, Soong became a party to the health study.

League Health Experts Assess China's Needs

In January 1929 the Chinese request had reached the League and by February the Health Section Director himself was appointed to head a mission of technical experts to China which would examine conditions and offer advice on modernizing public health services (The League from Year to Year, October 1, 1928 to September 30, 1929: Chapter VI, 125). Finally, on September 14, 1929 the Ministry of Foreign Affairs cabled the League that it would welcome a delegation of public health experts. Rajchman and Frank Boudreau, an American member of the League's Health Section, left Geneva in late October and on November 7 began a two month tour observing the current Chinese health practices and formulating ideas for reforms. After study in Shanghai, Nanjing, and Canton, Rajchman, T.V. Soong and Chinese medical leaders proposed a Three-Year Plan for a Chinese health system that would be headquartered in Nanjing. This began nearly a decade of League missions to China which eventually drew in over 50 Western experts who brought expertise not only in the area of public health, but also on a wide variety of the components for the infrastructure of a modern economy. Other Chinese projects with League experts advised on upgrading industries such as cotton and silk, agriculture, monetary policy, public engineering of flood control, railroad and highway construction, and public education. For the sake of brevity, this study will focus on the transfer of the technology of public health as a leading example of what became a generally successful collaboration between the League-designated experts and Chinese modernizers like T.V. Soong and, later, his National Economic Council.

During 1930 the Nanjing government decided to give continuity to the technological relationship with the League; requesting that the League send a "permanent" technological advisor to China that could match up Chinese needs with various technologies available through the several League Sections. The General Assembly and Council struggles against international conflict turned out to be their least effective function, and were surpassed by the Sections that disseminated technologies worldwide. The dynamic Rajchman played a leading role from Geneva, focusing attention on China and attracting leading experts into missions of exchange. The Three-Year Plan from 1929 for health and medicine initiated a national quarantine service by July 1930 in Shanghai to check cholera and small pox around the lower Yangtze. Ground was also broken for medical facilities:

the Central Hygiene Station and the Central Hospital in Nanjing from which a nationwide system would gradually radiate. The medical education system was to emphasize national coordination of existing Chinese medical schools with a new experimental medical school at the center and radio broadcasts on health issues.[2]

League experts emphasized equality between China and the League; thus, avoiding the servility of traditional imperialism. The collaboration between equals was symbolized by the League's appointment of a Harvard-trained Chinese doctor, Liu Ruiheng, as Vice-chairman of the League's Health Committee in Geneva. China's new Minister of Health spearheaded the National Health Administration as it evolved and was the first of a series of Chinese doctors to serve on special League committees under the Health Organization, parent of today's World Health Organization. The League in 1930 not only approved the ongoing technical support for China, it created the League Council's Committee on Technical Cooperation between China and the League.

Soong's National Economic Council Implements League Expertise

With regular meetings this committee devoted to exchange with a particular country was unique. With Rajchman as a vigorous catalyst and ringleader and T.V. Soong as an expediter, a high-powered team of Section Directors from the League joined Rajchman in China in late 1930 for fact finding and advising. Rajchman sponsored Dr. Berislav Borcic director of Zagreb's School of Hygiene who became in November 1930 the League's first permanent technical adviser to Nanjing's Ministry of Health. Within several years Borcic was referred to as the "uncrowned prince" of a new Chinese Health Service and Rajchman's man on the scene. Likewise, in late 1930 Robert Haas, French Head of the League's Communications and Transit Section, arrived to begin study and reporting on a centralized approach to highway and railroad building (League Council document 450. 4 Oct. 1934; Hoe 1933). Of greater consequence was the arrival of Rajchman's friend Sir Arthur Salter, British economist and the League's Director of the Economic and Financial Section whose expertise synchronized well with T.V. Soong's ambitions for economic development (Balinska 1998:86–88, Meienberger 1983, Monthly Summary of the League of Nations for 1934:114).

His close exchange with Salter and the two other League Directors crystallized in Soong's successful promotion at Nanjing in early 1931 of the National Economic Council (N.E.C.). This was to be a top level coordinating body that would

[2] League of Nations Council report of September 1931 included a report from the new Committee of Technical Cooperation Between the League and China. C.445.1934–General. Also see The League from Year to Year, October 1931–December 1932:128, and Hoe 1933.

cut across bureaucratic lines and expedite national plans for development, including the new national Health Service. By April 25, 1931 Soong as Vice-Premier of the Executive Yuan could state in a telegram to the League that Chiang Kai-shek wished to state that the Chinese Government was setting up the N.E.C. "for planning reconstruction [and] requests collaboration [with the] League" (League Council document C.405.M.208.1933).[3] Soong formally requested a League official to assist in creating the N.E.C. and provide liaison with the League technical organizations to obtain advisors for N.E.C.'s projects. As the infant National Government grew at Nanjing, the Ministry of Health was brought under the Ministry of the Interior which caused temporary anxiety to Technical Advisor Borcic and Rajchman who were reassured by Soong of continuing commitment to advancing public health.

The N.E.C. evolved along with the close friendship of T.V. Soong and Rajchman. In a letter back to Geneva, Rajchman explained that he was hopeful of the support of Chinese business and bankers for the N.E.C.'s plans "primarily because the Finance Minister (Soong) is a first-rate man who inspires confidence."[4] Rajchman recalled that it was T.V. Soong's specific request to the League that Rajchman be appointed as the Technical Agent to the Chinese Government that proved decisive. Soong actually lobbied with the British and French League representatives to gain Rajchman's appointment, despite some skepticism from the Japanese critical of his lack of objectivity on China (Balinska 1998:94–95 based on Rajchman's letters).

This was a foretaste in April 1931 of how League missions to China would become an irritant to those Japanese working to secure China as an economic dependency of Japan's economic empire. Soong and his N.E.C. were striving for economic independence and thus became hated threats to Japan. When the League accepted Soong's proposal in May, the Japanese delegate Yoshizawa agreed to the ideal of supporting Chinese reconstruction but thought Japan in its advanced state of development should be sending experts to China (League Official Journal 1931:1082). In May advisor Borcic participated in the inauguration of the Central Applied Hygiene Station at Nanjing as part of the Three Year Plan which the new N.E.C. had moved quickly to implement (The League Year to Year 1931–32:130). When Rajchman returned to China in early September it was in the throes of the Great Flood of 1931. However, the threat of epidemics had already been lessened by the work of the new Health Service with its large scale vaccinations.

---

3 Cited in Meienberger 1983, Hoe (1933) also quotes the "historic" telegram.

4 Balinska 1998:88 cites letter to William Martin in his private papers in Geneva.

Japanese Intervention in China

As China's great anti-Japanese boycott began in July and then in September the Manchurian coup erupted, the League faced its greatest challenge. After September 18, Rajchman, as Soong's chosen advisor and representative from the League, enthusiastically convinced Soong and Chiang Kai-shek to turn the problem of Japanese aggression over to the League rather than negotiate directly with Tokyo or declare war. "China would come out victorious."[5] Chiang remained skeptical when the buoyant optimist Rajchman claimed that with League intervention, "the Japanese will retreat."[6]

Within the League frustrations over its inability to restrain Japanese aggression gradually turned into a common desire to do whatever else could be done technologically to help China defend itself through the N.E.C. projects. The League effort to end the Shanghai War of 1932 may not have been decisive in the May truce, but most of those on the scene agreed that the Health Service and its new public laboratory at Shanghai had been crucial in curtailing cholera among the tens of thousands of refugees. Some two million vaccinations had been produced and distributed along with pure drinking water despite the temporary destruction by bombardment of the Shanghai lab. The League's Health Organization responded by gathering up serums, drugs, mobile labs and money to meet the challenge of the war and its aftermath. League health experts observed the expansion of health services from Guangdong north to the border of Manchuria. Teams of doctors and aids took the technology of sanitation and public health to sub-stations up river at Hankou, and north to Qingdao and Tianjin (The League from Year to Year, 1931–1932:130–31). By September 1932 the planned Central Field Health Station was operating out of Nanjing with N.E.C. funding, demonstrating public health techniques to the widening circle of sub-stations (ibid.).

1933 saw T.V. Soong carry his crusade for China's economic development overseas. In the U.S. he met with League expert and Rajchman cohort, Jean Monnet, who began brainstorming with Soong on various means for attracting Western financing of China's development that would break Japan's hold (Duchene 1994, Balinska:48, 95, 100). By mid-May, T.V. and Franklin Roosevelt worked out an American loan of surplus cotton and wheat which Soong could sell in China to fund the N.E.C. outside of China's military dominated budget.[7] From Washington, Soong went on to the London Economic Conference with the prior coaching

---

[5] Yen 1974:178–79.Yen was in the Foreign Ministry at Nanjing.

[6] Excerpts from the Chiang Kai-shek diary at the GMD Archives, September 21, 1931.

[7] Morgenthau Diaries, I:28 in the Farm Credit Diary, see Zanasi 1997.

of League financial expert, Rene Charron.[8] While in Paris attending a session of the League Committee on Technical Cooperation between China and the League with Rajchman, Soong listened to reports praising Chinese progress and informed the members that China would assume the salary and expenses of a designated Technical Agent for China. The committee had to argue with the Japanese that the work was strictly "non-political" and approved Rajchman to that position and arranged for yet another medical expert from Yugoslavia to assist with the needs of the N.E.C. for sanitation in road building and flood control work.[9] Soong's vision of 14 key projects in 1933 became a Ten-Year Plan for N.E.C. that would engage a wide range of League experts. They generally spent several months in China and produced studies, made proposals, and made valuable reports, such as those on the infant Health Service. A few stayed on as government advisors.

The Central Hospital in Nanjing opened in mid-1933, with 350 beds – another of the new national medical facilities. The over one million Mexican dollar construction had required a new power station, water and gas lines, and a sewage system. The League awarded new hospital staff with travel fellowships for specialized training at European hospitals. Some were graduates from the hospital's School of Nursing which had just graduated its first class (Monthly Summary, February 1934:36–37; Hoe 1933:21). In that summer of high expectations, Japanese banks successfully intimidated Western banks against joining with Soong and Jean Monnet's development scheme. When Soong returned with only the U.S. loan in 1933, he and Monnet were left with fewer prospects for funding Chinese development and had to turn to Chinese banks and eventually a more autarkic pattern called bureaucratic capitalism. Upon Soong's return the N.E.C. was reorganized to meet the Japanese economic threats with a more centralized system (Coble 1980:127, Duchene 1988:52; Zanasi 1997:111–12).

During 1934, the reorganized N.E.C. revived up its development efforts by ordering new commissions to focus China's scarce resources on the key components of China's vital textile industry – cotton and silk. League expert on sericulture, Benito Mari criticized China's obsolete fractionated silk industry and proposed in a valuable report a five year silk improvement strategy that was reminiscent of the Three-Year Plan for the Health Administration. League economist Salter's report in April 1934 also underscored the need for the silk and cotton commissions (Mari 1933; Salter 1934). These were slowed by the success of Japan's obstruction of Western investing. The formulation by League expert Monnet and Soong of the

---

[8] Rajchman's report to the N.E.C. and League in 1934 in Rajchman 1934 and in the China Yearbook of 1934 see also The International Who's Who 1938:192.

[9] Monthly Summary of the League of Nations, July 1933:170. Rajchman 1934:765. Hoe 1933:29 quotes the July 18 resolution.

China Development Finance Corporation as a means to bring foreign and Chinese capital together triggered a shocking reaction from Japan's Foreign Ministry.[10]

On April 17, the notorious Amo Declaration warned the West not to assist, even financially or technically in any way designs that would impede Japan's mission to bring order to East Asia (Toshihiko 1983: 79–80; Sun 1993:49). Neither Soong nor the League experts gave up. Salter's proposals for monetary stabilization and economic rationalization were released soon after in May 1934. During the rest of 1934 and into 1935, Soong's N.E.C. secretariat followed the several League plans for development, generally expanding programs from the Nanjing centers out into the surrounding provinces along the new roads and railroads. As of April 1, 1934 Rajchman's own detailed summation to the N.E.C. and League committees on all the development projects included specifics on the new public health system from 1931 onward. He proudly cited 35 new field health stations in 20 areas in six provinces, while studies of diseases took place at special offices over nine provinces. According to Rajchman the new major laboratory on epidemic diseases that opened in October 1933 "compare[ed] favorably with any of this type" anywhere. His inclusive report of 1934 (Rajchman 1934) was to be Rajchman's swan song as the Japanese diplomats, no longer at Geneva, were working in Western capitals against his reappointment as Technical Agent by threatening to shut off imports from trade partners.[11]

Final League Aid to China

In May 1934 Doctor Wu Liande reported to the Committee on Technical Co-operation Between China and the League at Geneva that progress could be proven on how fully the Three Year Plan on health were being implemented. The Central Field Health Station, the Central Hospital, the Experimental Medical School, the National Quarantine Service and the coordination of national public health in the Health Service were all operating successfully (Monthly Summary of the League of Nations, May 1934:114). This glowing Chinese observation was followed in 1935 and 1936 by further evidence of expansion from Nanjing out into a national network.

When League expert Robert Haas wrote his 1935 summary on progress with the plans, he noted that in the Health Service had "now firmly established" a new Central Laboratory and Schools of Hygiene and Midwifery at Nanjing (Haas

[10] Coble 1980:216 links Soong's investment corporation with the Amo reaction.

[11] The Japanese effort to remove Rajchman from China is surveyed in Balinska 1998:100–101 but only noted tersely in League Council document C.450.1934:18 that he returned from China to Geneva once again as Health Section Director.

1935:12). In gratitude for the numerous missions, Nanjing presented a gift to the League Library in Geneva – a complete copy of the Qian Long imperial collection in four divisions (Monthly Summary of the League of Nations, May 1934:138). Cooperation continued through 1936 until the outbreak of full-scale war in July 1937.

In 1937, the last year covered in this study, while the *political* sections of the League failed to end the China "Incident", the Health Organization under Rajchman acted on Wellington Koo's plea on behalf of the multitude of war refugees in China and the danger of epidemics. Great Britain, rather timid toward Japan, suggested an increase in League funding for the problem and the Polish representative, presumably Rajchman, suggested that 2 million Swiss francs go to the Red Cross of China (Ibid. September 1937:219–20). The League Council convened in October 1937 a special session to decide on health issues from the war raging in China. To support the Health Service that the League experts had worked so hard to create, the League voted to spend the 2 million francs on 12 medical trucks that would move to wherever health crisis erupted. Each truck would be stocked with Red Cross equipment and instructions, medicines and chemicals for sanitizing. Some of the trucks were to be mobile labs, and others would be fitted with showers for disinfecting large numbers (Ibid. October 1937:248–49). The health needs and situation in China became the responsibility of a special Epidemic Commission for China made up of teams of health experts. The teams were staffed according to language groups with a French team from Marseilles and an English speaking team that would work within Shanghai's International Settlement a refuge from the fierce battle raging in Chinese Shanghai. The German speaking team included Dr. H.M. Jettmar, an Assistant Professor at the University of Vienna, and an expert on the plague in China This steady support from the League reveals that while the body mainly created to promote peace had failed, China's interaction with League experts from all over Europe did help win world and American opinion over to the Chinese side in what became World War II. Rajchman's advice in 1931 for League intervention was good only in the long run. The Japanese had sensed this League preference for China before they walked out of the League in 1934. Without that war, it may be argued based on many reports by League experts that China up to 1937 was undergoing a comprehensive modernization such as in its League-inspired National Health Service.

Donald A. Jordan, History Department, Ohio University, Athens

References

Balinska, Marta (1998): For the Good of Humanity: Ludwik Rajchman medical statesman. Ithaca: Cornell University Press, 1998.

Benito Mari (1933): Summary Report on an Enquiry into the Reorganization of Sericulture. Shanghai: N.E.C.

Coble, Parks (1980): The Shanghai Capitalists and the Nationalist Government 1927–1937. Cambridge: Harvard University Press.

Duchene, Francois (1994): Jean Monnet, the First Statesman of Interdependence. New York: W.W. Norton.

Haas, Robert (1935): Report of the Secretary of the Council Committee on His Mission in China, January –March 1935) (September 1935). Geneva: Committee on Technical Co-operation Between the League of Nations and China.

Hoe, Y.C. (1933): The Programme of Technical Cooperation Between China and the League of Nations. Paper for August 1933 conference at Banff, Canada.

Hsia Chi-feng (1928): China and the League and my Experience in the Secretariat. Shanghai: Commercial Press.

League of Nations. Secretariat. Information Section: Monthly Summary of the League of Nations (different editions). Geneva: League of Nations.

League of Nations: Official Journal. Geneva: League of Nations.

League of Nations: The League from Year to Year (different editions). Geneva: Information Section, League of Nations.

Meienberger, Norbert (1983): China and the League of Nations. In: The League of Nations in Retrospect: Proceedings of the Symposium, Geneva, 6–9 November 1980 (organized by the United Nations Library and the Graduate Institute of Graduate Studies. Berlin: de Gruyter, 313–318.

Rajchman, Ludwik (1934): Report of the Technical Agent of the Council on his Mission in China from the Date of his Mission until April 1st, 1934. Geneva.

Salter, Sir Arthur (1934): China and the Depression – Impressions of a Three Month Visit. Shanghai: N.E.C.

Sun Youli (1993): China and the Origins of the Pacific War, 1931–1941. New York: St. Martin's Press.

The China Yearbook of 1934: London: Routledge.

The International Who's Who (1938). London: Routledge.

Toshihiko, Shimada (1983): Designs on North China. In: Morley, J. (ed.) (1983): The China Quagmire, New York: Columbia University Press.

Yen, W.W (1974): East-West Kaleidoscope 1877–1944: An Autobiography. New York: St. John's University Press.

Zanasi, Margherita (1997): Nationalism, Autarky, and Economic Planning in 1930's China. Columbia University dissertation.

John K. T. Chao

The Question of Chinese Representation in the UN

Introduction

The question of the Chinese Representation in the United Nations (UN) arose with the People's Republic of China (PRC) putting forward its demand for a seat in the Security Council on January 18, 1949. Since 1951, the government of the PRC annually applied to be seated instead of the government of the Republic of China (ROC) as the representative of China. With the adoption of General Assembly Resolution 2758 on 25 October, 1971 expelling the Nationalist government and recognizing the government of the PRC as the only legitimate representative of China, the issue of the Chinese representation came to a close.

The objective of this paper is to reconstruct and analyse the struggle over the issue of the Chinese representation in the UN. It will discuss the different solutions to the problem in light of USA's (United States of America) involvement with the security of Taiwan and suggest a realistic assessment of the ultimate outcome of the struggle from a ROC point of view.

The Question of China's Representation in the UN

China was one of the important states within the Anti-Axis Alliance of the Second World War and a founding nation of the UN. It was given the status as an original member state in the UN. In the UN Charter Article 23 states that the Republic of China, along with another 4 sponsoring powers, shall be permanent members of the Security Council. When the UN Charter was signed in 1945, the PRC did not yet exist and the government of the ROC was the only legitimate representative of China. After October 1, 1949, when the Central Government of the PRC was established, two governments represented China: the Kuomintang Government and the Chinese Communist Government. Both claimed to be the central government representing China. The former controlled only Taiwan, the Islands of Penghu, Jinmen and Mazu and the latter controlled Chinese mainland.

During the civil war in China, the Union of Socialist Soviet Republics (USSR) supported the Chinese communists and the US aligned with the government of the

Kuomintang offering a counter-balance to the USSR. In order to oppose the Soviet bloc, the USA continued to recognize the ROC and her right to represent China in the UN and to hold the seat of China in all bodies of the UN. But the ROC neither represented a great power nor could it coordinate international conflicts in the UN effectively, because it depended on the US to guarantee its seat as a permanent member in the Security Council. Instead of coordinating international conflicts, the ROC was troubled by the question of Chinese representation.

Representation of member states is not a customary issue within the UN. The delegations accredited by the governments of the member states are accepted by all bodies of the UN. Only if two governments exist in one territory and both declare their right of representation, the UN has to take action. The problem of representation arose because after the retreat of the ROC government to Taiwan it continued to claim the role as the central government representing China while the PRC had taken effective control of mainland China. From 1951 to 1971, the question of Chinese representation became an annual issue which had to be dealt with by the UN.

The Security Council

On 15 November 1959, the Foreign Minister of the PRC, Zhou Enlai, announced in a letter to the Secretary-General of the United Nations, Trygve Halvdan Lie, and the President of the fourth session of the General Assembly, Carlos P. Rumolo, that the government of the ROC should be replaced by the PRC. Consequently, according to Zhou, the delegations accredited to the UN by the government of the ROC were not approved (UN Doc. A/1123, 11/21/1949 (mimeo.)).

On 15 November, the representative of the Soviet Union, Andrei Vyshinsky, declared that the Soviet delegation had informed the General Assembly of its support for the government of the PRC denying the Chinese delegation headed by Jiang Tingfu (蔣廷黻) the right to represent the Chinese government and people. On the 458th meeting, the delegate of the Soviet Union in the Security Council, Yakov Malik, suddenly cited the letter of Zhou Enlai and denied the ROC the right to represent China. However, the President (Canada) of the Security Council did not put this resolution to a vote because by commenting on items not on the agenda Malik had violated the rules of procedures in the Security Council.

In the letter dated January 8, 1950 addressed to Trygve Halvdan Lie and the members of the Security Council, Zhou Enlai protested again against the Security Council's refusal to exclude the non-legitimate delegate of the government of the ROC, Jiang Tingfu. On January 10, Malik repeated his position and during the

459th meeting put forward a resolution demanding not to approve the credentials[1] signed by the government of the ROC and consequently excluded the delegate. Then the President of the Security Council, Jiang himself, put the resolution to a vote. It was rejected by eight votes against and by two votes in favor (Soviet Union and Yugoslavia) with one vote in abstention (India)[2].

The American delegate Ernest Gross argued that the question of Chinese representation was a matter of procedure: If seven of the eleven member states voted for it, the PRC could gain admission to the Security Council. Secretary of State, Dean Acheson, stated that the US could not vote in favor of the admission of the PRC as it did not recognize this state. However, if other states voted in favor of this resolution and it won seven votes, the US would be outvoted. In spite of sev-

---

1 Credential is provided in a document identifying a representative and authorizing him to act. It must be issued by the proper authority and comply with the requirements of the General Assembly rules of procedure allowing for the provisional admission of a representative. Credentials are usually verified by a credentials committee, which reports to the plenary meeting for approval (Feltham:131). A question of recognition that originally arose as a question of credential is that concerning the representation of China. China was a member of the United Nations and of many specialized agencies when, after the 1949 revolution, the Chinese communist government came in power and the previous nationalist government only remained in control of Taiwan. Both governments claimed that they were the legitimate representations of China as a member State of numerous organizations. Were the credentials signed by the Taiwan government still valid credentials for delegations from China after the communist government had taken over the mainland? Dr. T.F. Tsiang, representing the Nationalist Government, answered that for two years the Council had recognized his credential; if that were the issue that could be no question. He submitted, however, that the question was not one of credentials – which are a procedure matter – but one of great political importance. He would veto the Soviet resolution, if necessary. The US representative stated that since his government recognized the Republic of China, it considered the credentials of the present representative valid. Security Council, Official Records, V, 459 Meeting (01/10/1950). 1–4; 460 Meeting (01/12/1950):6. Within the Security Council, representation was treated as a matter of credentials and under Rule 17 a representative to whom objection has been made continues to sit until the Council, by a simple majority vote, decides to expel him. Hence the Nationalist representative continued to sit until nine Members were prepared to oppose him. During the period 1950–1971 the United Nations and the specialized agencies had taken the view that the Taiwan government had remained the lawful one and that credentials signed on its behalf were valid credentials for the delegations from China. Consequently, until 1971 credentials signed by the communist government was generally recognized as the legitimate representation of China in international organizations, and Taiwan government was excluded from further participation in the work of these organizations (see Schermers/Blokker 1995:261).

2 UN Doc. S/1462, 02/24/1950:2; Security Council, Official Records, 5th Year, 459th Meeting (01/10/1950):1–4. The Indian abstainer, Sir Benegal N. Rau, explained apologetically that he had abstained because he was such a newcomer to the United Nations that his experience of rules of procedure was only two hours old (Tetlow 1970:129–31).

eral consultations with the then ROC ambassador Gu Weijun (Wellington Koo), Secretary of the State John Foster Dulles did not retreat from this view (Jiang Tingfu 1967:129/130).

On January 13, the Security Council rejected the resolution of the Soviet Union by six against and three votes in favor. But in letters dated January 19 and 20 addressed to the Secretary-General of the United Nations Trygve Halvdan Lie and all members of the Security Council, Zhou Enlai announced the appointment of Zhang Wentian as the Chairman of the delegation of the People's Republic of China to the General Assembly of the UN (UN Doc. S/1462, 02/24/1950:2–3). This is how the controversy over "China's Right to Representation"[3] in the UN began.

In March 1950, the Secretary-General Trygve Halvdan Lie ordered the Law Department of the Office of the Secretary-General to circulate a memorandum titled "Legal Aspects of the Problem of Representation in the United Nations" (UN Doc. A/1466:2–3)[4] discussing the difference between recognition and representation of existing states. Lie pointed out that according to Article 4 of the Charter, the admission to membership in the United Nations was open to any states accepting the obligations contained in the present Charter and, in the judgment of the UN, are able and willing to carry out these obligations. The question of representation of a member state in the specialized organs should be decided in the organizations collectively. The General Assembly, other bodies and special agencies should recognize the credentials of representation of other states. Therefore, the solution of the dispute between the revolutionary and the existing government about which Chinese government should be recognized to represent China in the UN would, to his mind, have to be resolved as follows: If a government actually were able to maintain control over the people, it proved to have the ability to carry out the obligations of the UN.

Thus, Lie supported the PRC's claim to represent China (see Barros 1989:225–233). On March 9, 1950, Ambassador Gu Weijun officially protested against Lie's opinion on the grounds that it offended the UN Charter and that it amounted to complying to Soviet demands. Jiang Tingfu launched a formal protest against Lie on March 13.

---

[3] Liang Yunli 1951; Briggs 1952; Brown/Greene 1955: 3–30, 31–52; Brook 1956; China Institute of International Affairs 1956: Ch. 12, 252–62; Fitzmaurice 1952; Bloomfield 1966; Bailey 1970, Bailey 1988:150–57; Wang Kuo–Chang 1984; Zhu Jianmin 1964; Liu Zhigong 1985:120–153; Xu Boxiong 1973:149.

[4] Also a confidential memorandum on the legal aspects of the problem of the representation in the United Nations circulated to various members of the Security Council (Security Council, Official Records, 5th Year, Supplement for 1 January –31 May 1950, UN Doc. S/1466:18).

According to Security Council decisions on procedural and substantive and procedural matters were passed if seven states including the permanent members voted in favor. The President would decide about the character of an issue as of procedural or either substantive character.

Rule 30 of the rules of procedure of the Security Council states that if a resolution is challenged, the President shall submit his ruling to the Security Council for immediate decision and it shall stand unless overruled by seven member states.

According to Lie's analysis, the Soviet Union, Yugoslavia, Great Britain, Norway and India recognized the PRC. If they could find two additional states (e.g. France and Egypt) voting in favor of the PRC, the resolution would be passed with more than seven votes. Lie supposed that the USA, Cuba and Ecuador would not support the admission of the PRC, therefore the resolution had to be tabled when the state holding the presidency of the Security Council supported the recognition of the PRC. In that case the President would rule on the question of the Chinese credentials as a procedural question. Then the permanent members would not use their veto power.

Owing to the fact that the Soviet Union had the right to exercise a veto, the USA anticipated that the PRC would replace the ROC and get a seat as a permanent member of the Security Council. Therefore the US objected to the opinion of the General-Secretary. Instead, it argued that it did not suffice for a state to exercise effective power and to be able and willing to carry out the obligations of the UN Charter. It also had to respect human rights and fundamental freedoms. Later on, the USA argued that in addition, Communist China had no right to be admitted after having been accused of aggression by the General Assembly. It could not be considered as a "peace-loving" state.[5]

There were differences of view about the standards for admission between the USA and the General-Secretary. Whereas the former set a "subjective" criterion, Lie was promoting an "objective" criterion. As a matter of fact, both, the US administration and Trygve Halvdan Lie, confused the question of Chinese representation in the UN with the admission of China to the UN. The question of representation is a dispute of two governments about the seat of a member state in the UN that could be solved by half or two thirds of the majority in the General

[5] On 28 June 1957 the US Secretary of State, John Foster Dulles, in a public address, said "Diplomatic recognition is always a privilege, never a right. [It] gives the recognized regime valuable rights and privilege, and, in the world of today, recognition by the US gives the recipient much added prestige and influence at home and abroad." (Whiteman 1993:13) Mr. Victor Belaunde (Peru) addressed the General Assembly in these words: "We cannot forget that the Government of Communist China has been condemned by this Assembly for open aggression. […] That Government was therefore justly condemned for aggression." (General Assembly, Official Records, 12th Sess., 685th Plenary Meeting, 09/24/1957:118–119).

Assembly. For admission of new members to take place, the Security Council had to recommend a state for admission and gain two thirds of the votes in the General Assembly.[6]

The Member States of the UN

During the initial process of founding the UN, the eligibility for membership was a rather controversial issue. The ultimate goal of the UN is membership for all countries of the world, but as according to Article 4 of the UN Charter, which governs the requirements for states to join the UN and the pertinent approval procedure, the admission of states still contains elements of selectivity. Looking for an explanation, we find that whereas universal membership[7] had been unanimously advocated at the Moscow Conference and the Dumbarton Oaks Conference[8], things had changed by the time of the Yalta Conference[9].

The decisions made at the Yalta Conference changed the initially advocated model of universal membership into one of limited membership and forced neutral states to declare war on Germany and Japan as a prerequisite for joining the UN.

---

[6] The distinction between admission and representation is important in other respects, too. Legally speaking if communist China had been admitted as a new member State, nationalist China (Taiwan) could have remained a member of the UN and a permanent member of the Security Council even after the admission of communist China. If, however, the question is treated as one of the representation, the arrival of communist representatives must inevitably be accompanied by the departure of nationalist representatives from all the organs of the UN, because a state cannot be represented simultaneously by two rival governments in the organization. But the UN organization is indeed a political organ, all its decisions are taken by vote (Malanczuk 1997:372).

[7] The true meaning of universality consists not of a mechanical counting of heads. It must be a fellowship of kindred minds and spirits sharing the same fears, hopes, and aims. If this dream should come true, the United Nations would be able to include in its membership every nation on earth (Chen 1985:133–136).

[8] A meeting held in Georgetown, Washington, DC, between August and October 1944 to discuss the nature and functions of the UN organization. The main participants were the US, the Soviet Union, the U.K. and later China. The purpose was to hammer out agreement on the framework for post-war cooperation and to establish an effective security international community.

[9] An agreement reached in the Crimea in February 1945 between Roosevelt, Stalin and Churchill concerning the future conduct of the war and the shape of the post-war international order. The Conference made important decisions regarding the purposed UN organization, in particular that the great powers would be given the power of veto in the Security Council, and that the Soviet Union would receive three members, the Soviet Union, Byelorussia and Ukraine. Hu assesses the damage afflicted upon Asia by the Yalta agreement in a speech delivered on 4 February 1952, at Seton-Hall (Hu Shi 1952:374–381).

At the San Francisco Conference from April 25 to June 25, 1945 the representatives of the great majority of states approved an incorporation of the limited membership model into Article 4 of the Charter governing the requirements for the admission of states and the pertinent approval procedure (Nicholas 1959:164–179).[10]

The member states of the UN were divided into the "original members" and the "newer members", both being equal in terms of the Charter and in terms of their actual rights and duties, but being different in as far as a non-"founding member state" had to apply for membership and was subject to an approval procedure.

The Original Members

Article 3 of the Charter defines "all states which, having participated in the United Nations Conference on International Organization at San Francisco, or having previously signed the Declaration by United Nations of 1 January 1942, sign the present Charter and ratify it in accordance with Article 110" as the "original Members of the United Nations". By February 8, 1945, 36 states fell under the first category, 11 under the second.

After the Polish Government had been created and Ukraine, Byelorussia and Argentina had been admitted, the UN had 51 original members, which may be categorized as follows:

- the Five Sponsoring Powers: the Republic of China, the United States of America, the United Kingdom, France, and the Union of Soviet Socialist Republics;
- eleven European states (not already belonging to the first category – translator's note): Belgium, Byelorussia, Czechoslovakia, Denmark, Greece, Luxembourg, the Netherlands, Norway, Poland, the Ukraine, and Yugoslavia;
- five states of the Middle East / Arabian world: Egypt, Iraq, Lebanon, Saudi-Arabia, Syria;
- five states of the British Commonwealth of Nations: Australia, Canada, India, New Zealand, South Africa;
- two African states (not already belonging to another category – translator's note): Ethiopia, Liberia;

[10] China believed that a limitation of membership to "peace-loving states" would strike a desirable balance between the idea of a universal organization and that of a closed organization. When the suggestion was made at San Francisco Conference that the acceptance of the obligations of the United Nations Charter and the ability and willingness to carry out these obligations should be added as conditions for admission, China found itself in apposition to accept it (China Institute of International Affairs 1959:44; Liang Yunli 1958).

- three Asian states (not already belonging to another category – translator's note): Iran, the Philippines, Turkey;
- twenty Latin American states: Argentina, Bolivia, Brazil, Chile, Columbia, Costa Rica, Cuba, Dominica, Ecuador, El Salvador, Guatemala, Haiti, Honduras, Mexico, Nicaragua, Panama, Paraguay, Peru, Uruguay, and Venezuela.

Among the original members of the UN, the overwhelming majority had actually or nominally joined the Anti-Axis Alliance of WWII. At the end of 1955, the UN totalled 76 states, the added members for the most part[11] being newly emerged Asian or African countries. This trend later brought about a majority of seats for the newly emerged Asian and African states, sufficient to influence the casting of votes on any international issue.

The Newer Members

The requirements for admission of a state to the UN and the admission procedure are regulated by Article 4 of the Charter. According to paragraph 1 of Article 4, membership in the UN is open to all peace-loving states which accept the obligations contained in the Charter and, in the judgment of the Organization, are able and willing to carry out these obligations. This implies that, firstly, an individual, a tribe or an NGO is not eligible for UN membership. Secondly, a "non-independent country" cannot become a non-founding member of the UN. Whereas the group of original (i.e. founding) member states includes the then Soviet constituent republics of Byelorussia and Ukraine as well as the then not yet completely independent British colony of India, later applicants had to be completely sovereign states. All protected or vassal states were excluded from admission.

Whether or not a candidate is able and willing to carry out the obligations contained in the Charter is decided by the General Assembly and the Security Council. Therefore, while the substantive requirements for admission to the UN relate to the applicant states themselves, decisions concerning the procedural requirements rest with the Security Council and the General Assembly.

The Procedure for Admission to the UN

According to the Charter's Article 4, the admission of new member states is effected by a decision of the General Assembly upon the recommendation of the Security Council. Consequently, when the UN has to deal with the question whether or not a candidate meets the requirements specified in Article 4, paragraph 1, and

[11] Cf. http://www.un.org/Overview/growth.htm (July 31, 2005).

especially whether or not this candidate is able and willing to carry out the obligations contained in the UN Charter, two considerations concerning the admission procedure have to be taken into account:

Firstly, the application may only be forwarded to the General Assembly for discussion and voting after a favourable recommendation by the Security Council has been obtained. This recommendation for membership belongs to the non-procedural items. In order for it to be issued, nine Security Council members have to vote in favour, without any of the Council's permanent members voting against it. And since, according to the UN Charter, any state applying for membership has to obtain such a recommendation, the admission of a state is in fact controlled by the great powers enjoying the right of veto. Their recommendation can be taken as a good word put in for the candidate (as a matter of fact, the Security Council by no means always issues a "favourable recommendation").

Secondly, after the recommendation has been obtained, the application for membership has to be accepted by two thirds of the members of the General Assembly. But the Security Council's recommendation is the prerequisite for the application to be passed on to the General Assembly for discussion. Unless the Security Council issues a "favourable recommendation", the General Assembly has no right to vote on an application for membership.

In Resolution 36 adopted on November 19, 1946, at the first session of the General Assembly, the Security Council was requested "to appoint a Committee to confer with a Committee on procedure of the General Assembly, in view of preparing rules governing the admission of new Members [...]" (GA Res. 11/19/1946). Soon after this resolution was accepted by the Security Council, the General Assembly appointed the following members to serve on its committee on procedure: India, Australia, Cuba, Norway and the Union of Soviet Socialist Republics, with India serving as chairman. The countries appointed to serve on the Security Council's committee on procedure were China, Brazil and Poland, with China in chairing. From May 28 to June 21, 1947, the two committees met four times, and finally their resolutions were adopted by the General Assembly as its rules of procedure 134 to 138, and by the Security Council as its rules of procedure 58 to 60, respectively.

In 1947, no state except Pakistan and Yemen was admitted, because after none of the applications of Hungary, Romania and Bulgaria had achieved the nine-vote majority, the USSR vetoed the admission of Jordan, Ireland, Portugal, Italy, Austria, Finland, New Zealand, South Korea and Nepal. Thus, the General Assembly was simply not even given the chance to consider the applications of these nine states.

In 1948, the UK and the USA jointly declared that in case a candidate state's application should obtain the approval of at least seven Security Council members, they would abstain from vetoing. In 1949, the 4th session of the General Assembly adopted a resolution to request the five great powers to refrain from the use of the veto in connection with the recommendation of states for membership in the UN.

But although the number of applicant states gradually increased over the following years, the stalemate situation could not be overcome before 1955. After the admission of Israel in 1949 and of Indonesia in 1950, the USSR exercised its veto power 15 times in succession, with the result that not only the vetoed candidates, but its own favourites as well were denied admission.

Membership to the UN often becomes a political issue, and the only way to resolve it is compromise. For a long period of UN history, the members with the most conflicting views concerning membership were the USA and the USSR, and many small and medium-sized states took a keen interest in questions of membership, believing that the only way for weak countries to wield influence in the international community was by relying on their number. Quite naturally, they were generally most opposed to the use of veto power by the permanent members of the Security Council in membership matters.

The way the UN has dealt with the question of membership is manifested in its serious trend towards Afro-Asianization, which has as its most obvious consequence brought about a shift of the power centre. The developed countries have lost some of their power to control the international situation, and the multitude of small member states is being sought after by bigger nations to win support for their respective cases. After some of the newly emerged states had become independent, favourable circumstances facilitated their admission to the UN. Because of their sheer number of votes, their power to influence decisions soon became grossly disproportional to their otherwise humble stature in the international community.

The Advice of the International Court of Justice on the Conditions of Admission of a State to the UN and the Competence of the General Assembly

Interpreting the UN Charter, the International Court of Justice once issued its advisory opinions on the "Conditions of Admission of a State to Membership in the United Nations" (1948) and on the "Competence of the General Assembly for the Administration of a State to the United Nations" (1950). Let us look at them briefly.

On November 17, 1947 the General Assembly adopted a resolution which requested the International Court of Justice to give an advisory opinion on the "Conditions of Admission of a State to Membership in the United Nations".

This request is to be seen against the background of the confrontation between the camps of the free and the communist world. The free world could not only count on three permanent members of the Security Council (the USA, the United Kingdom, and France) enjoying veto power, but also controlled the majority of seats in the General Assembly, which altogether made it easy for it to prevent the East-European states supported by the USSR from joining the UN. So the USSR adopted the "package deal" method, by which a "package" of communist as well as non-communist states should be granted admission to the UN simultaneously. Refusal of the free world to accept this deal would result in the USSR's veto against the admission of the non-communist states.

The US and other western states, however, were of the opinion that a candidate's application for admission should be examined according to the applicant's specific situation. Since this conflict of views could not be resolved, the USSR for many years used its veto power to block the admission of Italy and other states, until finally in 1955 the free world countries accepted the deal. The advisory opinion requested from the International Court of Justice in 1947 concerned the following two legal questions:

(a) "Is a Member of the United Nations which is called upon, in virtue of Article 4 of the Charter, to pronounce itself by its vote, either in the Security Council or in the General Assembly, on the admission of a State to membership in the United Nations, judicially entitled to make its consent to the admission dependent on conditions not expressly provided by paragraph 1 of the said Article?"

(b) "In particular, can such a Member, while it recognizes the conditions set forth in that provision to be fulfilled by the State concerned, subject its affirmative vote to the additional condition that other States be admitted to membership in the United Nations together with that state?" (GA 11/17/1947)

Having dealt with this dual question according to the pertinent stipulations and rules, the International Court of Justice on May 28, 1948 rejected the motion by nine votes to six. In its advisory opinion, the Court recognized the exhaustive nature of the five conditions of admission enumerated in Article 4, paragraph 1, of the Charter, namely, that a candidate must be (a) a state; (b) peace-loving; (c) must accept the obligations of the Charter; (d) must be able to carry out these obligations; and (e) must be willing to do so. The interpretation that these conditions represent "an indispensable minimum in the sense that political considerations could be superimposed on them" was dismissed on the grounds "that it is inconsistent with paragraph 2 of the Article, which provides for 'the admission' of any *such* State", and "would lead to conferring on members an indefinite and practically unlimited power to impose new conditions", which could not be reconciled with the character of a rule which "establishes a close connection between membership and the observance of the principles and obligations of the Charter, and thus clearly constitutes a legal regulation of the question of admission". However, "the Article does not forbid the taking into account of any factor which it is possible reasonably and in good faith to connect with the conditions laid down. [...] No relevant political factor, that is to say, none connected with the conditions of admission, is excluded." The Court also ruled out that an argument against the exhaustiveness of the conditions in Article 4 could be drawn from paragraph 2 of the article, "which is only concerned with the procedure for admission", or "from the political character of the organs of the United Nations dealing with admission. For this character cannot release them from observance of the treaty provisions by which they are governed, when these provisions constitute limitations on their power."

As regards the second part of the dual question (concerning the subjection of a member's affirmative vote to the condition that other states be admitted to membership), the Court arrived at the conclusion that "such a demand constitutes a new condition; for it is entirely unconnected with those prescribed in Article 4. It is also in an entirely different category, since it makes admission dependent not on the conditions required of applicants, but on extraneous considerations concerning other states. It would, moreover, prevent each application for admission from being examined and voted on separately and on its own merits. This would be contrary to the letter and spirit of the Charter."[12]

The General Assembly of the UN

In August 1950, the holding president of the Security Council, the representative of the Soviet Union, proposed to put the recognition of the Central Government of the People's Republic of China as Chinese representation on the agenda of the Security Council. This was rejected by 5 votes in favor, 5 against and one abstention. In four later meetings (November 10, 1951; January 31, 1955; September 8, 1955 and May 24, 1967) the Security Council discussed the representation of China in the UN, too. The Security Council followed the suggestion of the United States not to consider any draft resolutions to exclude the representatives of the Republic of China or any draft resolutions replacing the representatives of the Republic of China by representatives of the Central People's Government of the PRC.[13] After careful consideration committee members reported that the

[12] http://www.icj-cij.org/icjwww/idecisions/isummaries/iasunsummary480528.htm (October 10, 2005).

[13] Security Council, Official Records, 6th Year, 566th Meeting, 11/10/1951:1; 10th Year, 689th Meeting 01/31 1955:1–27; 700th Meeting, 09/08/ 1955:1–5; 22nd Year, 1341st Meeting 05/24/1967:8–59.

General Assembly to be the proper institution to decide issues concerning the representation of China and to come up with suggestions for the Security Council. Later on, the Security Council accepted these recommendations and did not lead or push decisions concerning the representation of China. Until February 9, 1971, when Somalia raised the issue of excluding the representatives of the Republic of China and to replace them with representatives of the Central Government of the People's Republic of China, the discussions had not come to any conclusions.[14] During this time, the government of the ROC represented China in the main bodies of the UN and its special agencies, but the government of the PRC defied them the right of representation in the UN. In order to safeguard its position as the only legitimate representation of China, the government of the ROC used the "Stimson Doctrine of Non-Recognition"[15] in order to hinder other countries from recognizing the government of the People's Republic as legal representation of China. The ROC argued that Soviet aggressions and violations of the Sino-Soviet Treaty of Friendship and Alliance (GMD:295–300; Chiang Kai-shek:254–255) after the capitulation of Japan had threatened the political integrity of China, because their actions had strengthed the Chinese communists. This argument was asserted on November 29, 1949 by the General Assembly adopting a resolution based on the ROC's point of view.

From 1949 to 1951, the issue of the right for China's representation in the UN had become a regular issue in the UN. The 22 years of dispute after 1951 can be divided into three periods:

1951–1960: The Era of the Moratorium Device

After the retreat of the Republic of China to Taiwan, the political future of China remained unclear until 1953. The USA suggested a moratorium. The UN was to postpone all considerations and draft resolutions concerning the right to represent China. From 1954 to 1960 the General Assembly decided not to consider any draft resolution concerning the representation of China. This strategy of a "Moratorium Device" was relatively unquestioned, because the US had a strong

---

[14] Security Council, Official Records, 26th Year, 1565th Meeting 02/09/1971, paras.51–101; UN Doc. S/10378 10/26/1971 and S/10382, 11/02/1971 (both mimeo.).

[15] "The Stimson Doctrine is a policy of the US government, enunciated in a note of January 7, 1932 to Japan and China, of non-recognition of international territorial changes effected by force. Named after Henry L. Stimson (1867–1950), United States Secretary of State in the Hoover Administration (1929–1933), the policy followed Japan's unilateral seizure of Manchurian north-eastern China following action by Japanese soldiers at Mukden (now Shenyang), on September 18, 1931. For details see Langer 1969:50–66; Dugard 1987: 27–36, 133–135; Han Suk-jung 1995; Duara 2003: 59–61.

influence over the majority of votes in the General Assembly (Baehr/Gordenker 1999:47).

In 1960, when the number of member states had increased to 98, the resolution submitted by the USA to prolong the moratorium was adopted with 42 votes in favor, 34 against and 22 abstention votes. Thus the resolution was approved with a majority of only 8 votes.

1961–1970: The Era of an "Important Question"

By 1960, many countries were gaining independence and joined the UN. The US domination had diminished. Washington reversed its former strategy and in order to prevent the replacement of the ROC by the government of the PRC, it submitted a draft resolution every year considering the question of the representation of China to be handled as "Important Question" according to Article 18 of the UN Charter. Decisions were to be approved by a two-third majority of members present and voting. When the General Assembly decided on October 7, 1961 during its sixteenth session that any resolution to change the representation of China was an important question, this US-resolution passed with 61 votes in favour, 34 against and 7 votes in abstention. The resolution of the Soviet Union to expulse the Government of the ROC and replace it by the Government of the PRC was rejected by 48 votes to 37, with 17 abstentions.

In 1962 this resolution was submitted by Albania (the so called "Albanian Resolution") and rejected. Due to the financial crisis of the UN there was no discussion or voting regarding the question of the representation of China in 1964 after the general debate.

In 1965, after France had granted diplomatic recognition to the PRC, the situation in the General Assembly changed. During its 20th session of 1965 for the "Albanian Resolution" gained 47 votes in favor and 47 against with 20 abstentions, two members not voting (Benin and Thailand) and one member (The Congo) not attending.

Although the US resolution to affirm the existing resolution about the Chinese representation as an important question was adopted in 1965 with 56 votes against 49 votes, 11 abstentions and one non-voting, the draft resolution of Albania and Algeria "to restore all its rights to the PRC and recognize the PRC as the only lawful representative of China" received already 47 votes, with 20 abstentions. The number of votes for and against the "Albanian Resolution" was equal in number. In 1966 the Important Question Resolution was passed with 66 members in favor, 48 against by 7 abstentions. The "Albanian Resolution" was rejected with only 48 votes in favor, 57 against and 17 in abstention and one non-voting (Thailand).

During the 24th session of the General Assembly in 1969, the votings for the two resolutions were as follows: The Important Question Resolution was passed by 71 votes in favor, 48 rejected and three votes in abstention, 3 member states did not vote.

During the same session the "Albanian Resolution" to restore the legitimate rights of the PRC in the UN was rejected by 56, 48 states voted in favor, 11 in abstention and one non-voting (India).

The "Albanian Resolution" for the expulsion of the ROC and replacement by the PRC was already supported by a majority of the member states' votes, however their draft resolution did not gain a two-thirds majority of the members' votes. Therefore, there was an urgent need to revise the policy of an "Important Question".

In the beginning of 1967, the US changed their strategy towards the PRC: In a need to counter-balance the Soviet Union by establishing a Sino-US alliance, the USA now considered that they could not exclude the PRC completely from the international community. This change of strategy had a negative impact on the perspectives for the government of the ROC to represent China in the UN.

After the Ussuri River incident in 1969 the PRC and the Soviet Union had become enemies. The White House saw this as a golden opportunity to contact the government of the PRC. Based on global considerations, President Nixon ordered Secretary of State William Pierce Rogers in March 1970 to transfer the China issue from the State Department to the White House. The State Department could no longer intervene in the issue of Chinese representation in the UN.

In June of the same year, President Richard Nixon visited Beijing and discussed the issue of diplomatic relations. The US proposed to agree to admit the PRC to the UN. The right of representation of the ROC would be merely nominal, as Washington not only planned to admit the PRC to the UN and to the Security Council, but also to keep a seat for the ROC in the General Assembly.

After Canada and the PRC had established diplomatic relations on October 13, 1970, Italy announced on November 6 the establishment of diplomatic relations with the PRC. Both countries canceled their diplomatic relations with the ROC. During the 25th session of the General Assembly the communist and communist-friendly members proposed to decide on the resolution about the "Restoration of the lawful rights of the People's Republic of China in the United Nations". The voting results of the resolutions were as follows: The resolution to reaffirm the "Important Question" was approved by 66 votes in favor, 52 votes against, 7 votes in abstention, one member not attending (the Maldives) and one not voting (India).

The resolution to replace the government of ROC by the government of the PRC was approved by 51 votes in favor, 47 against and 25 votes in abstention, again the Maldives did not attend and India did not cast its vote. The situation for the ROC was deteriorating. However, the question of representation was put to vote before the "Albanian Resolution". Thus a two-third majority for the approval of the "Albanian Resolution" was needed. This resolution was rejected.

Previously the ambassador of the US, Walter McConaughy had held a reception celebrating the approval of the resolution every year in his residence located in Zhongshan Street in Taibei, but not in 1970 (Qian Fu 2005:145).

1971: The Question of Dual Representation of China

Since the dual representation of China in the UN had a bearing on US and Japanese interests, frequent consultations were held between Taibei, Washington and Tokyo. In early February 1971 Xue Yuqi (薛毓麒), the former permanent representative of the ROC to the UN, went to Tokyo for talks with top officials of the Japanese Ministry of Foreign Affairs on how to handle the representation issue. Japan still intended to stick to the "Important Question" approach, but during the talks Xue found out that the Japanese officials differed in their assessment of its chance of success – if they expressed a clear point of view at all.

By the end of February, the Department for International Organizations of the Ministry of Foreign Affairs in Taibei had made a catalogue of the most feasible strategies concerning the representation issue (Qian Fu 2005:145–146):

- The "Two-China Plan", proposed by both the USA and Japan. This plan maintained that China consisted of two sovereign political entities, each with its own territory, and that the UN, should therefore consider them as two separate states and consequently admit both to membership.
- A plan drafted by Belgium in 1970 (but not presented before the UN), according to which the PRC as well as the ROC, each representing the territory under its jurisdiction, should be granted membership to the UN, with the PRC replacing the ROC in the Security Council.
- A draft resolution deliberated by the Japanese Ministry of Foreign Affairs, in which was stated that in compliance with the UN's principle of universal membership all parts of a divided country should be admitted to the UN as long as they possessed the characteristics of a state.
- A resolution by the Tunisian government to request the Secretary-General to place the issue of the admission of the PRC on the provisional agenda of the next regular session of the General Assembly, to take on exploring possible paths for solving the issue and to submit the findings to the General Assembly.
- A resolution by the government of the Netherlands to leave discussion on the Chinese representation question to the Security Council, which

would hopefully first recommend to accept the ROC as a new UN member representing Taiwan and then recommend to admit the PRC representing China.

In mid-March the US expressed concerns regarding the possibility to sustain the status quo of the Chinese representation by merely relying on the "Important Question Resolution". Washington felt the need to come up with a "Dual Representation Resolution". Taibei, however, had objections to this idea and suggested that the White House should send a top official to discuss the matter (Qian Fu 2005:146).

When the US ambassador to the ROC, Walter McConaughy, met with Vice-Prime Minister Jiang Jingguo (蒋经国, Chiang Ching-kuo), he used this occasion to mention the issue of representation in the UN and the necessity to develop new strategies to prevent the adoption of Albania's draft resolution. He clarified that the "Dual Representation" formula should be given due consideration in this context. Jiang expressed neither disagreement with McConaughy's description of the situation nor the conviction that the old strategy would again lead to victory.

On April 9, the ROC foreign minister-designate Zhou Shukai (周书楷), accompanied by the ROC ambassador to the United Nations Liu Kai (刘锴), called on Marshall Green, the US Assistant Secretary of State for East Asian and Pacific Affairs. Green told Zhou that Washington had not yet made its final decision on its policy concerning the question of the Chinese representation, but also pointed out that the situation regarding the "Important Question" approach had continued to deteriorate and that, as all alternative measures to safeguard the ROC's seat in the UN were hard to go along with, one would have to find the least intolerable among the feasible ones.

Liu emphasized that no matter what kind of deal would finally be agreed on, the "Important Question" resolution should in any case be put forward again, for to act in accordance with the UN Charter was a matter of law, logic and the UN's usual practice (cf. Fitzmaurice 1952:135–150; Boeg 1954:5–23). He held that even in case a third resolution[16] aiming to seat both Taibei and Beijing in the UN (i.e. the "Dual Representation Resolution") was going to be the deal, one could still try to get the "Important Question Resolution" through.

Green drew attention to the fact that the main objective was to safeguard the membership of the ROC and that one should therefore not give priority to the "Important Question Resolution", but judge the hour and then decide on an appropriate strategy. If for instance the great majority of UN members regarded

---

[16] I.e. a resolution in addition to the "Important Question Resolution" and the resolution drafted by Albania – translator's note.

the “Important Question” approach as creating a stalemate to the solution of the problem, this might perhaps increase the chance of success for the Albanian and not for the third draft resolution.

Zhou requested having the latter put in writing and to present it to the ROC side. He promised to try to persuade Taibei to accept it if the adoption of the “Albanian Resolution” could be effectively prevented and the ROC, be granted the protection the Charter afforded to a member.

President Nixon sent Robert D. Murphy, a retired senior ambassador, on a special trip to Taiwan for talks on the question of representation in the UN. During his audience with President Chiang Kaishek (Jiang Jieshi) on April 23, he presented the US plan to replace the “Important Question” approach by a “Dual Representation” scheme, which did not contain any explicit reference as to which side was to be the sole representative of China. Thus, it was hoped, discussions about the Chinese seat on the Security Council could be avoided so that the ROC would be able to retain it. Confronted with this plan, Chiang pointed out that the admission of the PRC to the UN should be regarded as an important question and that the “Important Question Resolution” should be the main instrument for preventing the admission of the PRC. As to the “Dual Presentation” scheme, he insisted that it had to contain provisions to guarantee the ROC’s seat both in the General Assembly and in the Security Council, and suggested that the USA should rework it accordingly. Finally, Chiang candidly remarked that the various overtures the White House had made to placate Beijing had reached a point beyond which any further steps would bring disaster (Qian Fu 2005:147–148).

For more than a month after Ambassador Murphy’s return to the USA, the American side remained inactive. On May 25, Foreign Minister Zhou Shukai informed US Ambassador McConaughy about his government’s firm and uncompromising position that it would by no means agree to abandon its seat on the UN Security Council, he clarified that this was not mere rhetoric, but his government’s true position. On May 26, Zhou requested Ambassador Shen Jianhong (沈剑虹) to urge the USA to continue the talks.

On the same day, US Secretary of State Rogers met with President Nixon to present his recommendation on how to deal with the question of Chinese representation. He suggested to table a “Dual Representation Resolution” at the 26th session of the General Assembly, which was to call for seating the PRC and, in the same text, stipulate that any draft resolution to expel the ROC should require a two-third vote, a formula which would give the ROC the protection of the “Important Question” procedure and at the same time allow for Beijing’s admission. In Roger’s opinion, such a “Dual Representation Resolution” was the only remedy against the expulsion of the ROC at the 26th session through adoption of the “Albanian Resolution” and defeat of the “Important Question” strategy. As to the

Chinese seat on the Security Council, the State Department suggested not mentioning it in the resolution, but expected that an amendment would be put forward from the floor stating that the seat should go to Beijing.

On May 28, Rogers met with the ROC ambassador to the US, Shen Jianhong, to discuss the representation question. He confronted Shen with his assessment saying that no matter how much effort was put into it, the "Important Question" formula would be defeated at the 26th session and that for this matter his country was seriously considering a revision of its policy on the Chinese representation question. Upon Shen's question whether this was mere tactics or the US's genuine wish for the PRC to join the UN, Rogers emphasized that in the face of the current situation sticking to the present formula would lead to defeat. President Chiang had indicated, Shen went on to say, that if a failure of the "Important Question Resolution" was anticipated, the ROC would not stand in the way of a new resolution which preserved the essence of the "Important Question Resolution". For example, under a new formula the PRC might be admitted by majority vote, but a two-third vote would be required to expel the ROC. (Wang 2000:340)

On July 1, Ambassador Shen called on the Assistant for National Security Affairs to the US President, Henry A. Kissinger, for a discussion on how to preserve the ROC's UN seat at the 26th session of the General Assembly. Kissinger was about to leave for a trip to Asia, including a secret visit to Beijing. He did not disclose anything, but instead gave Ambassador Shen all kinds of guarantees. He reassured him that Washington's position on the representation issue was quite close to that of Taibei, and that the USA still intended to proceed in the way discussed during Ambassador Murphy's visit to Taiwan. But in reality, the USA had already made plans to transfer the ROC's UN seat to the PRC.

The same day, the ROC's deputy permanent representative to the UN, Ambassador Zhang Chunming (张纯明), returned to Taiwan to deliver his report. Upon his arrival, he was invited by Foreign Minister Zhou Shukai to take part in a consultation on the representation question, which was also attended by other top officials of the ministry. During the meeting, Zhang expressed his view that unless the seat on the Security Council was transferred to the PRC the "Dual Representation Resolution" would probably not be adopted, and Zhou was very concerned about Washington's persistent inactivity on the matter.

On July 3, McConaughy advised Foreign Minister Zhou to make timely preparations for a possible loss of the ROC's Security Council seat. In mid-July President Nixon informed the public that on July 11 Kissinger had returned from a visit to Beijing, and announced that he himself would visit the Chinese mainland before May 1972. Acting on behalf of Foreign Minister Zhou, who was away on official business, his deputy Yang Xikun (杨西崑) summoned Ambassador McConaughy to strongly protest against Nixon's planned trip, which the ROC regarded as a most unfriendly act. When Ambassador Shen called on Secretary of State Rogers on July 20, the latter did not offer any explanation concerning Kissinger's trip to the mainland. Instead he remarked that the ROC was bound to fail at the 26th session of the General Assembly if it attempted to retain its Security Council seat, but that otherwise the US might be able to lend Taibei a helping hand. Only now did the ROC government realize that the USA above all wanted to press the ROC to relinquish its Security Council seat to the PRC.

Shocked by Nixon's planned trip to the Chinese mainland and the US refusal to support Taibei in its defence of the Security Council seat, the ROC gradually changed its attitude and adopted a more moderate position. Ambassador Shen received a telegram approved by President Chiang, which contained the following key points: (a) The government has already revised its former proposition to safeguard its right to representation in the UN by use of the "Important Question Resolution"; (b) it agrees to the modified "Important Question Resolution" suggested by the US and Japan, which declares the expulsion of an original member of the UN to be an important question as defined in the Charter; (c) it requests the US to prevent the adoption of the "Albanian resolution" demanding the expulsion of the ROC and the admission of the PRC.

The telegram also contained the following three confidential points (i.e. the USA should treat them as confidential and not divulge them to other governments[17] – translator's note): (a) if there is a need to accompany the modified "Important Question Resolution" by a "Dual Representation Resolution" to ensure its adoption, the government insists that nothing be said in such a resolution concerning the Security Council seat; (b) if other states put forward amendments to such a resolution aiming at transferring the ROC's Security Council seat to the PRC, the government hopes that the US and Japan will not[18] co-sponsor or vote for such a resolution; (c) officially, the government will have to speak against any formula providing for dual representation. When Ambassador Shen Jianhong and Ambassador Liu Kai met with US Secretary of State Rogers on July 26, the latter responded quite positively to the content of the telegram. When he asked what the ROC's position would be in case the so-called "Dual Representation Com-

---

[17] "Shen stated that foregoing three points constituted GRC [= Government of the ROC] formal reply to USG [= US Government]. In addition, he was instructed to make following points which he asked be treated as confidential and not divulged to other governments." Cf. "Telegram From the Department of State to the Embassy in the Republic of China" (document number 382). http://www.state.gov/r/pa/ho/frus/nixon/v/42666.htm (August 19, 2005)

[18] "Shen replied that his instructions were [...] to ask US [...] not to co-sponsor or vote for resolution affecting GRC's [= Government of the ROC's] SC [= Security Council] seat." "Telegram From the Department of State to the Embassy in the Republic of China" (document number 382). http://www.state.gov/r/pa/ho/frus/nixon/v/42666.htm (August 19, 2005)

plex" (D.R.C.), i.e. that variant of the "Dual Representation Resolution" which would explicitly demand the transfer of the Security Council seat to the PRC, was adopted by the General Assembly, Ambassador Liu replied: "We shall fight on as long as the circumstances permit." (Qian Fu 2005:149–151)

On August 2, Rogers issued a statement in which he announced that in the General Assembly the US would support the admission of the PRC, but at the same time oppose any action aimed at depriving the ROC of its right of representation in the UN. The statement included the following formal declaration of the US position on the ROC's right of representation: (a) the USA will put forward a draft resolution called "Important Question Variation" (I.Q.V.), which will declare the expulsion of the ROC to be an important question, but will not touch upon the admission of the PRC; (b) the US will accompany the I.Q.V. by the "Dual Representation Resolution" to make the admission of the PRC possible; (c) the General Assembly shall decide by vote whether the PRC or the ROC shall occupy the Chinese seat on the Security Council (Qian Fu 2005:151).

The "Dual Representation Resolution" was intended not to mention the Security Council seat. In case other states should put forward amendments, the US planned to oppose them on the grounds that the General Assembly had no right to deal with the Security Council seat question. If the "Dual Representation Resolution" passed and the ROC, as a result, did not lose membership, Washington reckoned that Beijing would probably refuse to join the UN, which would give the US the opportunity to argue that the question of the Security Council seat did not arise.

In a subsequent meeting with US government representatives Shen pointed out that, in the opinion of the ROC, the Security Council seat was inseparably linked to the General Assembly seat and that Taibei hoped the US would preserve the Security Council seat for the ROC. At the end of the meeting, the US side summarized the discussion into four key points for consideration by the ROC government: (a) Without a change of policy, the "Important Question Resolution" will fail at the 26th session of the General Assembly; (b) the "Dual Representation Resolution" may perhaps be able to preserve the ROC's membership in the General Assembly; (c) as long as the ROC remains in the UN, the PRC will most likely choose to stay outside; (d) the US will do its best to safeguard the ROC's seat on the Security Council, but cannot guarantee success (Wang 2000:344–345).

On August 20, the Foreign Ministry of the PRC issued an official statement in which it reaffirmed its position not to accept a "Two Chinas" or a "One China, One Taiwan" arrangement, under either of which it would definitely refuse to be a member of the UN. The PRC reckoned that all it needed to bring about the failure of the US strategy was to wait another one or two years. In a conversation with the head of the ROC Foreign Ministry's Department for North American Affairs, Qian Fu (钱复, Frederick F. Chien), the US Embassy's deputy head of mission, William Gleysteen, conceded that Beijing's statement was obviously aimed at strengthening support for the "Albanian Resolution" and would probably cause some states to insist even more firmly on raising the Security Council seat question.

On August 26, Liu Kai met with the US representative to the UN, George HW Bush. He expressed his relief at the Secretary of State's plan to leave out the Security Council seat question for the time being, and disclosed that Taibei had instructed its embassies to request their respective host countries to support the "Dual Representation Resolution" – but not to require them to co-sponsor the said resolution, for Taibei deemed it more appropriate that the resolution be put forward by the US only.

On August 28, Qian told the US Embassy in Taiwan that his government had already given instructions to its embassies in Australia and New Zealand to request these countries to support the simple "Dual Representation Resolution" (which in contrast to the "Dual Representation Complex" mentioned earlier would not touch on the Chinese Security Council seat – translator's note). The instructions pointed out that by then several states which advocated the continuation of the ROC's membership were already vehemently opposing the "Dual Representation Complex". The inclusion of a provision on the Security Council seat would perhaps repel advocators of the simple "Dual Representation Resolution" and hinder the ROC from reaching its ultimate goal. The government of the ROC hoped that Australia and New Zealand could "at the present stage" support the simple "Dual Representation Resolution" – a position which was not meant to rule out later amendments to the resolution.

On August 31, Ambassador McConaughy warned Taibei in a meeting with Foreign Minister Zhou Shukai that although the USA did not wish to cover the issue of the Security Council seat in the initial resolution, it might perhaps be forced to do so, because it had to take into account the views of its major allies. So instead of a promise to avoid tabling the "Dual Representation Complex", all Zhou Shukai got was a guarantee from McConaughy to take the position of the ROC into consideration. Later in the conversation, McConaughy expressed his conviction that in case the US should conceive it unavoidable to include the Security Council seat question from the beginning and therefore decide to table the "Dual Representation Complex", the ROC would nevertheless be willing to tolerate such a move if properly notified in advance, the only reason being that Taibei would surely realize the bleak prospects of a draft which left the Security Council seat question to be introduced by way of amendment.

On September 8[19], Ambassador McConoughy received a telegram from the US Department of State, in which Rogers asked for immediate delivery of a message to Foreign Minister Zhou contained in the telegram. The message chiefly consisted of an explanation why the US had arrived at the conclusion that it would have to propose the transfer of the Chinese Security Council seat to the PRC, the information that the USA had already decided to muster co-sponsors for the "Dual Representation Complex", and a request for understanding and continued cooperation.

On September 10, Foreign Minister Zhou handed over his government's official written response, which called the American decision "particularly regrettable" and reiterated Taibei's position that admission of the PRC to the UN would violate the UN Charter. It also stated that once such a resolution was tabled, the government of the ROC would have to issue a public statement objecting to it. In addition to the written response, however, Zhou indicated that the Government of the ROC did want the US "Dual Representation Resolution" to succeed.

On September 11, Vice-Prime Minister Jiang Jingguo summoned Qian Fu for a discussion on the representation resolution. During this discussion, Qian received the following three instructions: (a) Investigate the sincerity of the US offer to help the ROC. (b) Keep a close watch on the moves of the USSR. (c) The position of the ROC is: if the US resolution succeeds and the PRC refuses to join the UN because of the ROC's membership, the ROC shall stand its ground; but if there are signs that the "Albanian Resolution" to admit the PRC and expel the ROC will be adopted, then the ROC shall withdraw from the UN on its own initiative before the "Albanian Resolution" is put to a vote. (Qian Fu 2005:152–153)

The same day, US Secretary of State Rogers presented a memorandum to President Nixon, in which he reported on the ROC's response to his new suggestions regarding the Chinese seat on the Security Council. He pointed out that although he expected pro forma opposition from the government of the PRC, he believed that Taibei would not oppose the US resolution on Chinese representation behind the scenes. He even felt that in case of a close vote Taibei might well support the US initiatives in its private representations to other governments.

Two resolutions concerning the question of Chinese representation were submitted for discussion on the occasion the 26th session of the General Assembly which began on September 21, 1971:

- The resolution tabled by 18 (later increased to 23) states including Albania and Algeria to restore all its rights to the PRC and to expel forthwith the

[19] http://www.state.gov/r/pa/ho/frus/nixon/v/42667.htm, "Telegram From the Department of State to the Embassy in the Republic of China" (document number 404) (August 23, 2005).

ROC from the UN. It was placed on the agenda by a vote of 17 to 2 with 4 abstentions.

– The "Dual Representation Resolution" tabled by 17 (later increased to 19) states including the USA and Japan demanding the admission of the PRC to the UN and its appointment as a permanent member of the Security Council without expelling the ROC from the United Nations, which would require the UN to recognize both the PRC and the ROC.

The US representative to the UN, George Bush senior, put forward an extempore resolution to combine the two above-mentioned resolutions into one big resolution with the sub-resolutions (a) restoration of the PRC's legitimate rights in the UN, and (b) maintenance of the ROC's right to representation. His resolution was however rejected by a vote of 9 to 12 with 3 abstentions (Qian 2005:154).

The "Important Question Variation" draft resolution, which declared the expulsion of the ROC to be an important question requiring a two-third majority (instead of the admission of the PRC as in the original "Important Question Resolution") was tabled by 19 (later increased to 22) states including the USA and Japan, made it into the agenda by a vote of 11 to 9 with 4 abstentions.

In a speech held on October 4 during the general debate of the 26th session, Secretary of State Rogers declared that his government had decided to support the admission of the PRC to the UN as a permanent member of the Security Council, because it deemed the long-time exclusion and isolation of a great power and a large portion of the world's population undesirable. Rogers added that he earnestly hoped that China would assume all responsibilities, obligations and rights of membership.

Although Mexico at that time still maintained diplomatic relations with the ROC, the Mexican president Luis Echevarria in his speech on October 5 expressed his hope that the PRC representing a quarter of the world's population would be admitted to the UN and appointed a permanent member of the Security Council in the 26th session. He reminded that his country had advocated the principle of universal membership ever since 1945, and presented his government's view that both the sovereignty and the territory of China were legally undividable wholes.

At five o'clock in the afternoon of the same day, Foreign Minister Zhou, accompanied by Qian Fu, went to the US delegation's office to meet with Rogers. He complained that Kissinger had scheduled his next visit to the PRC to take place in mid-October, which was exactly when the UN delegates would begin their discussions, criticized Kissinger's decision as inevitably damaging the joint efforts of the ROC and the US, and wondered why the US had to make this announcement now. Rogers answered insincerely that he also believed the discussions to be an important matter, and he assured Zhou that Kissinger's upcoming China visit would in no way affect the decision process concerning Chinese representation.

Later, facts proved the contrary. In Qian Fu's opinion, Rogers' words were either a sign of his exclusion from the inner policy-making circle or a deliberate, albeit by no means clever deceit (Qian 2005:155–156).

On October 14, Foreign Minister Zhou, the ROC representative to the UN, Liu Kai, and Qian Fu met with Rogers once again and suggested to him that President Nixon himself should publicly declare his government's active support for the preservation of Taibei's UN seat. Rogers agreed. When asked whether Washington had a fall-back position in case its draft resolutions failed to obtain the necessary number of votes, Rogers replied that such a position was currently under consideration at the highest level[20].

On October 16, Zhou, accompanied by Qian Fu and two secretaries, went to the Department of State for another meeting with Rogers. At this meeting, which was held in a rather unfriendly atmosphere, Zhou brusquely told the Secretary of State that in the eyes of some the US was in fact not fulfilling its responsibility when it declared, as it had repeatedly done before, Japan's position to be the key to resolving the issue (Qian Fu 2005:153).

On the same day, Kissinger deceived Ambassador Shen by telling him that the Taiwan issue was not on the agenda of the talks between Washington and Beijing and that the Taiwan-US relations were non-negotiable. During his conversation with Ambassador Shen, Kissinger pretended to be optimistic about the ROC's chances of retaining its UN seat, but actually he had long before informed Zhou Enlai of Nixon's intention to force the ROC in to a withdrawal from the UN. Kissinger feared that in case Taiwan was not expelled from the UN the PRC might perhaps detect the USA's double tactics. Therefore he urged Ambassador Shen to suggest to his superiors that the ROC should keep silent during the debate on the Chinese representation question at the UN General Assembly (Tyler 2000:132–133).

On October 18, the US Embassy in Taibei reported to the State Department that the US shift towards support of the "Dual Representation Complex" resolution had resulted in a low-key reaction of the ROC's government and media, with only some fairly mild criticism of the US. The report also mentioned a statement

[20] According to the pertinent US document, the "Secretary said he did not think there was one [i.e. a fall-back position]", but at the end of the conversation it "was agreed that we would give future consideration to possible fall-back positions if our present program fails". Cf. http://www.state.gov/r/pa/ho/frus/nixon/v/42667.htm (August 26, 2005), "Telegram From Secretary of State Rogers to the Department of State" (document number 419).

issued by the ROC's Ministry of Foreign Affairs which declared that the government firmly opposed the PRC's admission to the UN and any arrangement to transfer the ROC's Security Council seat to the PRC.

By October 21, the US State Department had devised a contingency plan, in which two scenarios were discussed:

- Adoption of the "Important Question Resolution", rejection of the "Albanian Resolution", but majority for "Dual Representation Resolution" was uncertain. Under this assumption, two actions were considered in the contingency plan: (1) a deferment of vote could be sought to allow time for further canvassing; (2) because the "Albanian Resolution" demanding the expulsion of the ROC would have been rejected in this scenario: the "Dual Representation Resolution" could be shortened rendering it into a resolution for the sole purpose of admitting the PRC.
- Rejection of the "Important Question Resolution". Under this assumption, the contingency plan considered: (1) seeking to adopt the amendments put forward by the UN representative of Saudi-Arabia, Jamil M. Baroody[21]; (2) seeking to delete the clause demanding the expulsion of the ROC from the "Albanian Resolution"; (3) following the ROC's proposal to rely on the Charter's Article 6 (recommendation by the Security Council required for the expulsion of a member persistently violating the principles of the Charter) and Article 18, (two-third majority of the members present and voting required for an important question such as the expulsion of a member). The US side held the opinion that in scenario (b) the ROC could live with the "Albanian Resolution" as amended by the Baroody proposals, which would allow for the preservation of the ROC's UN seat.

After the ambassador of the ROC to Canada Xue Yuqi had arrived at the estimation that the "Important Question Resolution" would be defeated by four votes, he tried to convince the US side that the time for a contingency plan had already come. But the members of the US delegation to the UN pretended that they were still striving for the success of the "Important Question" and "Dual Representation" resolutions, and that they had not yet decided on a contingency plan.

---

[21] Baroody proposed a series of amendments to the "Albanian Resolution". The most important of these would have the General Assembly decide on a „one-China, one-Taiwan" policy (admission of the PRC, transfer of the Security Council seat to the PRC, preservation of the ROC's UN seat) and would justify the latter on the basis of self-determination (by plebiscite). Cf. the author's note on Baroody in the Chinese original and http://www.state.gov/r/pa/ho/frus/nixon/v/42667.htm, "Telegram From the Mission to the United Nations to the Department of State" (document number 421) (September 10, 2005).

On October 21, the Japanese government announced that it was going to co-sponsor both the "Important Question Variation" and the "Dual Representation Complex" resolutions put forward by the US.

On October 22, when the agenda for the plenary session of October 25 was set by the General Committee of the General Assembly, it was decided that the voting on the "Albanian Resolution" should take place prior to the voting on the "Dual Representation Complex" resolution.

The same day, Secretary of State Rogers told Ambassador Shen during a meeting at the White House that in the afternoon President Nixon would order his press secretary to express the president's interest in safeguarding the ROC's right of representation in the UN. When asked by Ambassador Shen about contingency plans in case the "Important Question Variation" resolution should fail, Rogers indicated that it was impossible to make a perfect contingency plan (Qian Fu 2005:157–158).

On October 23, the US State Department sent an urgent telegram to 23 US missions abroad in which it informed them that the ROC government's statement criticizing the US "Dual Representation Resolution" was issued for domestic purposes only and should not be misinterpreted as an indication of any action on behalf of the ROC against the transfer of the UN Security Council seat to the PRC.

The PRC's news agency Xinhuashe, which covered and commented on the events for three consecutive days from October 24 to 26, declared that the PRC would by no means join the UN unless Chiang Kai-shek's delegates were expelled from the UN and the rights of the PRC were restored (ibid.).

On October 25, the "Important Question Variation" resolution, which the US had put forward in order to safeguard the ROC's seat in the General Assembly, was rejected by 55-59-15 (i.e. a vote of 55 to 59 with 15 abstentions).[22]

Then, in a last-ditch effort the US representative George Bush senior proposed to split up the "Albanian Resolution" and vote on the passage demanding Taibei' expulsion separately, but his motion was defeated by 51-61-16.

At 23:15, when it became evident that all attempts to prevent the adoption of the "Albanian Resolution" were bound to fail, Foreign Minister Zhou took the floor and declared ROC's immediate withdrawal from the UN.

Finally, after the delegation of the ROC had left, the "Albanian Resolution" was adopted by 76-35-17.[23] Thus, the 22-year struggle for the Chinese seat of the PRC in the UN finally drew to a close.

---

22 The delegates from two newly admitted members, Oman and the Maldive Islands, were absent.

23 Of 18 African states entertaining diplomatic and/or consular relations with the ROC, 15 supported Taibei in the votes on the "Important Question Variation" and the "Albanian Resoluti-

In its effort to maintain the ROC's right to representation in the UN by means of the "Dual Representation Resolution", the US had initially planned not mentioning the Security Council seat, but later found it necessary to include a passage demanding the transfer of the Chinese Security Council seat to Beijing ("Dual Representation Complex"). Because of its motto that "gentlemen cannot coexist with thugs" the ROC publicly opposed this variant of the resolution, but in the face of international trends favourable to the PRC eventually had no choice but to consent in secret (Qian 2005:146–148).

Taibei looked upon the "Dual Representation Complex" resolution from a tactical point of view. It hoped to preserve its right to representation in the UN by the manoeuvre of "admitting China without expelling Taiwan", and even speculated that the PRC's "One China" policy would hinder it from joining the UN, thereby enabling the government of the ROC to continue its exclusive occupation of the Chinese UN seat. But because the 26th session of the General Assembly adopted the "Albanian Resolution" demanding "the expulsion of Taiwan and the admission of China", the "Dual Representation Complex" resolution was never put to a vote.

After ROC's withdrawal from the UN the Nixon administration was somewhat plagued by a guilty conscience. On October 29[24], Secretary of State Rogers sent a telegram to Ambassador McConaughy, in which he instructed him to deliver the message contained therein orally to President Chiang Kai-shek (or in the case of his unavailability to Vice Premier Jiang Jingguo), to leave an aide-mémoire consisting of the orally presented text, and to conclude the oral presentation with the statement "I have been instructed to inform you that these views have the full support of the President of the United States" (lacking a reference as to who had authorized the message, and not to be included in the aide-mémoire).[25] One should suppose that if Nixon had really been sincere in his support of the views expressed in the message, he would have sent a telegram in his own name and

on" (General Assembly Resolution 2758), respectively. What enabled the General Assembly to adopt the "Albanian Resolution" was the growth in the membership of the UN. The Secretary General reported to the Security Council that he was satisfied under rule 15 of the Rules of Procedure, and the Council welcomed the PRC on 21 November 1971. *Security Council, Official Records*, 26th year, 1565th Meeting. 09/02/1971, paras. 51–101; see also UN Doc. S/10378 10/26/1971, and S/10382 02/11/1971 (both mimeo.).

24 Cf. http://www.state.gov/r/pa/ho/frus/nixon/v/42667.htm, "Telegram From the Department of State to the Embassy in the Republic of China" (document number 434) (September 18, 2005).

25 http://www.state.gov/r/pa/ho/frus/nixon/v/42667.htm, "Telegram From the Department of State to the Embassy in the Republic of China" (document number 434) (September 18, 2005).

would have ordered it to be dispatched to President Chiang Kai-shek. This not being the case, the formula "have the full support of the President of the United States" cannot but be regarded as mere diplomatic courtesy (although a copy of the draft telegram had been sent to the President's Deputy Assistant for National Security Affairs Haig, perhaps even Kissinger had not seen it, let alone that Nixon would have been asked to overlook it).

In his telegram, Rogers criticized the UN for depriving the ROC of its right to representation in the General Assembly, called this action a serious mistake and expressed the US government's deep regret about it. He claimed that the defeat of the "Important Question Resolution" had come as a surprise to the US government, guaranteed that the result of the UN General Assembly's vote would in no way affect the close Taiwan-US relations covering a wide variety of fields, expected these relations to continue to prosper, and also guaranteed that the defence commitment of the USA to the ROC would remain unchanged. He further stated that the representatives of the US government, who had worked closely with their colleagues of the ROC Government during the previous few months on this difficult question, had been uniformly impressed with both the adherence to principle and tactical flexibility reflected in the ROC government's decisions. Finally, McConaughy was instructed to take the opportunity of this representation to mention Rogers' personal appreciation for the great effort of Foreign Minister Zhou Shukai in their common cause at the UN. (The US intent to shift the responsibility for the decisions in the struggle for Chinese representation onto President Chiang Kai-shek is clearly revealed in the telegram.) (Wang 2000:390–391)

On October 26, Rogers told the press that the USA accepted the result of the UN General Assembly's vote and that the admission of the PRC to the UN was in keeping with US policy. He expressed his regret about the deprivation of the ROC's right of representation in the UN, but declared that the US neither intended to speak up against this development nor planned to stop payments to the UN in retaliation.

When conferring with Rogers on the questions of how to safeguard the ROC's membership in UN-related specialized agencies and how to maintain its bilateral relations with the US, he urged Rogers to make a public statement affirming the US unswerving support for the ROC promised by McConaughy on the occasion of his audience with Chiang Kai-shek on October 29[26]. Zhou felt that such a statement was necessary in the current situation, but Rogers did not respond enthusiastically (Qian Fu 2005:162).

[26] Cf. http://www.state.gov/r/pa/ho/frus/nixon/v/42667.htm, "Telegram From the Embassy in the Republic of China to the Department of State" (document number 437) (September 20, 2005).

From 4.15 to 6 p.m. on October 19, 1971, Zhou, Shen und Qian met Kissinger and John Holdridge, Director of the Office of Research and Analysis for East Asia and Pacific at INR (Bureau of Intelligence and Research) in the National Security Council in the basement of the White House. Analyzing the reasons for failure, Zhou asked what would happen? Kissinger assured: "The US will not abandon you, they will have to keep their treaty obligations and they will definitely not abandon their treaty obligations and hold normal and friendly relations with your country." Zhou pointed out that the US had to declare this guarantee in public in order to reassure the Taiwanese public. At this moment Kissinger looked around and said something else. Zhou said that President Nixon could make a strong declaration of continuous support of the ROC. Kissinger replied that the journalists would clarify all unnecessary misunderstandings within the next week to come (Qian 2005:162).

Bilateral relationships should not be influenced by multilateral decisions. But in reality, if one country leaves the UN, this has an immediate effect on bi-lateral diplomatic relationship: The withdrawal from the UN set off a chain reaction in diplomatic relations: Within one year 15 states broke off diplomatic relations with the ROC and established relations with the PRC: Belgium, Peru, Lebanon, Ruanda, Senegal, Cyprus, Malta, Mexico, Argentina, Greece, Togo, Japan, the Maledives, Madagascar and Luxembourg.

Conclusion

The UN officially came into existence in 1945. China is one of the original members and one of the permanent members in the Security Council. After the PRC was founded in 1949, the Communists requested the Chinese seat in the UN. From the 5th session of the General Assembly onward, the USSR, India and Albania submitted to every year's session a resolution concerning the Chinese representation trying to exclude Taiwan and admit the PRC. These efforts were opposed by the allies of the USA and other states. From the 6th session of the General Assembly in 1951 until the 15th session in 1960 the ROC using the "Memorandum" resolution prevented that the question of Chinese representation was put onto the agenda of the General Assembly. Starting with the 16th session in 1961, the ROC secured the adoption of a procedural resolution defining every draft resolution trying to change the current Chinese representation as an "important question". According to Article 18 of the UN Charter, this required at least a two-third vote for approval as opposed to a "non-important question resolution" which needed only a simple majority of member states present and voting.

It is not easy to understand why the ROC voluntarily left the UN. In fact, it was forced, because there is only one seat for China. After 22 years the PRC started to represent China as a consequence of a resolution adopted in the General Assembly during its 26th session. Since 1971 the PRC has represented China, has taken the Chinese seat in the UN and has gradually established diplomatic relations with the US. It is also becoming more and more important in several international issues.

Besides the approaches of a Memorandum, Important Question Resolution or the expulsion of the ROC and replacement by the PRC another alternative was put forward by Italy and other states proposing from 1966 to 1970 to establish a committee aimed at researching the question of Chinese representation. Taken into consideration the principle of universal membership and the real political situation, the aim of this committee would have been to find some fair and feasible way to include the PRC and not to touch the membership of the ROC. If this were submitted to vote to the General Assembly, this would imply two Chinas[27] within the UN. This alternative was heavily opposed by Taibei and three times rejected, so it was never submitted to vote.

Liu Kai, the ROC ambassador to the United Nations, acknowledged that the USA had not strongly supported the ROC and that the politics against the ROC had undergone obvious change. Additionally, more and more Asian and African countries as well as small states were admitted to the UN and their decision power started surpassing their actual weight in international politics. The result of this tendency in the UN is that old member states are loosing their power in international politics.

There are several reasons why communist-friendly states united with communists states voting in favor of the resolution of the expulsion of the ROC and of admission of the PRC:

---

[27] There were two Chinas, a "democratic China," meaning areas under Chinese Communist control, and a "feudalistic China," meaning areas under the Nationalist Government control. Thus, the refrain of "two Chinas" that one hears nowadays is the echo of an old tune first sung by the American Communists (see Bisson 1943; Chiang Kai-shek 1969:119). The Government of the People's Republic of China is the legal successor to the pre-1949 Government of the Republic of China, and of permitting its accredited representatives of China to sit among the Permanent Members of the Security Council; and admitting the Government of the Republic of China *de novo*, and allowing its accredited representatives to be seated in the various organs. The Italian Resolution, 1966–1968 which had US support, was deemed a way to gain formal consideration of a 'two Chinas' solution that would allow membership for both ROC and PRC with the PRC presumably in the Security Council seat. Not until the US in 1971 specifically put forward the resolution that there were 'two Chinas,' and that both in their respective territories should be members of the UN and both represented in that Organization. The solution of two Chinas is unacceptable to both the Nationalist Government and to the Soviet bloc. They asserted that there were not two Chinas, but only one, the rightful government of which was represented as the Central Government of China.

First, reality has to be acknowledged. The point of view of General-Secretary Lie concerning the Chinese representation was as follows: If a government could, within its borders, assume power and there is little resistance to its authority, the UN could admit this new government as national representative into the UN. This was a juridical argumentation, so the PRC was admitted. Lie's view has prevailed even since and is still one of the convincing reasons for the admission of the PRC into the UN.

Second, the actual political situation in the UN has to be considered. At that time, the government of the PRC represented 600 million people. China's population exceeded the total number of the population in the US, Great Britain and France, moreover the immense territory of China was as big as Europe. Asia and the Far East were seen as one of the strategic important areas in world politics and the participation and interests of China could no longer be neglected.

Third, the principle of universal membership of the UN must not be neglected. There was no reason to exclude the PRC, because among the UN member states there were communist and anti-communist nations, countries with different political, social and belief systems.

Regarding the UN Charter, the right to represent China in the UN involves many issues such as the question of membership and of assumed right to represent a state, the one-vote principle of every state, and the admission into or expulsion from the UN. International law differentiates between membership of states in the UN and the right of representation: membership in the UN relates to states and the right to representation relates to governments. In Article 2 of the UN Charter there are formulations regarding the membership, but there is no regulation concerning the right of representation. The question of Chinese representation in the UN is not a problem of the validity of credentials, but of the juridical status of the government issuing these credentials. Membership in the UN and the right of representation touch upon the "recognition of state", "continuity of states" (Swift 1969:68), "recognition of government" (Talmon 1992) and the "succession of government". The problem of Chinese representation is related to the two principles of the "continuity of a State" and the question of the "recognition of a new government".

The question of Chinese representation could be analyzed on the basis of the two principles of international law, "recognition of government" and "succession of government". According to international law, if a revolutionary government recognized by other countries establishes bilateral relations and has signed treaties with the old government, the new government inherits these rights or obligations. Here the principle of "succession of state" is to be applied. But there are two preconditions: First, the new government fully replaced the former government and is executing control over the whole territory. Second, this principle is limited to bilateral treaties; multilateral treaties are not considered. The problem of the Chinese representation in the UN does not meet these preconditions, because it is a case of a multilateral treaty (UN Charter) and the former government is still in existence.

In international organizations, the problem of recognizing a *de facto* government, as the representative of the member state within the UN, arises when two governments claim to represent it. The UN Charter does not provide any special procedure for ascertaining a state's succession in membership of international organization. In such cases, the problem may be treated as one of credentials. It is only with decisions regarding credentials in accordance with the rules of procedure of the various constituent bodies of the organization that the UN can resolve the problem whether one government may succeed to another. The UN recognizes as the government of the state in question the one that obtains the required majority of votes of the member states. Voting is a highly political solution, it is assumed that member States having voted in favor recognize the government for which they have voted, and, conversely, indicates that a vote against implies non-admission of the government accepted as the representative of that state. Indeed, the majority vote of the member states does not create an obligation to establish bilateral diplomatic relations. In law and practice, each body is entitled to come to a decision in accordance with its own rules of procedure, although, in general, it is the decision taken by the body in which all member states are represented and voted that is accepted. The only difficult that may arise is that the General Assembly and the Security Council, within their respective power to decide on credentials, may behave differently when faced with the same case, that is, they may each maintain that a different government has the right to occupy the same seat. This drawback will find a solution only in an agreement between these two organs. It is connected with a more basic theme, that of possible divisions between the Assembly and the Council due to the possible differences in the political forces that prevail at the same time in each of the two organs. Political, rather than legal, complications posed the main obstacle to the solution of the question of Chinese representation in the UN. The question of Chinese representation in the UN, on its merits, is neither a problem of the validity of credentials, nor of the juridical status of the government issuing these credentials, but is decided on the basis of power politics.

From 1950 to 1971 the ROC was recognized as the sole government representing China in the UN, but after the approval of General Assembly Resolution 2758, the representatives of the government of the PRC replaced the representatives of the ROC and have since held the seat in the General Assembly, the Security Council, as well as in all organs and specialized agencies of the UN.

This paper has shown that all strategies in dealing with the question of Chinese representation depended on the voting situation in the Security Council and the General Assembly. Even if an "Important Question Variation" or "Dual Representation Resolution" had been approved and the resolution promulgated by Albania would have failed, the PRC would have been seated in the General Assembly and in the Security Council. But as long as Taiwan retained a seat in the UN, the PRC would not join the UN (Mao Zedong 06/13/1961; Mao Zedong [no date]). Their allies, however, would continue to find ways to exclude the ROC from their right to represent China (Qian Fu 2005:166–167).

John K. T. Chao, Department of Diplomacy, National Chengchi University, Taibei.

References

Baehr, Peter R. and Leon Gordenker (1999): The United States at the End of the 1990s. London: Macmillan Press.

Bailey, Sydney D. (1970): Chinese Representation in the Security Council and the General Assembly of the United Nations. Brighton: Institute for the Study of International Organisation.

Bailey, Sydney D. (1988): The Procedure of the UN Security Council, 2nd ed. Oxford: Clarendon Press.

Barros, James (1989): Trygve Lie and the Cold War: The UN Secretary-General Pursues Peace, 1946–1953. DeKalb, Illinois: Northern Illinois University Press.

Bisson, T.S. (1943): China's Position in the Allied War. In: Far Eastern Survey, published by the Institute of Pacific Relations (14 July 1943).

Bloomfield, Lincoln P. (1966): China, the United States, and the United Nations. In: International Organization 20, 653–671.

Boeg, N.V. (1954): Review of the Charter of the United Nations. In: Transactions of the Grotius Society 40, 5–23.

Briggs, Herbert W. (1952): Chinese Representation in the United Nations. In: International Organization 6, 192–209.

Brook, David (1956): The U.N. and the China Dilemma. New York: Vantage Press, 1956, 77–82.

Brown, Benjamin H. and Fred Greene (1955): Chinese Representation: A Case Study in the United Nations Political Affairs. New York: Woodrow Wilson Foundation.

Chen, Tiqiang (陳體強) (1985): 聯合國的會員國應當具有普遍性 (Membership of the UN Should be Universal). In: Chen Tiqiang (陳體強) (1985): 國際法論文集 (International Law). Beijing: Falü chubanshe, 133–136.

Chiang, Kai-Shek (1969): Soviet Russia in China, Rev. ed. Taibei: China Publishing Co.

China Institute of International Affairs (1959): China and the United Nations. Report of a Study Group set up by the China Institute of International Affairs. New York: Manhattan Publishing Co.

Donner, Ruth (1988): International Adjudication: Using the International Court of Justice with special reference to Finland. Helsinki: Academia Scientiarum Fennica / Suomalainen Tiedeakatemia, 112–139.

Duara, Drasenjit (2003): Sovereignty and Authenticity: Manchukuo and the East Asian Modern. Lanham, Maryland: Rowman & Littlefield Publishers.

Dugard, John (1987): Recognition and the United Nations. Cambridge: Grotius Publications.

Feltham, R.G. (1988): Diplomatic Handbook, 5th ed. London & New York: Longman.

Fitzmaurice, G. G. (1952): The United Nations and the Rule of Law. In: Transactions of the Grotius Society 38, 135–150.

Fitzmaurice, Sir Gerald (1952): Chinese representation in the United Nations, in: Year Book of World Affairs, 636–55.

GA 11/17/1947: Resolution 113. Admission of New Members. http://daccessdds.un.org/doc/RESOLUTION/GEN/NR0/038/20/IMG/NR003820.pdf?OpenElement (October 6, 2005).

GA 11/19/1946: Resolution 36. Rules Governing the Admission of New Members to the United Nations. http://daccessdds.un.org/doc/RESOLUTION/GEN/NR0/032/87/IMG/NR003287.pdf?OpenElement (October 5, 2005).

GMD: Committee for the Party History of the Central Committee of the GMD (中國國民黨中央委員會黨史委員會)(ed.) (without date): 中華民國重要史料初編—對日抗戰時期第三編 戰時外交（二）(Collection of Important Documents of the Republic of China: The Period of the Sino–Japanese War, Vol. 3: Diplomatic Relation during the War, Part 2. Taibei: Committee for the Party History of the Central Committee of the GMD.

Han, Suk-jung (1995): Puppet Sovereignty: The State Effect of Manchukuo, from 1932 to 1936. Ph.D. dissertation University of Chicago.

Hu, Shi (1952). China Seven Years after Yalta. In: Zhou Zhiping (周質平) (ed.) (2001): 胡適未刊英文遺稿 (A Collection of Hu Shi's Unpublished English Essays and Speeches). Taibei: Lianjing, 374–381.

Jiang, Tingfu (蔣廷黻) (1967): Jiang Tingfu's Records and Life (蔣廷黻的志事與生平). Taibei. Zhuanji wenxue chubanshe.

Keith, J.K. (1971). The Extent of the Advisory Jurisdiction of the International Court of Justice; Leyden: A.W. Sijthoff.

Langer, Robert (1969): Seizure of Territory; The Stimson Doctrine and Related Principles in Legal Theory and Diplomatic Practice. Reprint ed. New York: Green Wood Press.

Li, Enguo (李恩國) (ed.) (1970): 聯合國憲章概論 (The UN Charter). Taibei: Zhengzhong shuju.

Liang, Yun-li (1951): Recognition by the United Nations of the Representation of a Member State: Criteria and Procedure. In: American Journal of International Law 45, 691–695.

Liang, Yunli [Liang Yuen–Li] (梁鋆立) (1958): 中國對聯合國之貢獻 (Contributions of China in the UN). In: Wang Yuxiu (王聿修) (ed.) (1958): 紀念崔書琴先生政治學術論文集 (Collections in Memoriam of Cui Qin about the Art of Politics). Taibei: Zhonghua congshu weiyuanhui yinhang, 89–95.

Liang, Yuen–Li (1949): Notes on Legal Questions Concerning the United Nations: Conditions of Admission of a State to Membership in the United Nations. In: American Journal of International Law 43, 288–311.

Liu, Zhigong (劉志攻) (1985): 中華民國在聯合國大會的參與－外交政策、國際環境及參與行為 (The Republic of China in the UN: Foreign Politics, International Environment and Participation. Taibei: Taiwan shangwu yinshuguan.

Malanczuk, Peter (1997): Akehurst's Modern Introduction to International Law, 7th rev. ed. London & New York: Routledge.

Mao, Zedong (毛澤東) (no date): 關於恢復中國在聯合國的合法席位問題 (The Recovery of the Legitimate Chinese seat in the UN). In: 中共中央文獻研究室 (Zhonggong zhongyang wenxian yanjiushi) (ed.)(1994): 毛澤東外交文選 (Selections of Mao Zedong's Texts about Foreign Policy). Beijing: Zhongyang wenxian chubanshe, shijie zhishi chubanshe, 263–274.

Mao, Zedong (毛澤東) (06/13/1961): 毛澤東同印尼總統蘇加諾談話 (Talk of Mao Zedong with Indonesia's President Suharto). In: 中共中央文獻研究室 (Zhonggong zhongyang wenxian yanjiushi) (ed.)(1994): 毛澤東外交文選 (Selections of Mao Zedong's Texts about Foreign Policy). Beijing: Zhongyang wenxian chubanshe, shijie zhishi chubanshe, 468–469.

Nicholas, H. G. (1959): The United Nations as a Political Institution London: Oxford University Press.

Pomerance, M. (1973): The Advisory Function of the International Court in the League and the United Nations Eras. Baltimore & London.

Qian, Fu (錢復) (2005): 錢復回憶錄, 卷一 (Memoirs of Qian Fu, Vol. 1). Taibei: Tianxia wenhua.

Rosenne, Shabtai (1973): The World Court: What it is and How it Works, 3rd ed. Leiden: A.W. Sijthoff, 1973, 80–84.

Schermers, Henry G. and Niels M. Blokker (1995): International Institutional Law, 3rd rev. ed.. The Hague: Martinus Nijhoff Publishers.

Swift, Richard N. (1969): International Law: Current and Classic. New York & London: John Wiley & Sons.

Talmon, Stefan (1992): Recognition of Governments: An Analysis of the New British Policy and Practice". In: British Year Book of International Law 63 (1992), 231–297.

Tetlow, Edwin (1970): The United Nations: The First 25 Years. London: Peter Owen.

Tyler, Patrick (2000): 中美交鋒 (A Great Wall: Six Presidents and China). Taibei: Lianjing chubanshe.

Vandenbosch, N. Army and Willard N. Hogan (1963): Toward World Order. New York: McGraw-Hill Book Co, 53–54.

Wang, Jinghong (王景弘) (2000). 採訪歷史：從華府檔案看台灣 (Interviewing History: The View on Taiwan from the Files in the White House). Taibei: Yuanliu.

Wang, Kuo-Chang (1984): United Nations Voting on Chinese Representation: An Analysis of General Assembly Roll-Calls 1950–1971. Taibei: Institute of American Culture, Academia Sinica.

Whiteman, M. (1993): Digest of International Law, Vol. 2. Washington, D.C.: Government Printing Office.

Xu, Boxiong (續伯雄) (1973): 在聯合國大會奮戰經過 (Documentation of the Political Struggle in the General Assembly of the United Nations). Hong Kong: Xinwen tiandishe.

Zhu, Jianmin (朱建民) (1964): 1950–1960 十年緩議案表決比較： 確保我在聯合國的合法地位－十四年的苦鬥經過 (Ten Years of the Moratorium Decision (1950–1960): The Question of the Chinese Legitimate Status in the UN). In: 國立政治大學學報 (Journal of the National Chengchi University) 5/1964 : 73–94.

Wang Dong

The Dissemination of International Law and the Study of the Unequal Treaties in China*

On June 29, 1929, at a time when the Guomindang Nationalist Government was making its most strenuous efforts to rescind foreign consular courts in China, *China Weekly Review* reported that the Municipal Council of the International Settlement had coincidentally launched a drive against gambling in the foreign quarters of Shanghai. Raids staged by the Shanghai foreign police on gambling dens popularly known as "wheels" resulted in the arrest of some three hundred people, both foreign and Chinese. *China Weekly Review* listed the greatly varying legal consequences of the very same crime for defendants of different nationalities:

> "The Chinese, of course, got the worst of it, because this type of gambling is clearly illegal under Chinese law and the Chinese were immediately arraigned in their Provisional Court where some 160 defendants received sentences ranging from 50 days imprisonment to fines ranging from $200 to $450, the total amount of the fines collected approximating $30,000. Of the foreigners who were caught as a consequence of the raids, mostly of British nationality, whose cases have been disposed of up to the present, were simply bound not to frequent such gambling institutions in the future. In order to convict them it was necessary for the local British Court to dig up an old law passed in the time Henry VIII. Those of Spanish nationality who were caught in the raids, were brought up in the local Spanish Consular Court and since this form of gambling apparently is not illegal under Spanish law, they were simply cautioned and released. One Portuguese who was arrested is said to have been fined $50 and one Japanese has had his case remanded for future hearing in the Japanese Consular Court […]. [T]wo unfortunate Russians, who have lost their extraterritorial rights [as a result of the 1924 treaty between China and the U.S.S.R.], were arraigned in the local Chinese Provisional Court and received sentences of 50 days in jail, plus a fine of $200." (Unknown 1929:186–188)

This incident illustrates well the conflicting jurisdictions and sovereignty and the concomitant inequalities and failures in the justice system suffered by all na-

---

* This text has been previously published as Chapter 5, "Universalizing International Law and the Chinese Study of the Unequal Treaties: The Paradox of Equality and Inequality" in Wang, Dong: "China's Unequal Treaties: Narrating national history", 2005. It is reprinted with the kind permission of Lexington Books, a division of Rowman & Littlefield Publishing Group.

tionalities under extraterritoriality (extrality or consular jurisdiction) in China. The story also reveals the paradox of equality and inequality which has been an ongoing feature of China's multi-faceted encounter with the West since the mid-nineteenth century.

This article explores aspects of the paradox of equality and inequality from the perspective of the dissemination of international law in China. The paradox has three levels of meaning. Firstly, the principle of extraterritoriality (or the practice of capitulations) was inserted into the "Unequal Treaties" which foreign countries imposed on China in the name of "justice and equality" in the aftermath of the Opium Wars (1840–42, 1856–60). However, as the above story illustrates, the actual legal consequences for different nationalities under extrality were all too unequal. Secondly, although sovereign nations are equal in principle, in reality they are politically and economically unequal. Thirdly, from the mid-19th century through the 20th century, the Chinese made considerable efforts to conform to international law in the hope of achieving an equal status in the world of power politics.

As China's first experience of international law, the Unequal Treaties were long a source of antagonism, working as a reminder of the mistreatment which was suffered on a large scale over many decades and which made the Chinese particularly sensitive to issues of sovereignty. It was to take many decades before the Chinese experience of international law could be transformed into a positive one. The modern literature on the subject either emphasizes China's passivity in the face of the "universalization" of international law, or stresses the trans-lingual promulgation of international legal theories in the late nineteenth century (Dudden 1999; Hsü 1960; Li Chao-chieh 1996; Liu Lydia 1995; 1999b, c; Zhang Yongjin 1991). In his carefully researched book, *China's Entrance into the Family of Nations: The Diplomatic Phase 1858–1880*, Immanuel Hsü raises a question about the "national humiliations" suffered by China (often equated with the Unequal Treaties) that has continued to loom large in the Chinese consciousness: "Why, after the introduction of international law into China, did she [China] fail to use it as an instrument to assert her sovereignty and recover her lost rights?"(Hsü 1960:121) Moving away from such questions, however, I focus instead on the positive role played by the Chinese in the spread and development of international law. I also aim to extend the study of international law in China to the twentieth century, an undeservedly neglected topic in the field. Finally, the emphasis on language and translation as a tool of cultural transmission – an approach so popular in literature and cultural studies – is expanded through an examination of a unique dual process, i.e., the Chinese study of the Unequal Treaties and the concomitant dissemination of international law from the nineteenth to the twentieth centuries.

Through an examination of the almost contemporary Chinese publications on imposed and unequal treaties, on the one hand, and public international law, on the other, I attempt to show that the interpretation of international law can take place only on the terms presented by a given nation's own culture and history. Interpreting the history of international law in China also involves the reinvention of China's political, diplomatic and cultural inheritance. China's strong interest in topics such as the Unequal Treaties, national humiliations and the indigenization of international law indicate that China today still believes it has a wrong to rectify, a bitter reminder of the nation's weakness and vulnerability to outside forces in the past. In the meantime, the numerous Chinese publications dealing with these topics and the evolution of international law itself point to both the challenges posed and the contributions made by Chinese to the theory and practice of international law.

To many Chinese, modern Chinese history has been naturally equated with the history of the Unequal Treaties. The realities of the Unequal Treaties have long framed the general reception and broader praxis of public international law in China. The transplantation of international law to Chinese soil can be divided into three phases. The first, which began in the nineteenth century and ended in 1912, marked the introduction of international law into China; the Chinese were forced to grapple with the paradox of the legal equality of sovereign nations guaranteed by international law and the inequality resulting from the Unequal Treaties. The second phase lasted from 1912 to 1949 when the Republic of China grafted international law onto the Chinese legal system as part of the search for solutions to the issue of inequality. During this period, international law was indigenized and struck firm roots in China. The final phase occurred in the latter half of the twentieth century, a period when China developed an original and innovative set of rhetorical formulas with which to interpret world events. The People's Republic of China made full polemical use of the concept of the Unequal Treaties, turning international law into an instrument of struggle against imperialism, colonialism and hegemony in the dynamics of international bargaining. In addition, to Chinese, the true "internationalization" of international law demanded that it transcend its Christian European origins and expand to accommodate the cultures of non-Western nations.

The Beginnings of International Law in China and the "Unequal Treaties"

In this section, I argue that of all the factors relevant to the origins and development of international law in China, the issue of the Unequal Treaties has had by far the strongest impact on its transmission, appropriation, and indigenization in modern China. When international law was first applied in China, the Chinese were perplexed by the paradox of the principle of equality between sovereign states and the unequal nature of the treaties imposed on China by the West.

In 1840, Qing imperial Commissioner Lin Zexu visited Guangzhou to crack down on opium consumption and the opium trade. Through the efforts of his interpreter Yuan Dehui (袁德辉) and Peter Parker, an American medical missionary, Lin became acquainted with *Le droit des gens*, the seminal work of the Swiss jurist Emmerich de Vattel (1714–1767) (Vattel 1760; Tian Tao 1999). The Chinese translation made by Parker and Yuan, however, was heavily glossed and scarcely intelligible to Lin. There is evidence that Lin was influenced by Vattel's work, translated as *Geguo lüli* (The laws and regulations of all nations, 各国律例), which was also excerpted in Wei Yuan's *Haiguo tuzhi* (An illustrated gazetteer of maritime countries; 海国图志). For instance, in a letter to Queen Victoria in 1839, Lin protested: "To clearly summarize legal penalties as an aid to instruction has been a valid principle in all ages. Suppose a man of another country comes to England to trade, he still has to obey the English laws; how much more should he obey in China the laws of the Celestial Dynasty?" (Teng/Fairbank 1954:26–27)

In 1864, under the auspices of the Tsungli Yamen, three hundred copies of the Chinese translation of Henry Wheaton's *Elements of International Law* (Wheaton 1855) by William A. P. Martin (丁韪良, an American missionary, Sinologist, and interpreter to William B. Reed, American Minister to China), were distributed to Chinese officials.[1] Martin's work was well received among leading ministers of the Qing Tsungli Yamen, especially Wenxiang and Prince Gong. "International law," now always translated as *guojifa*,[2] was rendered by Martin as *wanguo gongfa*.[3]

In 1877, Martin, with Wang Fengzao (汪凤藻), et al., co-translated T. D. Woosley's *Introduction to the Study of International Law* into Chinese, titled *Gongfa bianlan* (公法便览). Then, three years later, the Chinese version of the French translation of the German jurist's, Johann Caspar Bluntschli's *Le droit international codifié*, co-translated by Martin and Lian Fang, et al., was published under the title *Gongfa huitong* (公法会通). Obviously, great effort was made to translate international law into Chinese in the decade after its first introduction, from foreigners taking the lead in translation to Sino-foreign collaboration. Reversing their initial passive role, the Chinese increasingly got involved and eventually took over the process of transplanting international law in China.

---

[1] Chinese translation in Ding Weiling 1998. See further Chen Shicai 1932, 1954:5.

[2] *Guojifa* (国际法) is a term first adopted by Mitsukuri Rinsho in 1873, according to Immanuel Hsü.

[3] "The Public Laws of the Ten Thousand Nations", 万国公法. (Hsü 1960:129).

At the time of its introduction into China, a number of officials immediately recognized international law as an important mechanism of conflict resolution. The reformist official Xue Fucheng wrote with implicit trust: "Nations, whether large or small, strong or weak, are in every way dependent upon international law to balance their differences and to alleviate potential conflicts. As far as weak and small nations are concerned, they must rely on international law for their survival." (Xue Fucheng 1994:156–157)[4] However, in their encounter with the West in the late nineteenth century, the Chinese had to face up to the paradox that, while international law employed a formal concept of national sovereignty that made all nations equal, it could not guarantee that such equality would be respected or enforced in practice. Chinese were quick to learn that formal judicial equality between sovereign states was not to be confused with political equality. Thus while international law was universally regarded as reasonable and instrumental, it provided no remedy for political and economic inequality. This dilemma was only too well recognized by officials such as the reformist Zheng Guanying: "Although international law applies to all, it has not, by any means, always been observed. [My speculation is] that international law can govern the relationships between equally powerful states. However, if there is no equality of national power, then public international law will not necessarily work" (Zheng Guanying 1982).[5] Or, in the words of a Qing diplomat, "International law is […] reasonable but unreliable. If it is a case of right without might, then right will not prevail"(Cui Guoyin: Vol. 2, Journal entry for April 12, 1891).

Chinese officials also recognized that the *spirit* of international law was in conflict with the ways in which European powers – claiming the *name* of international law – had acted in their relations with China. In this connection, the "Unequal Treaties" are particularly important. On the issue of tariff rates, Guo Songtao, China's first minister to Britain and France (1876–1878), commented on the inequalities created by the series of treaties concluded between the Qing and various foreign countries. Compared with the uniform 5% *ad valorem* tariff charged on all foreign merchandise imported into China, he noted that countries such as England, France, and the United States levied much higher taxes (set at differential rates) on imported commodities. On some items, the tariff rate was as high as 100% (Ibid:706–707). The Qing diplomat, Zeng Jize, minister to Britain, France, and Russia (1878–1885), was later to express the same concerns. Draw-

---

4 The Chinese original reads "各国之大小强弱, 万有不齐, 究赖此公法以齐之, 则可以弭有形之衅. 虽至弱小之国, 亦得藉公法以自存." Xue Fucheng was considered to favor the adoption of international law in China (Liu Baogang 1999).

5 The Chinese original is "虽然公法一书久共遵守, 乃仍有不可尽守者. 盖国之强弱相等, 则籍公法相维持, 若太强太弱, 公法未必能行也."

ing a clear line between diplomatic immunity and non-diplomatic privilege, Zeng wrote, "In Western practice, the residential office of a foreign minister is regarded as the sovereign territory of that foreign country, over which the host country has no jurisdiction whatsoever." By the same token, all diplomatic personnel enjoyed special diplomatic immunity. However, "foreign citizens with no diplomatic status are not supposed to be exempted from the jurisdiction of local authorities and laws" (Yang Xianqun 1985:164–165). Hence, in Zeng's opinion, international law consisted of "empty principles" (虚理, *xuli*):

> "As far as public international law is concerned, weak nations make use of it for self-protection, while strong nations, nonetheless, often violate it [...] As to its workings among states, both far and near, they do not necessarily comply with international law. Today, Western nations tend to regulate others by means of public international law; tomorrow, whenever they see opportunities to exploit our China, they will explain away theories of public international law in order to make their case. Their arguments [for requests] will come like swarms of bees so that the situation [China's dealings with foreigners] will resemble a flight of steps overgrown with brambles" (Zeng Jize 1983:181–182).[6]

There was another view of the nature of international law. As one author pointed out in *Waijiaobao* in 1901, international law was just an instrument that required good skills to make it work better:[7]

> "Those compatriots who have commented on international law often hold international law accountable for its inefficacy in regulating encounters between strong and weak nations [... In my view,] [t]he function of international law is the same as that of warships and fortresses. If one is not adept at operating warships and defending fortresses and as a consequence suffers defeat at the hands of one's enemies, how come is it the fault of warships and fortresses [i.e., Can one really blame the warships and fortresses]?"

Historically, the Unequal Treaties were China's first exposure to international law, an experience which confounded the Chinese because of the very different implications it held for strong and weak nations. This was the difficult situation which confronted them in seeking to implement international law for themselves.

Studies of international law began to take shape at the turn of the 19th and 20th centuries, as an integral part of Chinese efforts to pursue wealth, strength and Western learning. In 1896, two translated works on international law were published – one was John Fryer´s and Wang Zhensheng's (1896) translated work

---

6 The Chinese original reads: "公法者, 弱国以自保, 而强国时时犯焉 [...] 而睦邻绥远之道, 亦未必与公法处处符合. 今日据公法以责人, 则他日西洋各国凡有可以取利于吾华者, 皆以曲援公法之说以相渎扰, 势将辩难蜂起, 步步荆棘."

7 The original text reads: "吾国论国际法者, 多以强弱相遇公法无效为公法之罪 [...] 公法之用与战舰炮台同, 不讲于驾舰守台之策, 而忽焉蹂躪于外敌, 岂台舰之罪吁." (Waijiaobao 1901)

Gongfa zonglun, the other was the Chinese version of Sir Robert Phillimore's (1810–1885) *Commentaries upon International Law*, *Geguo jiaoshe gongfa lun*, translated by John Fryer and Yu Shijue (1896). What was interesting from the late 19th century onward was that the Chinese seemed independently to take more initiatives to translate or initiate research about international law.There was a loose study group, *Gongfa xuehui* (公法学会), in existence from April to September 1898 in Changsha of Hunan Province. The bylaws of this study group indicates that topics such as international law, the treaties between China and foreign countries in connection with their biggest problems, small blemishes, issues to be added to negotiations with foreigners and issues to be negotiated for changes were highlighted for study and discussion (Duan Muzheng 1998). Meanwhile, some young Chinese intellectuals compiled translated works in Chinese on international law, and some translated Japanese books on international law into Chinese. Such examples were Tang Caichang's (唐才常, 1867–1900) *Gongfa tongyi* (公法通义) in 1897 and Cai E's (蔡锷, 1882–1916) *Guoji gongfa zhi* (国际公法志) in 1902 (Ibid).

Besides wealth, strength and Western learning, studying international law also served other political purposes. For instance, Hu Hanmin (1879–1936), one of the Tongmenghui's[8] leading polemicists, also disseminated knowledge of international law in order to arouse anti-Manchu sentiments among the Han Chinese. To justify the efforts made by the United League to topple the Manchu Qing government, Hu, in his treatise *Panwai yu guojifa* (Hu Hanmin 1957) published in *Minbao* from 1906 to 1907, singled out the treaties as well as the Qing government's legal mistakes as essential factors that gave rise to xenophobic feelings among the Chinese.

Finding a Basis for the Application of International Law in China (1912–49)

In the Republic of China (1912–49), the study of international law went hand in hand with the search for legal grounds on which to revoke the Unequal Treaties. The tensions between formal sovereign equality and actual political and economic inequality, which had been given scant attention within the traditional framework of international law, were extensively discussed by a variety of political and social agents in China. Furthermore, the perceived inadequacies of international law inspired scholarly interest in the subject, stimulating a body of literature on the Unequal Treaties and imperialist aggression in China. Thirdly, Chinese research on international law corresponded with the flourishing printing business in the

[8] Its English translation is the United League, the forerunner of the Guomindang founded in 1905 in Japan by Sun Yat-sen.

studies of international law as well as the unequal treaties. Finally, the indigenization of international law in China was characterized by the invocation of existing legal theories and practices in calling for changes to the status quo.

In the 1910s, Chinese knowledge of international law was rudimentary and one of the main channels of dissemination was through secondary works in Japanese, rather than through direct Chinese translations of original legal works. Translated publications of significance included an edited volume by Jin Baokang, *Pingshi guojifa* (1907) (Jin Baokang 1907), and a translation of the Japanese text *Pingshi guoji gongfa* (1911) by Chen Shixia (Chen Shixia 1911), as well as *Guojifa yaolun* by Shen Yushan (1914).[9] Evidence also confirms that the *Beiyang Fazheng Zhuanmen Xuexiao* in Tianjin[10] adopted works in Japanese as textbooks for students to study international law. One of the founders and early leaders of the Chinese Communist Party, Li Dazhao (1888–1927) studied law there.[11] In 1909–1910, as a third year student of the Preparatory School, Li spent considerable time studying his textbook in Japanese on the general theories of law, one chapter of which is about public and private international law (Li Dazhao 1999: Vol. 1, 1–161). A few years later while studying at Waseda University in Tokyo, Li, together with his classmate and friend Zhang Runzhi, translated Imai Yoshiyuki's *Zhongguo guojifa lun* with a focus on foreign extraterritoriality in China (Imai Yoshiyuki/Li Da-zhao/Zhang Runzhi 1915).[12]

The translated book of *Zhongguo guojifa lun* provides us with a window through which we can see five characteristics of the propagation of international law in China in the 1910s: Firstly, the Chinese should firmly believe in the authority of international law as the basis of international covenants. Secondly, the power of international law and national strength should be based upon the equality of international status. Thirdly, changes to or elimination of international compacts by invoking the power of law should be in the hands of the Chinese. Fourthly, Li Dazhao felt embarrassed with the fact that foreign legal scholars, such as Imai Yoshiyuki, took the lead in research about international law and international relations related to China, whereas the Chinese intellectuals, absorbed by the politics of saving China, had found little time to devote to academic research. Fifthly,

---

[9] See Lawrence 1910; Chen Shixia 1911; Gonghe fazheng xuehui bianjibu 1913; Shen Yushan 1914

[10] The Beiyang School of Law and Government, 北洋法政专门学堂.

[11] Li's pursuit of law has normally not been taken notice of by scholars because of his active part in leading the Communist movement in China (Boorman 1968: 329–333).

[12] Imai Yoshiyuki (1878–1951), a graduate in law from the Tokyo Imperial University, taught at the Beiyang University of Law and Politics in Tianjin from 1908 to 1913 (Li Dazhao 1999: Vol. 2, 1–296). Also see the translation Li Dazhao 1999: Vol. 2, 1–293; Han Depei/Luo Chuxing/Che Ying 1999.

obviously aware of the differences between the Chinese and Japanese translations of the English concept of foreign leased territory and possessions – 租界 in Chinese and 居留地 in Japanese – Li in his translation into Chinese of the Japanese translation preserved the Japanese use of the term.

The political instability of the 1920s did little to dampen Chinese enthusiasm for public international law, and the publication of both translations of original legal scholarship and Chinese indigenous writings flourished in this period. Observations which can be made about promotion of international law in the 1920s China are: Firstly, international law emerged as a mature field of study and as a formal academic discipline. Many of the Chinese publications on international law in this period were university textbooks, which was an obvious advance on the situation in the 1910s when Chinese textbooks were lacking (For example, Ning Xiewan 1919:808; Ning Xiewan 1923:1114). A greater number of translations appeared, including the translation of Lassa Oppenheim's (1858–1919) classic *The Future of International Law* by Chen Zongxi (Chen Zongxi 1928). Secondly, we see a group of European trained Chinese international lawyers devoting their entire life to the study and dissemination of international law in China. These people – Zhou Gengsheng, Zhou Wei, Wang Tieya, Chen Tiqiang, and Zhou Ziya, etc – were critical figures assuming the role of teachers of international law in 20th century China (Zhou Gengsheng 1923; Zhou Gengsheng 1929; Cen Dezhang 1931; Zhou Wei 1930). Thirdly, instead of simply reproducing what points made by Western jurists, the specialized monographs in Chinese on international law displayed a greater grip by the Chinese on the whole nature and development of the subject. For example, in lucid language, Zhou Gengsheng in *Guojifa dagang* stated with precision what contemporary international law courses should cover: the nature, subjects, sources, basic rights and jurisdictions of nation states, treaties, international negotiations, diplomatic representation, resolutions to international disputes and the nature of international organizations. With regard to equality and inequality between nation states, Zhou made it clear that national equality refers to legal equity in spite of the fact that the fact that nation states are politically unequal. Political inequality cannot eliminate legal equality. In his summary of the differences among naturalists, Grotians and positivists, Zhou apparently agreed that positivism was the main direction in which international law evolved (Zhou Gengsheng 1929:20–25).[13] *Xin guoji gongfa* by Zhou Wei, in a different style from Zhou Gengsheng's *Guojifa dagang*, engages in the discussion about the rubrics of international law with more emotions by introducing examples specific to China throughout the two volumes.

---

[13] For more on the different schools of international law, see next section of the Chapter.

Several other legal and historical works on international law and the Unequal Treaties also received attention. The nature of capitulations (extraterritorial rights) in connection with the Unequal Treaties, for example, was thoroughly discussed in Liu Shishun's (刘师舜, 1900-) *Extraterritoriality: Its Rise and Its Decline* (Liu Shishun 1925). In his comprehensive legal study of the Unequal Treaties (Tseng Yu-hao 1931), Zeng Youhao (曾友豪), then President of the High Court of Justice for Anhui Province, devoted the first chapter to the issue of capitulations and the Unequal Treaties.

In the history of international law, the terms extraterritoriality, extrality, and capitulations refer to the diplomatic immunities secured where one state permitted another to exercise the latter's jurisdiction over its own nationals within the former's boundaries. Today such a privilege is granted only to certain diplomatic agents exempt from both criminal and civil charges in the countries where they are accredited, as stipulated in the Convention on Diplomatic Relations signed in Vienna in 1961 (Encyclopedia Britannica 2003).[14]

Both Liu and Zeng argued that the historical practice of capitulations originated in the inadequacy of local laws reflecting ancient familial and agricultural practices to embrace the complex business activities undertaken by foreign merchants. Thus, in the 13th century BC, Memphis and other Egyptian cities allowed Phoenician and Greek merchants to be subject to their own laws. Similar treatment was given to Phoenicians in Greece, to non-Roman citizens in the Roman Empire in the third century BC, as well as to certain citizens of Italian city-states in Antioch and Jerusalem in 1098 and 1123. Both Byzantine emperors and the Ottoman sultans followed such practices to avoid administrative and legal burdens. In 1535, the Franco-Ottoman Treaty was signed between Francis I of France and Süleyman I of Turkey granting the French consuls jurisprudence over the criminal and civil affairs of French nationals in Turkey. Medieval Europe witnessed the establishment of permanent consulates by merchants of a particular city in other cities of the same country or in foreign countries; they settled business disputes and exercised jurisdiction over merchants sharing their nationality (Keeton 1928: Vol. 2, 155–163). Liu and Zeng argued that these examples were more a matter of convenience or the gratuitous granting of territorial powers than the surrender of sovereignty.

In the mid-seventeenth century, the modern conception of the sovereign nation state, one of the basic concepts of international law, took shape in Europe. This

[14] The first legal expression of this doctrine was formulated by Pierre Ayraunt (1536–1601), and later adopted by Hugo Grotius (1583–1645) and Samuel von Puffendorf (1623–1694). "Extraterritoriality" was introduced as a legal term by Georg Friedrich von Martens (1756–1821) in 1788 (Encyclopedia Britannica 2003).

concept emphasized reciprocity and equality among independent nation states, as embodied in the Peace of Westphalia in 1648. Liu and Zeng pointed out that the modern notion of sovereign supremacy and exclusiveness inevitably came into conflict with the precedents for extraterritoriality reviewed above. In the 1606 treaty between England and France, the 1787 treaty between France and Russia, the 1788 treaty between France and the U.S., and a series of treaties concluded between Portugal (1696), France (1701), England (1713) and Spain, reciprocal extraterritoriality was accorded (Liu Shishun 1925:35–43). While Europeans and Americans attempted to discontinue the ancient and medieval practice of capitulations among themselves, they happily imposed extrality on Turkey, China, Japan, and Siam, but with no corresponding rights given to nationals of those countries residing in Europe and the U.S. Extraterritoriality was brought to an end in Japan in 1899, in Turkey in 1923 (by the Treaty of Lausanne) and in China in 1943.

The work of the American historian Eileen Scully has added nuances to the picture of extraterritoriality in China. She challenges the common assumption that Western governments, consulate personnel, and their colonial nationals, as a monolithic unit, worked together harmoniously under the protection of extraterritoriality. "Far from being a blunt instrument imposed on a passive, victimized indigenous society by singled-minded imperialists, extrality was more in fact a complex balancing act in which metropolitan governments, colonial sojourners, indigenous elites, and opportunists of all nationalities battled for advantage." (Scully 2001:9) Nonetheless, for Liu and Zeng such subtleties were neither an historical nor a legal concern. On the contrary, what interested Chinese jurists the most was the legal validity of the Unequal Treaties.

In his work, Zeng recognized the conceptual vagueness of unilateral treaties and unequal treaties in international law and identified the Unequal Treaties with "those conventions and agreements concluded in the Orient with Christian powers when the idea of territorial sovereignty was not seriously defended." (Tseng Yuhao 1931:12, 17) Referring to China's Unequal Treaties as "decaying institutions," Zeng noted that the growing attention given to the topic had broadened research in the field of international law in the 1920s. He quoted the comments made by Raymond L. Buell at the 1927 meeting of the American Society of International Law: "There is a group of treaties which I imagine may be called unequal. You have treaties granting extraterritorial rights, of which the Chinese treaties are an example." (Ibid.:10) At the same time, Zeng drew attention to similar concerns about this contradiction in the world of politics, such as the Porter Resolution of January 1927 by the U.S. Sixty-first Congress.[15]

---

[15] The exercise in China of American extraterritorial rights as well as the established regime of customs duties was found to be inequitable and nonreciprocal in character. The Porter Reso-

The subject of a change of conditions relative to the termination of a treaty was given detailed attention in Tseng's book, which contended that the doctrine of *rebus sic stantibus* (conditions which warrant that the conclusions of a contract no longer exists) must be applied in the case of China, and thus would provide the necessary legal grounds for China to nullify certain treaties and to relieve itself of certain treaty obligations, including the Twenty-One Demands of 1915 signed with Japan (Ibid.:105–114).[16] Such examples illustrate the close connection of academic studies of the Unequal Treaties and international law in the Chinese context.

In the 1930s, the Chinese study of international law came to maturity and the transplantation of the theory of the subject was completed. This had involved a dual process – the translation of Western theory and original Chinese research into international law. In 1934, the first Chinese translation of Oppenheim's *International Law: A Treatise*, became available and has been the most popular and most frequently reprinted international law treatise in China (Cen Dezhang 1934). Influential indigenous Chinese writings included Zeng Youhao's compilation *Guoji gongfa li'an* (*Cases in Public InternationalLaw*), Zhou Gengsheng's *Xiandai guojifa wention* (*Questions of Modern International Law*) and Li Daren's and Yuan Guoqin's *Guojifa fada shi* (*The development of International Law*).[17] Approaching international law from a historical perspective, Liu Daren and Yuan Guoqin undertook a thorough examination of its definition, structure, nature, historical evolution, objects and subjects, neutrality and regulations – as well as the international diplomatic organizations and procedures that have arisen from it, and the solutions it offers for international disputes.

The proliferation of Chinese literature on the Unequal Treaties is characteristic of the spread of international law in China; to a great extent it overlaps with publications on "national shame" (国耻文学, *guochi wenxue*) and the literature on imperialist aggression against China.[18] In the words of Chen Tiqiang, "[…t]he

lution concluded that "the treaty relations between the two countries [China and the U.S.] shall be upon an equitable and reciprocal basis and will be such as will in no way offend the sovereign dignity of either of the parties or place obstacles in the way of realization by either of them of their several national aspirations or the maintenance by them of their several legitimate domestic policies." (Ibid:13; Congressional Report 1927).

[16] In international law, the doctrine of *rebus sic stantibus* is defined as "a name given to a tacit condition, said to attach to all treaties, that they shall cease to be obligatory so soon as the state of facts and conditions upon which they were founded has substantially changed." (Oppenheim 1912: Vol. 1, Section 539).

[17] Zeng Youhao 1934, a compilation of cases considered at the Hague Conference, League of Nations, and the International Court. Zhou Gengsheng 1931 is a collected volume of papers; Li Daren/Yuan Guoqin 1937.

[18] Paul A. Cohen (2002) has called for attention to be paid to the rich *Guochi* literature in China.

only field in which Chinese international lawyers made intensive study was the question of unequal treaties and special rights of foreign powers in China." (Chen Tiqiang 1984:8)

These two sub-disciplines of the history of modern China developed in the latter half of the 1920s, and became perennial topics of discussion for many different interest-groups in the 20th century. Nearly 100 entries can be found under the heading of *diguo zhuyi qinhuashi* in *Minguo shiqi zongshumu* (*A Comprehensive Bibliography of the Republican period*) (Beijing tushuguan 1985). From its first appearance in 1925 to 1930, Wang Jingwei's *Diguo zhuyi qinlue Zhongguo de qushi he bianqian lun* (*Characteristics and Evolution of the Imperialist Penetration of China)* was reprinted eleven times (Wang Jingwei 1925). The publication of more than a dozen books whose titles contain the key word *bupingdeng tiaoyue* underlines the point that the literature of the Unequal Treaties was flourishing by the mid-1920s (Beijing tushuguan 1985 under *Zhengzhi* 政治). Jin Baokang (1925) divided the Unequal Treaties into three categories – those treaties that should be terminated without consent; those that should be abrogated with bilateral agreement; and those that should be terminated unilaterally. Qiu Zuming (1926) offered a solid study of the Unequal Treaty system examining its origins, earlier critiques, and strategies for revision. He singled out the Treaty of Nanjing, Tianjin, the Boxer Protocol, and the Twenty-One Demands as the most "damaging to the existence of the nation".[19] Drawing on international legal theory, Qiu itemized those national rights lost through the negotiation of foreign treaties. Qiu thus argued that China's sovereignty and independence were contingent on the Unequal Treaties, and the chief task of China's diplomacy was to fight for national rights. With respect to international law, Qiu held that "public law can be used for constructing arguments but cannot be relied upon (公理可谈而不可侯) [...] Since it has been the case, ever since antiquity, that diplomacy is backed up by military power." (Ibid:51)

Zhang Tinghao's *Bupingdeng tiaoyu de yanjiu* (*A Study of the Unequal Treaties*) drew on the Leninist notions of imperialism and colonialism to interpret the phenomenon of the Unequal Treaties as an extension of developments in domestic capitalism (Zhang Tinghao 1926). As a consequence, Zhang wrote, "like a hunk of fat meat in Asia, China naturally fell prey to European and American imperialism. For the imperialists, the Unequal Treaties entailed rights for them to enjoy, whereas for us they meant obligations to be fulfilled." (Ibid:3) In this connection, Zhang characterized public international law as "an instrument for imperialists to deceive weak and small nations in protection of their illegal rights". (Ibid:143) A sample of the Unequal Treaties literature of the later 1920s thus illustrates the in-

---

19 The Chinese text reads: "四约不改, 国无幸存." (Ibid:3)

terest the subject evoked among scholars, jurists, government officials, and writers of all political inclinations (Waijiaobu tiaoyue weiyuanhui 1929; Zhou Gensheng 1929; Guomingdang Shanghai tebieshi dangwu zhidao weiyuanhui xuanchuanbu 1929; Wang Tieya 1943; CCP 1943).

The Chinese perception was that public international law primarily served the purposes of assisting Western expansionism. Their unease about the principle of sovereign equality and the extent to which it negated differences in power were evident in Chinese pronouncements on the function of international law in world politics. As we have seen, the principle of equality was not honored in most treaties signed between China and foreign countries. To what extent then, could sovereign equality be applied to China? Disparities in national power were a perennial issue in the dissemination of international law in China as well as in China's struggle with the Unequal Treaties.

As a result, the diffusion of international law cannot be simply understood as a matter of spreading the word of law in the sense of a mere transfer, but it also involves the assimilation of the appropriate legal framework and legal language into the indigenous culture of the host nation at a particular historical moment. One example can be given here. Historically, international law was composed of two parts, public and private.[20] Today, international law, also known as public international law or the Law of Nations, refers to standards of conduct and rules that apply between sovereign states. This is distinct from private international law, which deals with the conflict of laws, i.e. legal problems arising from the multiplicity of legal systems obtaining in different states.[21] For Chinese in the first half of the 20th century, private international law was of little interest since it had no relevance to the questions thrown up by their immediate historical context.

Indigenizing (本土化, *bentuhua*) International Law in the Chinese Context: the Second Half of the 20th Century

Over the last half century, the Peoples' Republic of China (PRC, 1949–) has developed set formulas and a systematic rhetorical vocabulary for interpreting world events. Here I argue that it uses this rhetoric to define its position on a variety of issues, to invoke public international law to serve its own purposes, and

[20] This view became standard after the term "private international law" was coined in 1841 by the German jurist Schaffner. "Conflict of Laws." (Encyclopedia Britannica 2004a)

[21] The study of the "conflict of laws" (private international law), an expression first used in 1653 by the Dutch jurist Christian Rodernburg (1618–1668), coincided with the beginnings of modern public international law. The doctrines of modern international law were first developed by the Anglo-Dutch School, especially Alberico Gentili (1552–1608) and Hugo Grotius (1583–1645) (Encyclopedia Britannica 2004b).

to modify internationally accepted interpretations of domestic and international events with which it does not agree.

In 1971, at the height of modern China's isolation from the outside world, Jerome Alan Cohen (1972) prophetically observed:

> "It would be surprising if the PRC did not make some distinctive impact upon international law in view of its Marxist-Leninist-Maoist ideology of struggle against imperialism; the fierce nationalism that derives from China's bitter heritage of foreign exploitation; the totalitarian order, 'socialist transformation' of the economy, and Cultural Revolution that have been instituted internally; the continuing civil war with the Nationalist forces; and the PRC's long-standing exclusion from many international organizations and bilateral diplomatic relationships."

Though Cohen's remarks were hardly propitious under the particular circumstances of the Cold War, they challenged the conventional (and still prevailing) wisdom which emphasized the passivity of China in its entry into the family of nations, the collapse of its traditional tributary system and its forced compliance with international norms (Hsü 1960; Zhang Yongjin 1991).

The great encounter between China and Europe between 1500 and 1800 made a significant impact on both sides. Yet it was in the period after the 1840s, with the new external threat posed by the West from the sea and the ongoing contest for legitimacy between rival governments (most notably the first Republic's warlord government in Beijing vs. the Guomindang (GMD) government in Canton; the GMD's Nanjing government vs. the CCP; and the GMD government in Taiwan vs. the PRC), that China and the world were confronted with a multitude of fascinating and challenging legal problems.[22]

We can distinguish five separate facets of the adaptation of international law to the Chinese context. First, China managed to resolve the paradox of sovereign equality and political and economic inequality that classical theories of international law had not been designed to deal with. Working in the positivist mode pioneered by Oppenheim, Chinese international lawyers treat major inequalities between powers as political rather than legal issues. They have staunchly defended the principles of sovereignty and legal equality as the basis for the regulation of state-to-state conduct, advocating enhanced opportunities for small or weak states to influence legal development and to "pursue agendas that are not simply those of the powerful."(Kingsbury 1999:621, see also Macdonald 1994) However, China's most prominent jurist, Wang Tieya, stresses that such arguments must not be equated with the doctrine of absolute or unrestricted sovereignty – under which

[22] David Mungello (1999) characterizes the three centuries of encounter between China and the West as a reciprocal process of acceptance and rejection, at different times and in different ways.

nation states enjoy freedom to act at will, perhaps leading to the emergence of a single ”superpower” or even “world government” (超世界政府) – which would only lead to anarchy. This is the kind of situation which the PRC has perceived as paving the way for past imperialist expansionism and aggression (Deng Zhenglai 1993:355–358; Zeng Lingliang 1994). The Chinese argument is that:

> “The principle of equality does not mean that states are all equal in fact. The fact that states are different in size and population – large or small – and in terms of power – strong or weak – cannot be ignored. However, this actual inequality should not be a reason for the denial of the legal equality of states as the basis of interstate relations and a fundamental principle of international law.” (Deng Zhenglai 1993:363)

Wang viewed this underpinning legal equality as “a safeguard” for the small and the weak “against encroachments on their rights by larger and stronger powers” Deng Zhenglai 1993:363). Chinese international lawyers also argue that the limited enforceability of international law should be regarded as a potential strength rather than a deficiency (缺陷). The source of authority in international law lies in “equitable coordination” (平等协作) among sovereign states in the international legal order rather than in the ability of any one state or grouping of states to act as the world’s policeman (Jiang Guoqing 2000).

The second way in which international law has been adapted to the Chinese context results from globalization and multi-nationalism. These ubiquitous features of the contemporary world have confirmed Chinese jurists in opposing the radical change in the modern conception of national sovereignty proposed in some recent work in international law. Their objection derives from China’s “bitter experience” of the Unequal Treaties in the past, as well as from the conviction that the doctrine of sovereignty is “the only foundation upon which international relations and international law can be established and developed” (Leng Shaoquan 1965:260–261).

The history of international law demonstrates broad support for national sovereignty as “territorial supremacy” and for sovereign equality as a fundamental principle of an international legal system (Oppenheim 1905:171). Nonetheless, there was no consensus on its theoretical basis, and “unease about it persisted in practice” (Kingsbury 1999:603). Among international law theorists, three positions predominate with regard to the paradox of equality and inequality. Benedict Kingsbury (1999:603–604) summarizes them as follows:

> “Vattel’s naturalistic approach, with its remarkable analogy between equality of individuals and equality of states, has remained influential […]. It persists in assertions that the exclusion of individuals from democratic participation in local and national government is the same injustice as exclusion of large third world states from permanent membership in the Security Council.[…] The positivist alternative, well represented by Oppenheim, sees equality as a logical corollary of sovereignty. A third explanation, reciprocity, is preferred by structural realists in international relations (for whom particular configurations of power

among states will largely determine the patterns of inter-states interactions), as reciprocity potentially accounts for the otherwise puzzling acceptance by states of formal equality despite disparities of power."

Chinese international lawyers have been more at ease with positivists (Oppenheim) than naturalists (Grotius, Puffendorf, and Vattel), a stance clearly related to China's experience with the Unequal Treaties.[23] Provoked by the discrepancy between the principles of international law which Western nations preached and what they actually practiced, Chinese viewed the transplantation of international law to their country as a bitter and humiliating experience involving the cynical separation of theory and practice (He Qinhua 2001). Nonetheless, despite the fact that international affairs were often not conducted in accordance with the principle of equality between sovereign states, Chinese international lawyers accepted the practical value of international law in providing the legal framework for a coherent world order.

As a third major point of distinction, Chinese discourse on international law displays a universalistic rhetoric that demands that the subject be sufficiently elastic to adapt itself to a constantly changing world environment. From time to time, this universalistic rhetoric appears self-contradictory. On the one hand, Chinese scholars stress that international law dealt initially with only a few European states. Developments since World War II, however, have created a legal system that applies to all nations universally. On the other hand, Chinese legal scholars argue that, given China's size and importance, "the extent to which contemporary international law can really be said to be universal in character depends largely on China's attitudes towards international law." (Li Zhaojie 1993)

Fourthly, having accepted the efficacy of international law, China has exerted considerable pressure on traditional international legal doctrine. As a result of their violent history, the Chinese came to believe that public international law could be an effective instrument of struggle against imperialism, colonialism and hegemony.[24] In nearly all the textbooks on international law published in the PRC,

---

[23] Important naturalist writers agreed that the source of national and international laws were derived, "not from any deliberate human choice or decision, but from principles of justice which had a universal and eternal validity and which could be discovered by pure reason; law was to be found, not made." (Malanczuk 1997:15–17) By the 18th century, the theory of the law of nature was challenged by positivism, which argued that law was largely positive and man-made. In other words, positivism held that law and justice were not the same thing, and international law was credited through states' behavior and practice. Concerning treaties, positivists normally "assert legal rules can be found by consulting provisions of treaties that have entered into force. Among these scholars, there seems to be a great deal of sanctity accorded to the written text." (Ku/Diehl 2003:25)

[24] A good example is Chen Tiqiang 1985.

a prominent place is given to the Five Principles of Peaceful Co-existence as leading principles of international law (Liang Xi 1993; Wang Tieya 1998). The Five Principles were first formulated and proclaimed as the basis of international relations in a treaty known as the Agreement between the Republic of India and the People's Republic of China on the Trade and Intercourse between the Tibet Region of China and India signed on April 29, 1954. This agreement was later reconfirmed in several international documents, including the "Ten Principles" adopted at the Bandung Conference in 1955, and the Charter of Economic Rights and Duties of States approved by the UN General Assembly on December 12, 1974 (Chen Tiqiang 1984).[25] The five principles are: mutual respect for each other's territorial integrity and sovereignty; mutual non-aggression; mutual non-interference in each other's international affairs; equality and mutual benefit; and peaceful coexistence.

China's reading of international law and the Unequal Treaties has been seminal in shaping both academic perspectives on the subject and its stance on foreign relations, resulting in an emphasis on incorporating international law into research on modern China's foreign relations. An important example is Cheng Daode's *Jindai Zhongguo waijiao yu guojifa* (Modern Chinese foreign relations and international law), which examines such issues as foreign extrality in China, the concession system, tariffs, and the Treaty of Friendship and Alliance between China and the U.S.S.R. of 1945 (Cheng Daode 1993).

Conclusion

The issue of legal equality versus political and economic inequality engages with a broad range of debate in China on the meaning of modernity (expressed in the desire for international standards) and nationalism (molding and reconstructing national identity through the story of the Unequal Treaties and national humiliations), whether in the age of imperialism, the period of nationalist movements, or the post-imperialist period.

The conclusion that emerges from a study of the dissemination of international law in China and its links with the story of the Unequal Treaties is that the tangled web of connections between two significant collective impulses – the desire to conform with international standards and the concomitant molding and reconstructing of cultural, ethnic, and historical memories – should not be overlooked as a factor in the development of Chinese nationalism in the twentieth century. The issues of the Chinese development of international law and the Unequal Trea-

[25] In this article, Chen details the origins, development and significance of the Five Principles from the perspective of the PRC.

ties display a triple concern for internal unification, international status, and the reinforcement of Chinese identity. This supports my argument that the age of globalization, far from diminishing the influence of nation-states, has in reality made the role of sovereign nations more diverse and complex (Smith 2001:135–139; Duara 2002).[26]

The paradox of equality and inequality enters into the discussion of Chinese nationalism on two levels. Firstly, there is the narrative of the past that constitutes cultural and historical memories. The working of memory in popular consciousness, as Paul A. Cohen (2001) remarks, is primarily about defining identity and "framing the past interpretively" in such a way that it ultimately makes the past square with a preferred present. In the case of China, memories of the Unequal Treaties and the one-sided application of international law reinforce a deep sense of injustice, or fear of injustice in a world of power politics, that is central to modern Chinese identity. This fear, bordering on paranoia, is well illustrated in the following two examples.

At the end of 8 months of negotiations over the 16-article Sino-MacKay Treaty of 1902, as detailed in Chapter 1, China's chief negotiator Zhang Zhidong commented that, for fear of losing more *zhuquan* (主权 sovereignty), rights related to *zhiquan* (治权 extraterritoriality), *caiquan* (财权 rights related to finance), and *liquan* (利权 interests), the Chinese "had met [with the British] more than 60 times, and bargained over and over again about every single detail of each treaty clause till their tongues and lips were parched."[27] My second example is taken from a series of seminars on international law run by the CCP Central Committee in 1996. On December 9, 1996, at the end of one of the seminars, the then Chinese President Jiang Zeming warned the participants that, owing to their lack of knowledge of international law, some local and departmental cadres were severely disadvantaged in their work. Therefore, Jiang urged, "our leaders and cadres, especially those of high rank, ought to take note of international law and enhance their skills in applying it [...] We must be adept at using international law as 'a weapon' to defend the interests of our state and maintain national pride." (Renmin Ribao 12/10/1996) Jiang's talk was later characterized by Wang Tieya as a "second spring" in twenty years of international law in China (the "first spring" being the launching of reform in China in 1978, Wan Xia 1996; 1999). In addition to the element of anxiety, these examples also illustrate China's search for a balance between the acceptance of international legal standards (by reasoning things

[26] For more about different aspects of Chinese nationalism and transnationalism, see http://cio.ceu.hu/.

[27] The Chinese text reads: "聚议六十余次之多, 舌敝唇焦. " (Wang Yanwei/Wang Liang 1987: vol. 162, 2602)

out, *shuoli* 说理) and vigilance over any verbal or actual provocation that might pose a threat to its sovereignty.

The second level at which the paradox works in the context of nationalism is seen in the formulation of a distinctive language of controversy and polemic used to communicate China's interpretation of current events to the wider world. On March 21, 2003, on the eve of the U.S. attack on Iraq, Chinese jurists met and agreed that the impending war had no legal basis and was in violation of both international law and the United Nations Charter. The President of the Chinese Association of International Law, Wang Hongli, commented: "The American war on Iraq is the result of the bad reasoning of 'Monopowerism' and unilateralism (一强独大和单边主义). Subjecting international law to 'the law of the fist' will surely bring about a catastrophe for humanity." (Renmin Ribao 03/22/2003)

This line of argument resonates with what China defines as the true "internationalization" of international law after WWII. For China, the fundamental changes in international relations that characterized the post-war period included the abandonment of the principles and rules that justified imperialism and colonialism and their replacement by the principles of self-determination and sovereign equality among all nations (Ibid.:195). Disputing the existence of what some commentators have called "a crisis" of international law as a result of the "disappearance" of "cultural unity," Wang Tieya described the task of international lawyers as "taking account of [the] different histories and cultures of various countries" and seeking principles of law and justice which are common to all (Wang Tieya 1990:356). What this means for China is that any application of international law in matters where China is concerned must take into consideration its historical situation as well as its national culture.

Wang Dong, Department of History, Gordon College, Wenham

References

Beijing tushuguan (北京图书馆) (ed.) (1985): 民国时期总书目, 1911–1949 (A Comprehensive Bibliography of the Republican Period: 1911–1949). Beijing: Shumu wenxian chubanshe.

Boorman, Howard L. (ed.) (1968): Biographical Dictionary of Republican China. 3 vols. New York: Columbia University Press.

CCP (1943):中英中美签订新约: 百年桎梏一旦废除 (The Signing of the New Sino-U.S. and Sino-British Treaties: Smashing the Shackles of a Hundred Years) (Place unknown: Huabei xinhua shudian.

Cen Dezhang (岑德彰) (transl.) (1931): 国际法典 (Code of International Laws) [Chinese translation of the English translation of Hugo Grotius 1625's War and Peace.] Shanghai: Shangwu yinshuguan.

Cen Dezhang (岑德彰) (transl.) (1934): 奥本海国际法 [Chinese translations of: Oppenheim, Lassa, Ronald Roxburg (ed.) (1934): International Law: A Treatise, vol. 1: Peace; vol. 2: Disputes, War and Neutrality]. Shanghai: Shangwu yinshuguan.

Chen Shicai (陈世材) (1954): Bismarck and the Introduction of International Law into China. In: Chinese Social & Political Science Review XV (1931–1932), 98–101.

Chen Shicai (陈世材) (1954): 国际法学 (International Law). Taibei: Jinghua yinshuguan, 1954, vol. 1.

Chen Shixia (陈时夏) (transl.) (1911): 平时国际公法 (Public International Law in Peacetime) [Chinese translation of Nakamura Shingon (中村进午)] Shanghai: Shangwu yinshuguan.

Chen Tiqiang (1984): The People's Republic of China and Public International Law. In: Dalhousie Law Journal 8:1.

Chen Tiqiang (陈体强) (1985): 国际法论文集 (A Collection of Papers Related to International Law). Beijing: Falü chubanshe.

Chen Zongxi (陈宗熙) (1928): 国际法之将来 (The Future of International Law). Shanghai: Taidong tushuju.

Cheng Daode (程道德) (ed.) (1993): 近代中国外交与国际法 (Modern Chinese Foreign Relations and International Law). Beijing: Xiandai chubanshe.

Cohen, Jerome Alan (1972): Introduction. In: Cohen, Jerome Alan (ed.) (1972): China's Practice of International Law: Some Case Studies. Cambridge, MA: Harvard University Press.

Cohen, Paul (2002): Remembering and Forgetting National Humiliation in Twentieth-Century China. In: Twentieth-Century China 27:2 (April 2002).

Cohen, Paul A. (2001): Introduction: Politics, Myth, and the Real Past. In: Twentieth-Century China 26:2 (2001), 1–15.

Congressional Report (1927): Revision of Treaties with China, House of Representatives, Report No. 1891. In: *Congressional Record*, February 21, 1927, 4347.

Cui Guoyin (崔国因) (1995): 出使美日秘日记 (Diary of my Mission to the U.S., Japan and Peru). Shanghai: Shanghai guji chubanshe.

Deng Zhenglai (邓正来) (ed.) (1993): 王铁崖文选 (Selected Works of Wang Tieya). Beijing: Zhongguo zhengfa daxue chubanshe.

Ding Weiliang (transl.) (1998): 万国公法 (International Law). Unknown place: Chongshi guan 1864. Taibei: Zhongguo guojifa xuehui, [1864 reprint of work published by Chongshi guan with introduction by Hungdha Chiu (丘宏达)].

Duan Muzheng (端木正) (1998): 中国第一个国际法学术团体 - 公法学会 (The First Chinese Scholarly Organization of International Law) In: 中国国际法年刊 (Chinese Yearbook of International Law). Beijing: Falü chubanshe, 105–111.

Duara, Prasenjit (2002): The Legacy of Empires and Nations in East Asia. Frankfurt /Oder, Budapest: Central European University (Budapest) and Viadrina Europe University, 2002, available from http://cio.ceu.hu/ (March 26, 2004).

Dudden, Alexis (1999): Japan's Engagement with International Terms. In: Liu 1999a

Encyclopedia Britainnica (2003): "Extraterritoriality." Encyclopedia Britainnica 2003, Encyclopedia Britannica Premium Service. http://www.britannica.com/ed/artiche?=eu=34058 (April 04, 2003).

Encyclopedia Britannica (2004a): Conflict of laws. In: Encyclopedia Britannica Premium Service. http://www.britannica.com/eb/article?eu=117329 (February 20, 2004).

Encyclopedia Britannica (2004b): International Law. In: Encyclopedia Britannica Premium Service. http://www.britannica.com/eb/article?eu=109303 (February 20, 2004).

Fryer, John (Fu Lanya,傅兰雅) and Wang Zhensheng (汪振声) (transl.) (1896): 公法总论 (General Introduction to Public Laws). Place unknown: Hongwen shuju.

Fryer, John and Yu Shijue (俞世爵) (transl.) (1896): 各国交涉公法论 (On public laws of all nations). Place unknown: Hongwen shuju.

Gonghe fazheng xuehui bianjibu 1913 (共和法政学会编辑部) (transl.): 国际公法、国际私法问题义解 (Explaining Public International Law and Private International Law) [Chinese translation of Riben pu wenxuehui (日本普文学会) (eds.)]. Shanghai: Gonghe fazheng xuehui.

Guomingdang Shanghai tebieshi dangwu zhidao weiyuanhui xuanchuanbu (国民党上海特别市党务指导委员会宣传部) (1929): 不平等条约研究集 (Studies on the Unequal Treaties). Shanghai: Minguo Ribao

Han Depei（韩德培）, Luo Chuxiang (罗楚湘), and Che Ying (车英) (1999): 李大钊的国际法思想 (The International Legal Thought of Li Dazhao). In: 武汉大学学报 (Journal of Wuhan University) 243:4 (1999), 3–6.

He Qinhua (何勤华) (2001): 略论民国时期中国移植国际法的理论与实践 （Short Studies on the Chinese Transplantation of International Legal Theories and Practices during the Republican Period). In: 法商研究 (Studies in Law and Commerce) 84:4 (2001), 136–144.

Henry Wheaton (1855): Elements of International Law. 6 ed. Boston: Little, Brown and Company.

Hsü, Immanuel C. Y. (1960): China's Entrance into the Family of Nations: The Diplomatic Phase 1858–1880. Cambridge, MA: Harvard University.

Hu Hanmin (胡汉民) (1957): 排外与国际法 (Xenophobia and International Law). In: 民报 (Minbao), No. 4, 6, 8, 9, 10, & 13. Reprint of 1957, 3 vols. Beijing: Kexue chubanshe.

Imai Yoshiyuki (今井嘉幸), Li Dazhao and Zhang Runzhi (张润之) (transl.) (1915): 中国国际法论 (On Chinese International Law) .Tokyo: 健行社.

Jiang Guoqing (江国青) (2000): 论国际法与国际条约 (On International Law and International Treaties), In: 真理的追求 (Looking For Truth) 9 (2000), 33–37.

Jin Baokang (金保康) (1925): 解决不平等条约的步骤 (Steps Toward Solving the Unequal Treaties). Beijing Huabei pingmin Chaoyang: Zhongguo minguo wu sili daxue, June 1925.

Jin Baokang (金保康) (ed.) (1907): 平时国际法 (International Law in Peacetime) Shanghai: Bingwushe or in: 法政讲义（Zhengfa jiangyi）1:17, 234).

Keeton, George W. (1928): The Development of Extraterritoriality in China. 1969 edition ed., 2 vols. New York: Howard Fertig.

Kingsbury, Benedict (1998): Sovereignty and Inequality. In: European Journal of International Law 9.

Ku, Charlotte and Paul F. Diehl (eds.) (2003): International Law: Classic and Contemporary Readings, 2nd ed. Boulder, CO: Lynne Rienner Publisher.

Lawrence, Thomas Joseph (British), Dan Tao (但焘) (1910) (transl.): 国际公法提纲 (An Outline of Public International Law). Shanghai:Changming gongsi.

Leng Shaoquan (冷绍泉) (1965): Chinese Law. In: Arthur and C. Wilfred Jenks Larson et al. (eds.) (1965): Sovereignty within the Law. Dobbs Ferry, NY: Oceana Publications.

Li Chao-chieh (Li Zhaojie) (1996): International Law in China: Legal Aspect of the Chinese Perspective of World Order. PhD dissertation, University of Toronto.

Li Dazhao (李大钊) (1999): 李大钊全集 (The Complete Collection of Li Dazhao’s Works) Shijiazhuang: Hebei jiaoyu chubanshe.

Li Zhaojie (1993): Teaching, Research and the Dissemination of International Law in China: The Contribution of Wang Tieya. In: The Canadian Yearbook of International Law XXXI.

Liang Xi (梁西), (ed.) (1993): 国际法 (International Law). Wuhan: Wuhan daxue chubanshe.
Liu Baogang (刘保刚) (1999): 论晚清士大夫公法观念的演变 (Changing Perceptions of Public International Law among the late Qing Literati). In: 浙江学刊 (Zhejiang Studies) 3, 152–156.
Liu Daren (刘达人), Yuan Guoqin (袁国钦) (1937): 国际法发达史 (The Development of International Law). Shanghai: Shangwu yinshuguan.
Liu Shishun (刘师舜) (1925): Extraterritoriality: Its Rise and Its Decline. In: The Faculty of Political Science of Columbia University (ed.) (1925): Studies in History, Economics and Public Law. New York, NY: Columbia University.
Liu, Lydia H. (1995): Translingual Practice: Literature, National Culture, and Translated Modernity – China, 1900–1937. Stanford, CA: Stanford University, 1995.
Liu, Lydia H. (eds.) (1999a): Tokens of Exchange: The Problem of Translation in Global Circulations. Durham, NC: Duke University.
Liu, Lydia H. (1999b): Introduction. The Question of Meaning-Value in the Political Economy of the Sign.In: Liu 1999a.
Liu, Lydia H. (1999c): Legislating the Universal: The Circulation of International Law in the Nineteenth Century. In: Liu 1999a.
Macdonald, Ronald St. John (ed.) (1994): Essays in Honour of Wang Tieya (Boston: M. Nijhoff Publishers, 1994.
Ning Xiewan (宁协万) (1919): 国际公法 (The Public International Law of the Ten Thousand Nations) Changsha: Hunan sheng lifazheng zhuanmen xuexiao.
Ning Xiewan (宁协万) (1923): 先行国际法论 (Introduction to International Law). Lectures at Beijing Zhengfa daxue.
Oppenheim, Lassa (1905): International Law: A Treatise (London: Longmans Green & Co., 1905), vol. 1.
Qiu Zuming (邱祖铭) (1926): 中外订约失权论 (On Lost Rights in the Negotiation of Treaties between China and Foreign Countries). Shanghai: Shangwu yinshuguan.
Renmin Ribao 03/22/2003: 拳头法不能高于国际法 (The Law of the Fist Cannot Supersede International Law). In: 人民日报 (People's Daily) 03/22/2003, No. F.
Renmin Ribao 12/10/1996: 中共中央举行国际法知识讲座 (International Law Seminars Held by the CCP Central Committee). In: 人民日报 (People's Daily) 12/10/1996, No. A.
Scully, Eileen P. (2001): Bargaining with the State from Afar: American Citizenship in Treaty Port China, 1844–1942. New York: Columbia University Press.
Shen Yushan (沈豫善), (transl.) (1914): 国际法要论 (Essential International Law) [Chinese translation of 远藤源六著]. Zhenjiang: Qinrun shushe.
Smith, Anthony D. (2001): Nationalism. Cambridge: Polity Press.
Teng Ssu-yu and John K. Fairbank (1954): China's Response to the West: A Documentary Survey, 1839–1923. Cambridge, MA: Harvard University Press, 1954.
Tian Tao (田涛) (1999): 丁韪良与《万国公法》(William Martin and 'The Public Laws of the Ten Thousand Nations). In: 社会科学研究 (Sociological Studies) 5, 107–112.
Tseng Yu-hao (1931): The Termination of Unequal Treaties in International Law: Studies in Comparative Law of Nations, 1 ed. Shanghai, China: The Commercial Press, Limited.
Unknown (1929): Gambling and the Extraterritorial Question. In: The China Weekly Review June 29, 1929.
Vattel, Emmerichs de (1760): The Law of Nations, or Principles of the Law of Nature Applied to the Conduct and Affairs of Nations and Sovereigns [Translated from French], vol. 2. London: Printed for J. Newbury and J. Coote.

Waijiaobao 1901: 论公法与强权之关系(On the Relations between International Law and Power). In: 外交报 (Waijiaobao) 1 or: 公论 (Public Opinion), 1901. In: 外交报汇编 (Collections of Waijiaobao) [Reprint of the 1914 collection from Waijiaobao issued 1901–1910]. Taibei: Guangwen shuju vol. 1, 1–3.

Waijiaobu tiaoyue weiyuanhui (外交部条约委员会)(ed.) (1929): 不平等条约表 (Charting the Unequal Treaties). Beijing: Waijiaobu.

Wan Xia (万霞) (1996): 北京大学国际法研究所学习江泽民主席讲话座谈会 (The Forum Held by the Institute of International Law at Beijing University on President Jiang's Speech). In: 中国国际法年刊 (Chinese Yearbook of International Law) 1996, 450.

Wan Xia (万霞) (1999): 回顾与展望:改革开放20年国际法在中国的发展 (Looking Forward and Backward: the Development of International Law in China in the 20 Years Since China's Opening-up). In: 外交学院学报 (Journal of Foreign Affairs College) 2 (1999), 62–66.

Wang Jingwei (汪精卫) (1925): 帝国主义侵略中国的趋势和变迁 (Characteristics and Evolution of the Imperialist Penetration of China). Unknown place: 国民革命军总司令部政治部 (Guomin gemingjun zong silingbu).

Wang Tieya (1990): International Law in China: Historical and Contemporary Perspectives. In: Hague Academy of International Law, Recueil des cours 221:II.

Wang Tieya (王铁崖) (1943): 新约研究 (A Study of the New Treaty of 1943) Chongqing: Qingnian chubanshe.

Wang Tieya (王铁崖) (ed.) (1981): 国际法 (International Law). Beijing: Falü chubanshe 1981).

Wang Tieya (王铁崖) (ed.) (1998): 国际法引论 (A Primer of International Law). Beijing: Beijing daxue chubanshe.

Wang Yanwei (王彦威) and Wang Liang (王亮) (eds.) (1987): 清季外交史料 (Diplomatic Sources from the Late Qing). Beijing: Shumu wenxian chubanshe.

Xue Fucheng (薛福成) (1994): 筹洋刍议 (A Brief Discussion of Tactics for Fealing with Foreign Countries). Shenyang: Liaoning renmin chubanshe.

Yang Xiangquan (杨向泉), et al. (ed.) (1985): 曾纪泽出使英法日记 (The Diary of Zeng Jize in England, France, and Russia). Changsha: Yuelu shushe.

Zeng Jize (曾纪泽) (1983): 曾纪泽遗集 (The Posthumous Works of Zeng Jize). Changsha: Yuelu shushe.

Zeng Lingliang (曾令良) (1994): 评梁西主编之'国际法' (A Review of Liang Xi's *Guojifa*). In: 法学评论 (Law Review) 3, 85–88.

Zeng Youhao (曾友豪) (1934): 国际公法例案 (Cases in Public International Law). Shanghai: Shanghai faxue shuju.

Zhang Tinghao (张廷灏) (1926): 不平等条约的研究 (A Study of the Unequal Treaties). Shanghai: Guanghua shuju.

Zhang Yongjin (1991): China in the International System, 1918–1920: The Middle Kingdom at the Periphery. New York: St. Martin's Press.

Zheng Guanying (郑观应) (1982): 盛世危言 (Warnings to a Prosperous Age), Gongfa [公法 Public international law], in Xia Dongyuan (夏东元) (ed.) (1982): 郑观应集 (Collected works of Zheng Guanying), vol. 1. Shanghai: Shanghai renmin chubanshe.

Zhou Gengsheng (周鲠生) (1923): 领事裁判权问题 (The Question of Extraterritoriality). Shanghai: Shangwu yinshuguan.

Zhou Gengsheng (周鲠生) (1928): 不平等条约十讲 (Ten Lectures on the Unequal Treaties) Shanghai: Taipingyang shudian.

Zhou Gengsheng (周鲠生) (1929): 国际法大纲 (An Outline of International Law) Reprinted in 1935, 1941, and 1989. Shanghai: Shangwu yinshuguan.
Zhou Gengsheng (周鲠生) (1931): 现代国际法问题 (Questions of Modern International Law). Shanghai: Shangwu yinshuguan.
Zhou Gengsheng (周鲠生) (1935): 国际法大纲 (An outline of International Law). Shanghai: Shangwu yinshuguan.
Zhou Wei (周纬) (1930): 新国际公法 (New International Public Law). 2 volumes. Shanghai: Shangwu yinshuguan.

Agnes Schick-Chen

The Conceptualization of '*fazhi*' – Towards a 'Rule of Law' in China?

Introduction

The story of China's encounters with the West over the past century is also the story of it getting to know – one way or the other – the power of law in the Western world. Foreign relations from the late Qing Empire to the "reign" of Deng Xiaoping and his successor Jiang Zemin, as well as China's changing position in the international community resulting from the ups and downs in those relationships, have been going along with the sometimes pushed and sometimes slowed down process of approaching and partly adapting to the Western concept of legality. Simultaneously, the question of establishing a post dynastic order and reforming China's political system, which was a revolving issue for the entire 20th century, was answered in great part by philosophical and ideological concepts imported from the West. The legal and political concept of constitutionality which had provided a model of modern statehood in the first half of the century was jeopardized by the communist idea of the law being subordinate to politics for most of the Maoist era, and only the last two decades of the century saw new approaches to defining the status of law in the context of governance. This tendency for new methods to contain factional struggles was greatly influenced by the idea that economic reforms were in need of stability of the social and political system. Furthermore the importance of new and substantial legal settings for both international and domestic business soon became an uncontested demand.

The difficulty to simultaneously strive for legality and legitimacy of the communist regime became especially poignant in situations of political crisis. Chinese intellectuals' attitude towards law and legality ten years after starting Deng Xiaoping's reform project was made visible, to the Chinese public as well as to the outside world, by wall posters and posters carried by protesters in May and June 1989 calling for 'the rule of law' as a saviour from turmoil and political arbitrariness (e.g. Shell/Shambaugh 1999:197–198). This was a clear indication for law not just being approached on a theoretical level, but as an emotionally accepted component of the intellectuals' renewed perception of Chinese society and culture. The (re-) establishment of a legal component in Chinese culture at the end of the 20th century is reflected by the increasing representation of legal issues in Chinese arts and media (books, movies etc.), a tendency that raises the question of a cultural component of law and a legal culture.[1] Both fictional and real life stories like those about customers suing producers of harmful consumer articles, companies suing media critics for defamation, citizens trying to defend individual property rights against state agencies which for their part are also using legal remedies to limit such attempts[2], show that legal culture is about the way in which interaction between political and/or social actors is shaped or even determined by the regulatory guidelines of a legal system.

Consequently, legal culture would have to be monitored or assessed in the following fields of interaction:

- foreign relations, i.e. the encounters of the nation state with the outside world;
- governance, i.e. the interaction between state and society, including both the attitude of government towards people (with intellectuals as a special category among them) and the reaction of people to be felt by the government;[3]
- and socio-economic relationships between individuals.

The standard by which legal culture is usually assessed in or by the Western world is 'the rule of law'. The corner stone of this concept is a set of rules that, although possibly having been created by the ruler(s), should finally have a status of its own and stand above the political and social hierarchy, in order to legitimize the binding character of decisions derived from it.[4] If taken as a standard to be attained or kept to, the 'rule of law' is measured against the degree to which decisions in political, social, intellectual, economic or cultural controversies or conflicts are made according to this established and acknowledged set of rules instead

1 For a Chinese view on legal culture see Liu Zuoxiang 1999; Yu Ronggen 2003; Liang Zhiping 1994; Li Jiaofa 2004; Xie Hui 2001. From the Western side a comprehensive introduction to Chinese legal culture was provided by Robert Heuser 1999.

2 Accounts of incidents of this kind are to be found in foreign magazines like the Far Eastern Economic Review (FEER) (examples given here: Forney 1998; Lawrence 1998; Saywell 1999, but the developing of a culture of litigation in general is also portrayed in Chinese daily newspapers, some of them explicitly focussing on legal matters, with the 法制日报 (*Legal System Daily*) as the most prominent example.

3 Reciprocity also marks another aspect of legal culture which is the relationship between positive law and the external factors of legal culture: While on the one hand legal guidelines have an obvious impact on life and society, social development has an equally strong influence on legislation.

4 For an overview of the historical emergence and development of this concept in the West and its status in East Asia in the 1990s see Clark 1999.

of being provided by the conflicting parties themselves. The following text shall explore the application of this standard to the situation in the People's Republic of China in the reform era, and point to the complexity of the underlying conceptual transfer as well as of the related question of terminology.

'FAZHI': 'RULE OF LAW' – 'RULE BY LAW'

When Western legal knowledge was exported to late imperial China, experts in charge of introducing those partly new and mostly alien ideas to Chinese legal theory and practise were prone to use Chinese translations of foreign scientific terms that were already known or at least did not sound completely unfamiliar to people who were supposed to use them.[5] In the case of transferring the concept of 'the rule of law' to the Chinese context, '法治 (fazhi)', a term that had connotations going back to Chinese legalist tradition with a clearly instrumentalist approach to law (Wu Shuchen 1999:32–33), was chosen. As a consequence, the process of integrating the idea of law ruling over government into Chinese thought which has been going on for more than a hundred years, as well as the reception of this process in Western sinology and legal studies, was continually accompanied by a flavour of law being used by rulers as an instrument of government instead.

The concept in direct opposition to '*fazhi*' (法治) is '*renzhi*' (人治, the rule of men), which has had a long history in China as well, reaching a climax versus the end of the Maoist era. The central discussion on legal reform in the PRC in the first years after 1979 therefore revolved around these two opposite concepts.[6] Deng Xiaoping who himself had been a victim of Mao's ruling without law before was eager to find an alternative to the arbitrary 'rule of men' and thereby safeguard national stability. Alongside political, economic and social changes that he orchestrated in the 1980s there was also a change in the general attitude towards legality, and in the 1990s the greater part of foreign and domestic evaluations of the process and results of Chinese legal reform were based on the assumption that '*fazhi*' was, or at least should be, the ultimate goal of all efforts made in this respect (Zheng Yongnian 1999:32).

Astonishingly enough, experts who contrast '*fazhi*' with '*renzhi*' and/or claiming '*fazhi*' as the ultimate model to be followed do not always deem it necessary to consider and comment the fact that the structure of wording in Chinese makes two translations of the term '*fazhi*' possible – and that as a consequence the term

---

5 For information on the history of translating Western legal knowledge into Chinese in the late Qing period see Wang Jian 2001.

6 For an account of the early period of this controversy see Keith 1991.

can stand for two different concepts: as the nature of synthesis between the characters '*fa*' (法, law) and '*zhi*' (治, rule) is not as clearly determined as in English,[7] the 'of' between 'rule' and 'law' can be replaced with 'by' – and the 'rule of law' becomes a 'rule by (way of the) law'.[8] This distinction becomes visually discernible when recurring to the more complete phrase '依法治国' (*yi fa zhi guo*, rule the country in accordance with the law) and its counterpart '以法治国' (*yi fa zhi guo*, rule the country by means of the law) – still identical in the oral form (with exception of the intonation of the syllable '*yi*'), but drawing a clear distinction by using two different characters as co-verbs or prepositions to 'law (*fa*)'[9]. While the latter clearly indicates an instrumentalist approach and was to be found in many texts on the reform process at its very beginning, the terminology of 'ruling in accordance with the law' has become prevalent in recent years and even found its way to the top of the legal system when written into the Fourth Constitution of the PRC of 1982 in 1999.[10]

This tendency towards a 'rule of law' notwithstanding the question of how to interpret the ambiguity of the Chinese term '*fazhi*' and how to handle its implications for the analysis of legal development in the PRC remains a complex one – especially if research on this subject is done in the West where the idea of a clear distinction between the 'rule of law' and the 'rule by law' prevails. Another way to see the relationship between the two concepts is the definition of the 'rule by law' as an earlier or lower stage of legal reform that has to be passed through on the way to the final level of 'the rule of law'. It is equally questionable even though proposed by researchers both of Chinese and Western origin[11]. In order to

---

[7] '*Fa*' can function both as subject and as definition to the verb '*zhi*'; while in the first case law is acting, it is just a more precise definition of the action performed by someone or something else in the second case.

[8] Some scholars taking the differentiation between 'rule of-' and '-by law' into account refer to Baum 1986. For another depiction of this differentiation see Peerenboom 2002:64–65. In a chapter on "'The concept of *fazhi*' and 'socialist fazhi' in China" Shen Yuanyuan (2000:24) points to the fact that the Pinyin transliteration '*fazhi*' has a third meaning (notwithstanding with a different character for '*zhi*', 制) which is 'legal system'.

[9] In the first case 'yi 依' has a first tone and the central meaning of 'use, take', in the second '*yi* 以' has a third (second) tone and means 'depend on, comply with, according to'.

[10] 中华人民共和国宪法第五条第一款 (Constitution of the PRC, Art. 5, 1): "中华人民共和国实行依法治国, 建设社会主义法治国家 (The People's Republic of China practices ruling the country in accordance with the law, in order to establish a socialist country of law [Rechtsstaat].) "

[11] One text attempting to 'show why rule by law is an unavoidable development stage in China's legal progress, and also to analyse the difficulties of the transition from rule by law to a rule of law' is Zheng Yongnian 1999:32. In Wei Pan 2003 the distinction between 'rule of and by law' is not drawn clearly throughout the whole of the text, but in a reply to Wei's argu-

demonstrate that the above named approaches are to be revised and how in the reality of today's legislation, jurisdiction and legal science in China the border line between the two concepts gets blurred, the text uses the examples of Internet regulations and administrative review.[12]

RULE BY LAW: THE EXAMPLE OF INTERNET REGULATIONS

The relevance of this example is due not only to the important role that the Internet plays in the lives of an ever growing part of the Chinese population (Lawrence 1999), but is also given by the impact that the existence and implementation of legal measures in this field has on every one of the fields of interaction defined as parameters of legal culture in the introductory part of this text: the accessibility of information and services formerly unknown to the Chinese public have changed both the way people interact on an equal basis, as well as the hierarchical relationship between the "ordinary citizen" and the political elite "educating, guiding and protecting" them. Getting linked online is not only about communicating facts or selling information, but clearly facilitates the expression of thought, which offers a new perspective to Chinese citizens in general, and is of extreme importance to Chinese intellectuals. Furthermore an exchange of views and ideas is not limited to Chinese sources, but revolutionizes contacts with the outside world.

Forming part of the World Wide Web, which in theory was to tear down any kind of information and communication barrier, had to be a shock, both in the positive and negative sense of the word, in a country where little more than ten years earlier any activity of this kind would have been handled as an affair of public security (Hartford 2000). Apart from widening the view on what was to be known or learned from the outside world, the internet and electronic mail provided a new device for exchanging news of what was going on in other parts of China and thus contributed to the forming of a preliminary stage of civil society (Yang Guobin 2003). The awareness of new forms and possibilities to associate and reunite made activities possible that had formerly been blocked or severely impeded by legal regulations like the "PRC Law of Assembly, Procession and Demonstration" – another piece of legislation often linked to the concept of 'rule by law' (Hintzen 1994). This process has been closely monitored and encouraged by the Western world because of its being considered essential for democratisa-

---

ments (not to be further discussed in this context) Randall Peerenboom (2003:45) quotes Wei as setting up a timetable in three stages, the first of them being a "rule by law period".

12 The decision to choose both examples from the field of administrative law was influenced by the fact that the difference between ruling by law and a rule being limited by the law becomes most obvious – and most controversial – when applied to the state-society relationship, visible in everyday life of the Chinese people.

tion in the PRC (Goldman/Perry 2002; Brook/Frolic 1997; White Howell/Shang 1996). In the eyes of the CCP leadership, even though Party committees in charge of information policy and propaganda themselves did not miss the chances offered by the new media, the obvious risk of political dissent developing on internet sites or user platforms, and then possibly spreading over the whole of the Chinese internet community was a clear indication to curtail the reach of this flow of information. As a consequence of this official attitude a race of users against institutions trying to control them took off soon after the Chinese mainland was linked to the internet: while the former kept trying to expand the range of information they could access via the net, the latter wanted to at least track or trail these new channels that could very easily lead to "dangerous" sources of information, such as homepages of exiled Chinese dissidents, organisations promoting Tibetan or Taiwanese independence, Falun Gong (Thornton 2000) or others and provide a forum for on-line discussion on subjects like corruption scandals or atrocities of the Cultural Revolution (Holland/Saywell 2000).

The Party and the government would have previously applied political and social repression to controle the use of information, but after 1979 the PRC leadership started developing new means of prevention and punishment, or prevention by punishment, to achieve the same result: activities in the fields of publishing, journalism, trading in copyrights and similar activities were now to be held under control by way of laws and regulations (Chan 2003; Alford 1995:65–94; Schick-Chen 2001:37–47) issued by the People's Congresses or governments, implemented by the law courts or government agencies and leaving space for censorship and propaganda if deemed necessary. The degree of technological specialisation and extremely fast development of the electronic media made respective legislation and implementation a difficult task for legal experts and politicians[13], not only in the PRC. It took the Chinese authorities a number of years before the first rather comprehensive set of regulations, the "Measures for the administration of Internet information services (互联网信息服务管理办法)" together with the provisions of the new "Regulations for Telecommunications of the PRC (中华人民共和国电信条例)", was issued by the State Council in 2000 (Giese 2000), but the overall amount and speed of Internet-related legislation[14], as well as trials and verdicts

[13] In order to improve the efficiency of Internet supervision departments established under the Public information network supervision departments, collage graduates with special skills in computer and telecommunications were "invited" to work as "public functionaries" in those public security institutions. In: Summary of World Broadcast/BBC. 11.12.2000:FE/4020 G/6.

[14] Information on up-to-date legislation in this and other business-related fields of law is provided by: Baker & McKenzie: China Legal Development Bulletin 3:10 (March 1996), 3–4 (Internet regulations); 3:6 (July 1996), 9–11 (Internet Channels, Computer Network Security); 4:5

covered by the domestic and international press seem to convey two different messages to two different groups of addressees: they reassure the international business community of Beijing's will to join world-wide efforts to provide a legal framework for this new, virtual reality, while at the same time demonstrating to users all over China as well as providers and users outside of the PRC of Beijing's vigilance concerning any exchange of information or ideas.

Cases like the one of a young entrepreneur in the software and internet business who was sentenced to a prison term of two years plus a fine of 10,000 RMB for forwarding Chinese e-mail addresses to "hostile foreign" organisations (Hartford 2000:261; China Aktuell 1999), or a Chinese web master prosecuted for publishing sensitive information on an internet site named after June 4 (Taipei Times 08/19/2001), as well as the repeated fining, confiscating and closing down of internet cafes and provider companies because of "improper" usage[15] identify the fear of loosing control over social currents and possible political consequences as the main force behind official China's taking legal action (Chase/Mulvenon 2002). They also seem to confirm critical voices claiming that the "ambiguity around the term *fazhi* reflects a continuing reluctance in China to have laws curb the discretion of the government" (Woo 2000: 165). Nonetheless, other cases like the conviction of a Chinese company by an Intermediate People's Court for unlawfully registering the trademark of an international brand as domain name and similar lawsuits (Saywell 2000) are signs of the Chinese legislation, administration and judiciary getting orientated towards international standards of Internet security. However, as news of legal victory against unlawful conduct as understood by the Western rule of law philosophy are outnumbered by reports on the interpretation and implementation of Internet-related regulations and laws that displays a lack of strictly legal motivation, the overall picture is still one of law being used for the political purpose of state control.

Rule of law: the example of Administrative review

The dispute between advocates of complete liberalisation in the virtual world and supporters of certain limitations set by safety measures in favour of public and personal interests is not unique to the case of China; neither is the danger of authorities making use of respective legal provisions in order to exercise some sort

(6/1997), 12–13 (Amendment to Computer Networking Regulations); 7:5 (6–9/2000), 14–20 (Measures for the Administration of Registration of Website Names, Implementing Rules for Measures for the Administration of Registration of Website Names); 8:1 (1–2/2001), 1–3, 9–11 (Administration of Chinese-Language Domain Names, Resolution of Internet Domain Name disputes, Internet Security Decision).

[15] Summary of World Broadcast/BBC. 11.12.2000:FE/4020 G/8.

of control over the net community. Nonetheless, as even those parts of the world where law is supposed to rule might not be immune from misuse of power, a genuine rule of law should at least provide for legal ways to defend oneself against such abusive behaviour on the part of the rulers. Administrative review and administrative appeal enable citizens to ask administrative bodies for reconsideration and possible reversal of former decisions, or even sue officials that have caused harm by "misinterpreting" or just plainly misusing administrative regulations or laws. The introduction of this concept is linked to the question whether the ruler is to be above or below and therefore constrained by the law and was the point of departure for the development of the rule of law in the West (Clark 1999:30). The rule of law debate in the PRC under Deng Xiaoping and Jiang Zemin paid special attention to the reform of the administrative law and focused on administrative law in general[16] as well as the problem of administrative appeal and/or review specifically. About the passage of the Administrative Litigation Law (行政诉讼法) in 1989 Pei Minxin says that "[…] it was hailed in the Chinese legal community. Optimists felt it had the potential to be the key legal instrument for protecting human rights and laying the foundation of the rule of law in China" (Pei Minxin 1997:835). The idea of one or several individuals, or even a juridical person, taking a representative of the state to court seemed outrageous in view of past usages in state-society relations and was therefore likely to have the greatest impact on the attitude towards law and legality of individuals and officials alike. At the same time the lack of familiarity with and immensity of the very thought of self-defence in the form of legal action against state authority impeded an instant and overall acceptance and implementation of this legal measure. The second form of legal protest against inappropriate use of official power, which is administrative reconsideration, consisting of a formal appeal to the superior administrative agency,[17] is met with a higher degree of acceptance, as the number of cases clearly show. It seems to correspond better to the Chinese tradition of complaining to the superiors of misbehaving officials or cadres and therefore to contain less of a psychological barrier.[18] And while the Regulations on Administrative Reconsideration (行政复议条例) of 1990 still limited the scope of control and interference from above, the

[16] The necessity of administrative reform was addressed frequently, not only in the political debate, but also in the academic field; the outcome of discussions on "the overall strategy and objective of 'rule the country according to law, build a country ruled by socialist law'" usually being that 'administration according to law is the key to ruling the country according to law'" (Guo Daohui 1999:91).

[17] In most cases this procedure is to be passed through before litigation (中华人民共和国行政诉讼法第37条 (Law of administrative procedure of the PRC §37)).

[18] For some of the cultural aspects of administrative law reform compared to the administrative law system in the United States, see Rubin 1997.

Law of Administrative Reconsideration (行政复议法) passed in 1999 exposes the majority of administrative actions to administrative review.[19]

Nonetheless, actual limitations to effective implementation still result from the "human factor" on the side of both the plaintiff and the accused. As the fictional *Story of Qiuju* (秋菊打官司) described in rather drastic, but not that unrealistic images in Zhang Yimou's film[20] of the early 1990s, administrative agencies still had to get used to their new responsibilities before the law, ordinary people still had to learn what defending their rights with the help of the law was really about, law courts were not vested with judicial independence as provided by separation of powers in Western democracies, and as a consequence, administrative review and appeal still could not guarantee a satisfying outcome of a crusade led by the principles of 'the rule of law'.[21]

A survey on support for anti-corruption campaigns conducted in various provinces in 1997/98 included an "evaluation of local officials' performance in governing by law". The result of only a quarter of the interviewed villagers defining themselves as "fairly confident in filing administrative law suits" (Li Lianjing 2001:582) showed that even after several years of legal practice, the Chinese population, especially in rural areas, was not completely convinced of the effectiveness of administrative legal measures.[22] On the other hand accounts of singular cases like the one of a township official encouraging people to sue under ALL provisions after having failed in administrative reconsideration (O'Brien/Li 1995:766), as well as an increasing number of administrative law suits and even more applications for administrative reconsideration in general[23], are clear indications of the fact that Chinese citizens at least *do know about and consider* these possibilities of protecting their individual rights when confronted with negligence or maltreatment from officials.[24]

---

19 The respective regulations in force in 2000 can be found in Xingzheng sugong fajiqi peitao guiding 2001.

20 For a short review of this film see Silberberg 1999 amongst others. For an analysis of the novel by Chen Yuanbin on which the film is based see Kinkley 2000:348–357.

21 While those principles are unknown to the heroine of the story, their impact on the author's, director's and maybe even producers' motivation seems obvious.

22 In the survey cited (Li Lianjing 2001) the confidence in administrative lawsuits (apparently including both administrative review or reconsideration and appeal) is contrasted with confidence in lodging complaints (individual complaints: 12.8%, collective complaints: nearly 40%).

23 For both implementation problems and success stories, as well as statistical data on administrative litigation see Pei Minxin 1997.

24 The results of a survey conducted by researchers from several Chinese universities in 1992 in several provinces, targeting relevant segments of the Chinese population (judges, lawyers,

Knowledge of the relevant legal provisions stems to a considerable extent from educational measures such as related newspaper articles, TV-shows or specialised seminars for professionals. Such endeavours, forming part of a campaign-like movement orchestrated in the form of five year plans under the name of '普法' (*pufa*, disseminate law = "law for everybody")[25] make it clear that political authorities not only allow, but even want people to know about means to question or even counter government action. In view of the political implications of this development – underlined by, among others, the number of intellectuals putting their belief in the rule of law into practice and fighting politically motivated censorship and other attempts at silencing dissident activities with the help of administrative law suites (Pei Minxin 2000:33–34) – this might be an astonishing strategy to be followed by an authoritarian regime. Still, realizing that it is not only plaintiffs who are driven by their frustration caused by unlawful behaviour of cadres, especially at the lower levels of administration, but that both the CCP leadership and the Central government themselves are desperately looking for new institutions to fight maladministration and corruption, administrative review and appeal present themselves as perfect means to give a new quality to the interaction between officials and people (= state-society relationship) and thereby diminish the danger of social instability and threats to the political legitimacy of the CCP government.

In fact, in 2001 an article in "Qiushi", the Party's ideological mouthpiece, claimed that "from real life and their own experience people know that without exerting control on the circumstances of cadres' official activities and performance of their duty, [those officials'] exercising their power might leave the path of democracy and legality", and that "as a result of this the image of the Party is certain to get damaged, the life of the Party endangered, and the foundations of the socialist state shaken". This text, pointing at the importance of administrative law without explicitly naming it, hints to an instrumentalist approach when it quotes Jiang Zemin saying that "it is necessary to build a sound mechanism of restraint and control on the execution of power in accordance with the law by way of intensifying internal party control, legal control and the control of the masses" (Chen Zheman 2001:31). Seen from this perspective, even administrative review and appeal, hailed as proponents of the 'rule of law', still contain the inherent trace of law being used for political purposes.

---

plaintiffs, administrative personnel, citizens, i.e. workers, peasants, intellectuals etc.) were published in Long Xiangrui 1993.

25 The first of these five year plans for the dissemination of legal knowledge was implemented in 1986. For more detailed information on this educational aspect of legal reform politics in the PRC see Exner 1995.

Conclusion

Both the 'rule by law' element in administrative law reforms and the intention of the PRC government to converge with the international 'rule of law' regime in the realm of Internet crime prevention and sanctioning are indications of the difficulty in identifying clear and unquestionable examples for the 'rule by law' or the 'rule of law' in China. In view of the concurrence and even mingling of these two theoretical concepts in legal practice the assumption of 'ruling *by* law' being just a preliminary stage of 'the rule *of* law' has to be discarded. Similarily, it seems diffcult to grant exclusiveness to 'the rule of law' as being the sole aim of legal reform, especially, when being aware of the fact that the instrumentalist element can not be completely discarded from the interaction between 'rule' and 'law' in a Western context neither.[26] A researcher rooted both in Chinese and Western (legal) culture seems to summarize the problematic issue in the statement that "Too many assumed conceptual categories and theoretical presuppositions have been used so often within the paradigm of thought known as 'legal culture' in Chinese society" (Ren Xin 1997:7).

The finding of factual and conceptual overlapping, as well as the problem of a correct handling of relevant terminology,[27] might lead to the conclusion that the terminological ambiguity of '*fazhi*' is nothing but an adequate reflection of the ambiguous reality denominated by it, which might further promote the idea of operating with the Chinese term itself instead of linking it to just one or the other English translation. This approach on the one hand would still allow for an individual interpretation of the word '*fazhi*' according to one of the two lines of Western thought, while at the same time function as a constant reminder of the fact that the process or situation addressed by this term is embedded in China's

---

[26] The instrumentalist aspect of the Western 'rule of law' approach becomes visible when Western researchers write with regard to Western political theory: "The law is regarded both as an instrument for guiding behaviour and as a safeguard, providing citizens with enforceable rights." (Jagtenberg/de Roo 1994:28) Another comment shows that Chinese researchers may be aware of this, but still see a difference between the Chinese and the Western situation: "I do not mean to deny the instrumental function of law in all societies. It is worth noting, however, that in modern Western societies the relatively high degree of law's authority is based not so much on its instrumental capabilities as on its degree of autonomy." (Shen Yuanyuan 2000:28)

[27] A quotation from the English abstract of a Chinese article may illustrate the problem of inexact terminology: in this text the term "*xifang fazhi*" is translated as "western rule *by* law", even though the article's content deals with the state-society relationship based on the "rule *of* law" in Western countries. (Ma Changshan 2001:3) At the same time researchers of Chinese origin working in the West are aware of the fact that "the Chinese language is another formidable obstacle in establishing reliable and accurate categories of legal propositions for a sound comparative study". (Ren Xin 1997:7) See also Shen Yuanyuan 2000:24.

political, social and legal culture and therefore prone to "challenge" or even "resist" foreign conceptualization and categorization.

Agnes Schick-Chen, Department of East Asian Studies, University of Vienna

References

Alford, William P. (1995): To Steal a Book is an Elegant Offense. Stanford, Stanford University Press 1995.

Baum, Richard (1986): 'Modernization' and Legal Reform in post-Mao China: the Rebirth of Socialist Legality. In: Studies in Comparative Communism XIX:2 (Summer 1986), 69–103.

Brook, Timothy and B. Michael Frolic (eds.) (1997): Civil Society in China. Armonk: M.E. Sharpe.

Chan, Joseph Man (2003): Administrative Boundaries and Media Marketization. In: Lee, Chin-Chuan (ed.) (2003): Chinese Media, Global Contexts. London/New York: Routledge Curzon, 159–176;

Chase, Michael S. and James C. Mulvenon (2002): You've Got Dissent! Chinese Dissident Use of the Internet and Beijing's Counter-strategies. Santa Monica: Rand, 49–63.

Chen Zheman (陈浙闽) (2001): 为什么要建立健全依法行使权力的制约机制和监督机制? (Why is it necessary to build a sound mechanism of restraint and control on exercising power in accordance with the law?) In: 求实(Seeking Truth) 24, 31–32.

China aktuell (1999): Staatssicherheit und Internet: Politische Risiken für Netzdienstleister (National Security and the Internet: Political Risks for Network Providers). In: China aktuell 1/1999: 11.

Clark, David (1999): The Many Meanings of the Rule of Law. In: Jayasuriya, Kanishka (ed.) (1999): Law, Capitalism and Power in Asia. The Rule of Law and Legal Institutions. London/NewYork: Routledge, 28–44.

Exner, Mechthild (1995): The Convergence of Ideology and the Law: the Functions of the Legal Education Campaign in Building a Chinese Legal System. In: Issues and Studies 8, 68–102.

FEER: Far Eastern Economic Review. Singapore.

Forney, Matt: Voice of the People. In: FEER (05/07/1998), 10–12.

Giese, Karsten (2000): Das gesetzliche Korsett für das Internet ist eng geschnürt (The Internet Constricted by Legal Regulations). In: China aktuell 10, 1173–1181.

Goldman, Merle and Elizabeth J. Perry (eds.) (2002): Changing Meanings of Citizenship in Modern China (Cambridge, Mass./London: Harvard University Press.

Guo Daohui (郭道辉) (1999): 法治行政与行政权的发展 (Rule of Law Administration and the Development of Administrative Rights). In: 宪法学, 行政法学 (Constitutional Law, Administrative Law) (China Renda social sciences information center D411) 3, 91–96.

Hartford, Kathleen (2000): Cyberspace with Chinese Characteristics. In: Current History 9, 255–262.

Heuser, Robert (1999): Einführung in die chinesische Rechtskultur. Mitteilungen des Instituts für Asienkunde Nr. 315 (Outline of Chinese Legal Culture. MIA No. 315). Hamburg: Institut für Asienkunde.

Hintzen, Geor (1994): Protest Your Loyalty: An Analysis of the Right of Assembly Procession and Demonstration in the People's Republic of China. Leiden: CNWS Publications.

Holland, Lorien and Trish Saywell (2000): Plugging a Sieve. Beijing Faces Frustration in its Bid to Regulate the Internet. In: FEER (02/10/ 2000), 20–21.

Jagtenberg, Rob and Annie de Roo (1994): Dispute Settlement in China: Law or Policy. In: Dong, Lisheng (ed.): Administrative Reform in the People's Republic of China since 1978. Leiden: IIAS, 27– 41.

Keith, Ronald C. (1991): Chinese Politics and the New Theory of "Rule of law". In: The China Quarterly 125 (Mar. 1991), 109–118.

Kinkley, Jeffrey C. (2000): Chinese Justice, the Fiction. Stanford: Stanford University Press.

Lawrence, Susan V. (1999): Widening Web. In: FEER (11/18/1999), 54–55.

Lawrence, Susan V.: Gagged by big business. In: FEER (08/01/2002), 24–27.

Li Jiaofa (李交发) (2004): 法律文化散论 (Writing on Legal Culture). Beijing: Renmin fayuan chubanshe.

Li Lianjiang (2001): Support for Anti–Corruption Campaigns in Rural China. In: Journal of Contemporary China 10: 29, 573–586.

Liang Zhiping (梁治平) (ed.) (1994): 法律的文化解释 (A Cultural Explanation of Law) Beijing: Sanlian shudian.

Liu Zuoxiang (刘作翔) (1999): 法律文化理论 (A Theory of Legal Culture). Beijing: Shangwu yinshuguan.

Long Xiangrui (龚祥瑞) (ed.) (1993): 法治的理想与现实: '中华人民共和国行政诉讼法' 事实现状与发展方向调查研究报告 (Ideal and Reality of the Rule of Law: Report on the Actual Situation and the Direction of Development with Regard to the 'Law of Administrative Procedure of the PRC'). Beijing: Zhongguo zhengfa daxue chubanshe.

Ma Changshan (马长山) (2001): 西方法治产生的深层历史根源, 当代挑战及其启示 – 对国家与市民社会关系视角的重新审视 (The Deep Historical Roots of (the Making of) the Rule of Law in the West, Present Challenges and Inspirations – a Re-evaluation of the View on the Relationship between State and Civil Society). In: 法律科学(Law Science) 6, 3–15.

O'Brien, Kevin J. and Li Lianjiang (1995): The Politics of Lodging Complaints in Rural China. In: The China Quarterly 143 (Sept. 1995), 756–783.

Peerenboom, Randall (2002): China's Long March Toward Rule of Law. Cambridge: Cambridge University Press.

Peerenboom, Randall (2003): A Government of Laws: Democracy, Rule of Law and Administrative Law Reform in the PRC. In: Journal of Contemporary China 12:24 (February 2003), 45–67.

Pei Minxin (1997): Citizens v. Mandarins: Administrative Litigation in China. In: The China Quarterly 152 (Dec. 1997), 832–862.

Pei Minxin (2000): Rights and resistance. The Changing Contexts of the Dissident Movement. In Perry/Selden, 20–40.

Perry, Elizabeth and Mark Selden (2000): Chinese Society, 2nd Edition; Change, Conflict and Resistance. London/NY: Routledge.

Ren Xin (1997): Tradition of the Law and Law of the Tradition: Law, State, and Social Control in China. Westport/London: Greenwood Press.

Rubin, Edward L. (1997): Administrative Law and the Complexity of Culture. In: Seidman, Robert B.; Seidman, Ann and Janice Payne (eds.) (1997): Legislative Drafting for Market Reform: Some Lessons from China. Basingstoke: Macmillan Press, 88–108.

Saywell, Trish: "Virtual Victory. Ikea's Success Against a Cyber-squatter is just the Latest Encouraging Sign from Chinese Courts". In: FEER (07/06/2000), 38.

Saywell, Trish: Demanding action. In: FEER (05/13/1999), 42–43.

Schick-Chen, Agnes S. (2001): Urheberrecht an der Taiwan-Strasse (Copyright at the Taiwan-Straits). Hamburg: Institut für Asienkunde.

Shell, Orville and David Shambaugh (eds.) (1999): The China Reader: The Reform Era. First Vintage Books Edition.

Shen Yuanyuan (2000): Conceptions and Receptions of Legality. Understanding the Complexity of Law Reform in Modern China. In: Turner/Feinerman/Guy 2000, 20–44.

Silberberg, Jerome (1999): China into Film: Frames of Reference in Contemporary Chinese Cinema. London: Reaction Books, 120–131.

Taipei Times (08/19/2001): China Goes After Online Dissenters, 1.

Thornton, Patricia M. (2000): The New Cybersects. Resistance and Repression in the Reform Era. In Perry/Selden 2000, 247–270.

Turner, Karen, G. (2000): Introduction. In: Turner/Feinerman/Guy 2000, 3–19.

Turner, Karen G./James V. Feinerman/R. Kent Guy (2000): The Limits of the Rule of Law in China. Seattle, Washington: University of Washington Press.

Wang Jian (王健) (2001): 沟通两个世界的法律意义: 晚清西方法的输入与法律新词初探 (Legal Translation between the East and the West: A Survey of the Introduction of Western Law in Nineteenth Century China). Beijing: Zhongguo zhengfa daxue.

Wei Pan (2003): Toward a Consultative Rule of Law Regime in China. In: Journal of Contemporary China 12:24 (Feb. 2003), 3–34.

White, Gordon / Jude Howell / Shang Xiaoyuan (1996): In Search of Civil Society. Market Reform and Social Change in Contemporary China. Oxford: Clarendon Press.

Woo, Margaret Y.K. (2000): Law and Discretion in Contemporary Chinese Courts. In: Turner/Feinerman/Guy 2000,163-195.

Wu Shuchen (武树臣) (ed.) (1999): 中国传统法律文化辞典 (A Dictionary of Traditional Chinese legal culture). Beijing: Beijing daxue chubanshe.

Xie Hui (谢晖) (2001): 法的思辨与实证 (Essays on Law: Speculative and Positive Studies). Beijing: Falü chubanshe, 388–412.

Xingzheng sugong fajiqi peitao guiding 2001: 行政诉讼法及其配套规定 (The Law of Administrative Procedure and Relevant Regulations) (2001). Beijing: Zhongguo fazhi chubanshe.

Yang Guobin (2003): The Internet and Civil Society in China: A Preliminary Assessment. In: Journal of Contemporary China 12:36 (August 2003), 453–475.

Yu Ronggen (俞荣根) (2003): 文化与法文化 (Culture and legal culture). Beijing: Falü chubanshe 2003.

Zheng Yongnian (1999): From Rule by Law to Rule of Law? A Realistic View of China's Legal Development. In: China Perspectives 25 (Sept./Oct. 1999), 31–43.

Contributors

John K. T. CHAO, MA, LL.B, LL.M. (Cantab.), Ph.D. Law (Edin.) is professor of International Law and Diplomacy at the Department of Diplomacy of National Chengchi University in Taiwan and an adjunct professor of International Law at the Chinese University of Political Science and Law in China. He is also a member of the board of examiners at Examination Yuan in Taiwan. His publications cover a range of topics on international law including "Chinese Membership Problems at Asian Development Bank", "On United Nations and Permanent Neutrality States", among others.

Margareta GRIESZLER graduated in Chinese Studies, General Linguistics and History and received her PhD from the University of Vienna. Her research focus is on late Qing Dynasty (Empress Dowager Cixi), foreign relations of China, and discourse between East and West. Since 2003 she is a Research Fellow at the Department of East Asian Studies at the University of Vienna.

A. Tom GRUNFELD is SUNY distinguished teaching professor at Empire State/State University of New York. He is a historian who specializes in modern China, and Southeast Asia. He is the author of over 100 articles; book reviews and contributions to edited books as well as several on his own including "The Making of Modern Tibet". He is currently a Fulbright Senior Specialist.

Judith HUFNAGEL studied Modern Chinese Studies, Economics, and Spanish Linguistics in Heidelberg and Shanghai, focusing on 20th century Chinese politics, cognitive and social linguistics (Spanish), and international economic policy (Economics). In 2004 she obtained her master's degree for a thesis on international law in cross-strait relations. At present she is working in Munich as a researcher for an international design agency.

Donald A. JORDAN is a professor of East Asian History at Ohio University in Athens. He received his PhD from the University of Wisconsin. Jordan specializes in Sino-Japanese relations in Republican China and the career of T. V. Soong as a modernizer. Publications include: "The Northern Expedition: China's National Revolution 1926–28" (University Press of Hawaii, 1976); "Chinese Boycotts versus Japanese Bombs; the Failure of China's Revolutionary Diplomacy

1931–32" (University of Michigan Press, 1991); and "China's Trial By Fire, the Shanghai War of 1932" (University of Michigan Press, 2001).

Nele NOESSELT, MA, is a doctoral candidate of Chinese Studies at the University of Vienna. Her Research interests include the modern Chinese state, China's foreign policy and international relations.

Agnes SCHICK-CHEN is assistant professor at the Department of East Asian Studies at the University of Vienna. She writes on Chinese law, politics and society. Her book "Urheberrecht an der Taiwan-Strasse [Copyright at the Taiwan Straits]" was published in 2001, a book on the discourse on Chinese legal culture in the PRC after 1979 will follow in 2006.

WANG Dong is associate professor of history at Gordon College and research associate of the Fairbank Center for East Asian Research at Harvard University. At Gordon College, she also directs the East-West Institute of International Studies. She is the author of "China's Unequal Treaties: Narrating National History" (Rowman & Littlefield Publishers, Inc., 2005). Her other English monograph on the cultural encounters between U.S. and China and Lingnan University (Canton Christian College) is under editorial consideration.

Susanne WEIGELIN-SCHWIEDRZIK is professor for Sinology at the Department of East Asian Studies at the University of Vienna. Her main field of research is modern Chinese history and historiography as well as Chinese politics. She was the organizer of the conference "As China meets the world – China's changing position in the international community", Vienna May, 2004).

XU Xiaoqun teaches history at Christopher Newport University in Virginia, USA and is the author of "Chinese Professionals and the Republican State: The Rise of Professional Associations in century China. Shanghai, 1912–1937" (Cambridge University Press, 2001) and numerous other articles. His research interest is in the institutional, social, and cultural history of twentieth-century China.